New Technologies in Developing Societies

WITHDRAWN
UTSA LIBRARIES

Palgrave Studies in Communication for Social Change

Series Editors: **Pradip Ninan Thomas**, the University of Queensland, Australia and **Elske van de Fliert**, the University of Queensland, Australia

Advisory Board: **Silvio Waisbord**, George Washington University, USA, **Karin G. Wilkins**, University of Texas at Austin, USA, **Thomas Tufte**, Roskilde University, Denmark, **Zaharom Nain**, University of Nottingham, Malaysia Campus, **Rico Lie**, Wageningen University, the Netherlands, **Claudia Mitchell**, McGill University, Canada, **Jo Tacchi**, RMIT University, Australia, **Nicholas Carah**, the University of Queensland, Australia and **Zala Volcic**, Pomona College, Claremont, USA

Communication for Social Change (CSC) is a defined field of academic enquiry that is explicitly transdisciplinary and that has been shaped by a variety of theoretical inputs from a variety of traditions, from sociology and development to social movement studies. The leveraging of communication, information and the media in social change is the basis for a global industry that is supported by governments, development aid agencies, foundations, and international and local NGOs. It is also the basis for multiple interventions at grass-roots levels, with participatory communication processes and community media making a difference by raising awareness, mobilising communities, strengthening empowerment and contributing to local change.

This series on CSC intentionally provides the space for critical writings in CSC theory, practice, policy, strategy and methods. It fills a gap in the field by exploring new thinking, institutional critiques and innovative methods. It offers the opportunity for scholars and practitioners to engage with CSC as both an industry and as a local practice, shaped by political economy as much as by local cultural needs. The series explicitly intends to highlight, critique and explore the gaps between ideological promise, institutional performance and realities of practice.

Titles include:

Tina Askanius and Liv Stubbe Østergaard (*editors*)
RECLAIMING THE PUBLIC SPHERE
Communication, Power and Social Change

Levi Obijiofor
NEW TECHNOLOGIES IN DEVELOPING SOCIETIES
From Theory to Practice

Pradip Thomas and Elske van de Fliert
INTERROGATING THE THEORY AND PRACTICE OF COMMUNICATION AND SOCIAL CHANGE
The Basis for a Renewal

Palgrave Studies in Communication for Social Change
Series Standing Order ISBN 978–1–137–36166–0 (hardback)
(*outside North America only*)

You can receive future titles in this series as they are published by placing a standing order. Please contact your bookseller or, in case of difficulty, write to us at the address below with your name and address, the title of the series and the ISBN quoted above.

Customer Services Department, Macmillan Distribution Ltd, Houndmills, Basingstoke, Hampshire RG21 6XS, England

---

New Technologies in Developing Societies

From Theory to Practice

Levi Obijiofor
University of Queensland, Australia

First published 2015 by
PALGRAVE MACMILLAN

Palgrave Macmillan in the UK is an imprint of Macmillan Publishers Limited, registered in England, company number 785998, of Houndmills, Basingstoke, Hampshire RG21 6XS.

Palgrave Macmillan in the US is a division of St Martin's Press LLC, 175 Fifth Avenue, New York, NY 10010.

Palgrave Macmillan is the global academic imprint of the above companies and has companies and representatives throughout the world.

Palgrave® and Macmillan® are registered trademarks in the United States, the United Kingdom, Europe and other countries.

ISBN 978–1–137–38932–9

This book is printed on paper suitable for recycling and made from fully managed and sustained forest sources. Logging, pulping and manufacturing processes are expected to conform to the environmental regulations of the country of origin.

A catalogue record for this book is available from the British Library.

A catalog record for this book is available from the Library of Congress.

For my mother, Esther Obijiofor

Contents

Acknowledgements

I would like to acknowledge the immense support, advice and encouragement I received from a number of people right from the conception of this book to its completion. The enthusiastic and outstanding support I received inspired and sustained my interest in this endeavour. I am grateful to my wife, Edith, and my daughters, Chidinma and Elochukwu, for their extraordinary spirit of understanding and encouragement. When I needed quality time to concentrate and write, they understood and provided me with that important private time and space to continue my work. A writer requires a period of privacy, isolation and personal reflection. Without their support and understanding, I could not have completed this book. They sacrificed many social events and weekends that we would have spent together outdoors because they understood my time commitment to this project. They also understood that I needed to be secluded from activities around me to be able to advance work on this book. In this context, I owe a debt of gratitude to all of them.

I am also grateful to my father, Caleb Ezeogu Obijiofor, for the wonderful support and encouragement he gave to me throughout my educational career. He supported me and taught me, right from my childhood, to appreciate the value of education. I dedicate this book to my mother, Esther, who passed away in November 2013. I will never forget the love, care and solid support she gave to me even in times of difficulties. Men and women are usually evaluated on the basis of the contributions they made to their society and the values they espoused and upheld during their lifetime. My mother will always be remembered because of what she embodied during her lifetime – honesty, diligence, integrity, service to humanity and her community, as well as commitment to her Christian religious principles.

There are people within and outside my family who have shown extraordinary love and kindness to me. I would like to acknowledge them. I refer in particular to my sisters, Christiana and Nneka, my elder brother, Nate Obijiofor, and his wife, Ify. My cousins, Justice Cecilia Uzoewulu and her brother Kofi Obijiofor (*Ajie Nanka*), are also acknowledged. I sincerely appreciate the remarkable support, advice and encouragement they have given to me. I am equally grateful to Poly I. Emenike (*Odenigbo Nanka*), who has been a mentor, a friend and a pillar of support to me in many ways. I appreciate his valuable advice and his exceptional magnanimity to me and my family. I wish to thank Dr Ben Emechete and his wife, Obiageli, for their wonderful friendship, encouragement and support.

I am thankful to Felicity Plester (Publisher and Global Head of Film, Culture and Media Studies, Editorial Department, Palgrave Macmillan) and Editorial Assistant Sneha Kamat Bhavnani, for granting me the important extension of time I needed to complete this book when I was held back by ill health. I deeply appreciate their understanding and the guidance they provided to me during the time of writing this book.

1
Introduction

Of all the innovations that have affected human lives in the 21st century, none has been as far-reaching as new technology. This is particularly true for people in the industrialised world. Their lives are affected in one way or another by technology. Whether they are awake or asleep, whether they are at work or at play, whether they are adults or infants, they interact with technology in some way. The infant who plays with toys connects with technology in a different way. As Last Moyo (2009a, p. 122) noted with particular reference to developed countries, new technologies such as computers and mobile phones have a profound impact on 'how people communicate, vote, buy, trade, learn, date, work or even play'.

In the health sector, technology is the engine that drives many services. Doctors use technology to communicate with nurses, patients and paramedical staff. Patients with access to technology do not have to wait to consult their doctors before they can get some idea about their ailments. They can google the symptoms of their illness in order to find information on the possible causes of their conditions. Availability of modern technology facilitates telemedicine or telehealth, through which patients in isolated and remote communities are connected to medical specialists in cities with better medical facilities for assessment of their medical condition. This is usually done through videoconference or teleconference technology.

Telehealth is deemed valuable in many ways because it saves money previously spent on air travel, accommodation and food, which patients had to pay for to be able to meet their specialist doctors in distant locations. It also reduces or, in some cases, eliminates the time that patients devote to travel to keep their appointments with specialists. In addition, telehealth offers several other benefits, such as providing web-based health education for community members; it facilitates greater inter-action among health workers in and outside local communities; it also makes it possible for patients to access specialist medical services. In the HIV/AIDS prevention campaign, technology is helping people living with the virus to access relevant information online about how to manage their condition and adopt appropriate behaviour to prevent the spread of the virus. In the campaign to stop the further spread of HIV/AIDS, there has been a shift in strategy from use of the mass media to use of social media and other digital technologies to reach the youth, to create awareness and to sensitise the public to the disease.

In the education sector, technology has transformed the mode of teaching and learning at the primary, secondary and university lev-els. University students need not be present physically in lecture halls to access lecture notes, to understand what was taught or to interact with lecturers. In various universities, especially in developed western countries and in some technologically resourced developing countries, students can access the audio version of lectures, as well as PowerPoint slides of lectures. With access to printers at home or at the univer-sity library, students can print learning material. Similarly, students can submit assignments online. Not only is technology facilitating dis-tance education, it is also making it possible for children in remote and isolated communities with limited educational facilities to remain in their communities and to continue their education through the Inter-net. This is what is known in some parts of the world, such as the northern Ontario province of Canada, as the Internet High School. The Internet High School shows that, in isolated communities that suffer from economic and social deprivations, education doesn't have to be delivered through a face-to-face medium. Technological transformations have affected the mode of teaching and learning.

While technology is affecting people in many ways in many countries, there are a large number of people in developing countries who lack access to basic technology, not to mention access to digital media. How-ever, despite the dearth of digital technologies in various parts of the world, the widespread diffusion of mobile phones has helped many peo-ple to close the gap between the technology 'haves' and the 'have-nots'. In rural and remote parts of the developing world, villagers are using mobile phones to communicate and connect with their relatives in dis-tant places. In the past, messages, news and information were passed on mostly by word-of-mouth communication in the rural communities of developing countries, but the situation is changing noticeably. Now technology is the main tool for news and information dissemination.

Villagers use the mobile phone, for example, to relay important and urgent messages to relatives who reside in city centres and other distant locations. Small and medium-sized business owners, fish farmers in remote locations, men or women involved in the marketing of local textiles, carved wood and other art and craft can all expand their businesses to reach customers in far-flung locations they would never have been able to reach without technology. Mobile phone technology and the Internet have made it possible for these people to create awareness about their products on a global scale and therefore extend the reach of their products to buyers in many parts of the world. This is the value of new technology.

In some cases, technology has enabled low and medium-scale business people to cut out the middlemen and women who often constitute obstacles in the business chain. Cutting out middlemen and women has also led to increase in profits. With technology, these business people can deal directly with their customers. They are also able to access information about prices of their products in markets near and far rather than rely on information provided by middlemen and women. In many impoverished communities in developing countries, the mobile phone has empowered women in various ways and is helping them to access information that enables them to break out of the cycle of poverty and to improve their socioeconomic conditions.

There are other ways in which new technologies are helping people to improve their living conditions through provision of employment opportunities, knowledge acquisition, cultural preservation and promotion of lesser used or minority languages. For example, Internet technology such as multimedia web service provides a forum where Indigenous people from different countries can meet online to share ideas, to tell their stories and to share experiences. The ability to meet and communicate online allows Indigenous people to enact and maintain their cultural practices, and to share ideas about the common challenges that affect them in different parts of the world. When Indigenous people in remote and isolated communities create and communicate through their home pages on the web, they use these not only to reduce the impact of isolation, distance and idleness in their communities but also to provide insights into the lives of many of their families, including their ancestral history and their relationship to the land (Ramirez, Aitkin, Jamieson and Richardson, 2004; Jansen and Bentley, 2004).

It is important to point out that technology does not have a homogenising effect in terms of the way people use it in developing and developed countries. In diverse cultures, new technologies are helping people to monitor their health, to undertake careers in education and to advance their businesses and their economic activities. In other words, technology use and adoption are occurring in different contexts and cultures under different conditions. Therefore, to understand the way people in Africa and other developing regions use technology, it is important that we understand the specific contexts. That is why the focus of this book is on technology use in Africa in particular and in developing countries in general. Even in our modern world, some communities are technologically well served but others are poorly equipped and lack access to technology, and so find themselves lagging behind other communities.

This resonates with the concepts of digital divide and poverty divide that exist within countries and between countries. The digital divide can be explained as the inequalities that exist between those who have access to new technologies and therefore have greater access to information and those who lack access to new technologies and are therefore disadvantaged. Norris (2001) describes the digital divide as a concept that should be understood in three distinct forms, namely as the global divide, the social divide and the democratic divide. 'The global divide refers to the divergence of Internet access between industrialized and developing societies' (2001, p. 4). The social divide refers to the information gap that exists between rich and poor people within every country, while the democratic divide refers to the difference between those who use and those who do not use the range of 'digital resources to engage, mobilize, and participate in public life' (Norris, 2001, p. 4). Like the digital divide, digital poverty refers to various aspects such as the inability of people to afford information and communication technology services, as well as the lack of skills to use new technologies. It also refers to the lack of infrastructure to deliver the information and communication technology services (May, 2012).

There is poverty in remote and rural communities. There is also poverty in metropolitan cities in industrialised western countries. It was generally thought that people in developing countries lack access to new technologies such as mobile phones, the Internet and social networking sites. While this is arguably true in comparison to the situation in developed countries, the situation is rapidly changing. Research shows that Africa is now the world's fastest-growing market for mobile phones, followed by Asia in second position (Aker and Mbiti, 2010; Chéneau-Loquay, 2010; LaFraniere, 2005). While technologies are transforming human activities in Africa and other developing regions in positive ways, it is important to acknowledge that they have their shortcomings. Some people use technologies as tools to commit crimes such as financial fraud and identity theft. In this way, new technologies have brought new challenges to human societies.

The analysis presented here focuses on information and communication technologies and their impact on the everyday lives of people in Africa and other developing regions. The analysis shows the interconnections between new technologies and the socioeconomic development of Africa, in the area of health (e.g., the fight against the spread of the HIV/AIDS virus) and in terms of how technologies are used by African youth to engage in participatory communication in the public sphere. It examines the challenges that new technologies pose to Indigenous people in terms of their rights to protect their traditional knowledge and their right to protect and preserve their intellectual property. The role of public service broadcasting in the socioeconomic development of Africa and other developing regions, as well as how public service broadcasting is being used to promote and preserve minority languages, is analysed. Also discussed is how technological changes and the growing involvement of people in online activities have transformed the way ethnographers conduct research in people's natural environment and in their online social spaces.

This chapter provides an important link to the rest of the chapters, not only in terms of the overarching ways that new technologies inform development activities but also in terms of the interconnection between theory and practice. Arguments have also been advanced to justify the focus of this book on practice rather than on theory, as is common in other texts. Each chapter is primarily concerned with or explores assumptions about the use of new technologies in different contexts.

Technology as the key concept that connects all chapters

Technology adoption and use is the common thread that links the chapters. Each chapter is primarily connected with theoretical explanations and practical examples of how people use new technologies in different cultural, political, social, structural and educational contexts. The point is made that, in the development of human societies, technology is the instrument that propels economic growth. It is the tool that helps to advance education and healthcare. Therefore, in all the chapters, technology is positioned as the agent of change. Each chapter questions and synthesises divergent theoretical assumptions relating to the role of technologies in human societies. In general, the diverse ways in which people use technologies constructively – to improve their health, to engage in politics and facilitate participatory democracy, to conduct ethnographic research, and to promote economic growth and language development via public service broadcasting – are analysed. The link between uptake of technology and development is widely discussed in the development communication literature.

In the field of development communication, a number of dominant theoretical paradigms stand out. These include but are not limited to the modernisation, dependency and culturalist paradigms (Houston and Jackson, 2009) and the social entrepreneurship approach (McAnany, 2012). McPhail (2009, pp. 8–9) summarised the principal arguments of modernisation theorists thus:

> modernization theory took hold and carried with it an element of economic determinism along with a parallel drive to expand democratic concepts and practices, such as the importance of voting behavior. Although the theories all recognized, to varying degrees, the role and importance of communication, they came from a number of social science disciplines. Sociologists, economists, anthropologists, political scientists, psychologists, social workers, media scholars, and others touched on aspects of modernization approaches. Many also took ideas and strategies from developed, industrialized nations and applied them with some fine tuning to the southern hemisphere. But the long range goal was similar. To make the inhabitants of poorer nations in the South more like the wealthier peoples of the North.

The modernisation theory, which was dominant between 1945 and 1965, is regarded as the first theory that was associated with the transfer of technology. Western scholars such as Lerner (1958), Schramm (1964) and Rogers (1969), who pushed this theory, regarded technology, including media technology, as the key facilitator of socioeconomic development in developing societies (Houston and Jackson, 2009). The modernisation 'model of change is based on the notion that there is a direct causal link between five sets of variables, namely, modernizing institutions, modern values, modern behavior, modern society and economic development' (Houston and Jackson, 2009, p. 107). In their view, therefore, 'modernization tends to support the agenda to transfer not only technology to "traditional" societies, but also the sociopolitical culture of modernity' (2009, p. 107). One of the key assumptions of this paradigm was that exposure to mass media would lead to an increase in the literacy rate, the growth of cities and industrial development. In the modernisation paradigm, development was conceived as and equated with economic growth as determined by a country's gross national product (GNP). As a reflection of the mood of that era, the post-World War II policies of many developing countries mirrored such an assumption. Based on experiences in the west soon after World War II, western scholars recommended that countries aspiring to achieve socioeconomic growth should invest in new technologies as a solution to problems of underdevelopment. Where this was not feasible, developing countries were advised to use foreign assistance packages to initiate economic development.

The emphasis on technology adoption is understandable. Many western countries had lived through the period of industrialisation, witnessed its impact on their economies and believed it to be a vital instrument that propels socioeconomic growth. The argument then was that, if technology assisted in the economic development of western countries, it would unquestionably engender a similar outcome in developing countries. Communication technology became a catchphrase for national socioeconomic development. Communication technology, particularly mass media technology, was strongly perceived as a major stimulus for economic growth. Accordingly, acquisition of mass media technology became a major objective of developing countries. Nevertheless, one critique of the modernisation theory is that it regarded 'modern life style' to be of better quality, so that development is seen as an effort to help the Third World 'catch up' (Houston and Jackson, 2009, p. 109). Another theoretical perspective – the dependency paradigm – that arose in the 1960s symbolised

> the goals of emerging nations for political, economic and cultural self-determination within the international community of nations. Much of the development promoted in this perspective is concerned primarily with political decisions focused on relationships between and within societies in regard to social, cultural, political and economic structures.
>
> (Houston and Jackson, 2009, p. 113)

It is within the dependency perspective that the concepts of cultural dependence and media imperialism are explored. It is argued that multinational corporations that manufacture mass media hardware and software dump these products – especially the software – at cheaper prices in developing countries where a local audience craving continuous enter-tainment actively consumes them. The media imperialism thesis is also seen as contrary to the dominant perspective on the role of the media in development (Fejes, 1981). Theoretically, media imperialism repre-sents the 'rejection by many Third World countries of Western models of modernization of which the earlier communication models were a part' (Fejes, 1981, p. 281). In the media imperialism thesis, the mass media were seen not as an instrument for national development, but – 'in a transnational context' – as instruments for the domination of the developing nations (Fejes, 1981, p. 281).

A related theoretical model of technology is the Marxist perspec-tive. The Marxist view on the role of the mass media perceives the broadcast media as an arm of the 'ideological state apparatus' and western capitalism. The Marxist view argues that the broadcast media, in concert with the bourgeoisie, the elite and the multinational cor-porations, promote needs, appetites, tastes and consumption habits that help to sustain capitalism and the status quo. This argument is fully represented in the dependency theory of development. Despite its attraction to critical scholars in developing countries, the depen-dency model was criticised for 'focusing too heavily on externalities and for being exaggerated in its claims that dependent development is always caused by outside investment' (Houston and Jackson, 2009, pp. 113–114). Nevertheless, one positive feature of the model is that it has enhanced public knowledge of the 'negative effects of tech-nology transfer' (Houston and Jackson, 2009, p. 114). Contrary to modernisation and dependency models of development, participatory development theory highlights the importance of empowering local people to initiate and engage in development projects at their own pace. According to scholars such as Servaes, Jacobson and White (1996), participatory development encourages the empowerment of ordinary people in developing countries to promote democracy and socioeco-nomic development of their societies (see Houston and Jackson, 2009). In participation, 'issues of cultural identity and context take precedence' (2009, p. 114).

In order to understand the extent to which new technologies have been adopted into local cultural practices, four important conditions have been outlined. The conditions are

a) the use of a given technology for purposes other than those for which it was originally intended; b) adaptation of local materials to meet the recurrent resource requirements of imported ICTs; c) modification of the technologies themselves to meet local needs; and d) modifications in personnel requirements, operational processes, and the like to suit local conditions.

(cited in Houston and Jackson, 2009, p. 114)

One benefit of participation theory is that it encourages the involvement of local people. Within the participation model, development projects are initiated and implemented by local people. Participation theory therefore 'emphasizes the ability of local communities for self-determination' (Houston and Jackson, 2009, p. 115). Nevertheless, participation theory is not without its drawbacks, one of which is that it 'glorifies and idealizes local relations, yet they may be laden with exploitation. It assumes that the local community will act equitably and efficiently, yet this is not always the case' (2009, p. 116). One of the weaknesses of the participation model of development is 'idealism..., which often assumes that development is an end point – higher standards of education or living will tie up all the loose ends in the social structure and create a global player' even if that may not be the case (Houston and Jackson, 2009, p. 116).

In the development communication literature, Contractor, Singhal and Rogers (1988, p. 129) described four theoretical models:

the utopian view that technology is intrinsically good for humankind, the dystopian view that technology is an unmitigated curse, the neutral view that technology per se has no important effects on society, and the contingency view that the potentially desirable and undesirable impacts of a technology are differentially determined by the context in which the technology is introduced at a particular time.

Contractor et al. found that utopians were generally predisposed to perceive technology as a solution to some of India's problems such as illiteracy, overpopulation and geographical distance, as well as economic and social gaps in the society. Beyond these, McPhail (2009) identified three other main lines of theoretical frameworks relating to technology and development. These include 'cultural imperialism, participatory communication, and entertainment-education' (McPhail, 2009, p. 16). These are similar to the earlier perspectives summarised above.

Not surprisingly, most of the studies on which western scholars based their arguments about modernisation or development were conducted in western countries. The scholars believed nevertheless that their research evidence was relevant to other societies irrespective of geographical location, cultural practices and level of development.

Major shifts in theoretical formulations

Despite the support given to the dominant perspectives of development communication in the 1950s, 1960s and early 1970s, the major epistemological basis of the perspectives was, by the mid-1970s, being questioned because of their inability to address the problems of developing countries. Rogers (1989) documented the shifts in theoretical formulations on development communication from the dominant perspectives to issues involving local participation, access to media and self-reliance in development planning and project implementation. According to Rogers (1989, p. 70), the dominant perspective was 'One-way in nature, from government-to-people; mass media-centered, especially featuring such big media as television; creating a "climate for development" through the mass media.' Contrary to this, alternative approaches to development feature 'participation, knowledge-sharing, and empowerment to the people; more attention to such little media as radio; equality achieved by focusing development programs on the weaker sections of a national population, including the poor, women, villagers' (Rogers, 1989, p. 70; Servaes, 2003).

McAnany (2012) has proposed a new paradigm for a new era, a practical approach to development that he calls 'social entrepreneurship'. He identifies two advocates of the idea: Muhammad Yunus, the founder of the renowned Grameen Bank in Bangladesh, and Bill Drayton, who is more commonly known for his work in the environmental protection agency (EPA) in Washington, DC, USA. Yunus's endeavour to assist impoverished women in Bangladesh eventually led to the development of microfinance ('very small nonsecured loans to poor people') across the world (McAnany, 2012, p. 109). Drayton founded the nongovernmental organisation (NGO) known as Ashoka in the 1980s. To put his ideas into practice, Drayton identified individuals whom he saw as capable agents of change and supported the development of their ideas through provision of funds. McAnany describes the social change practices that Yunus and Drayton advanced in their various endeavours as 'social entrepreneurship'.

Although less clearly defined, social entrepreneurship, according to McAnany, comes close to the participatory paradigm of communication for development because 'it tends to start locally to solve a problem with an innovative approach, and once the idea has been tested and shows positive results, it attempts to spread the approach to more people until it reaches a large scale' (McAnany, 2012, pp. 107–108). He explains that social entrepreneurship is a method that examines social problems that are not being dealt with in order to uncover local solutions. He admits there is no agreement among communication for development scholars about the idea of social entrepreneurship and points out that what is lacking in the approaches adopted by Yunus and Drayton is that neither of them addresses communication as an important element in the process of change. He states that Drayton does not acknowledge the important contributions that communication technologies have made to business growth. As he puts it,

> A current change to be noted is the rapid emergence of newer ICTs that include the internet, cell phones, social networking, and their applications in development and social change. One current example is the rapid diffusion of cell phones in Africa and Asia that has happened in the past six years and the various uses they have been put to by even the poor in these regions.
>
> (McAnany, 2012, p. 112)

One idea that communication for development shares with social entrepreneurship is that *'all change is local'* (McAnany, 2012, p. 113). He points out that what Yunus achieved in his Grameen Bank project and what Drayton is striving to encourage in his Ashoka project is 'a grassroots approach to social change' (McAnany, 2012, p. 113).

The diverse views in the literature and the different contexts in which new technologies are seen as influential in developing societies are critically analysed in this book.

Why the focus is on practice rather than theory

This book is unique in various ways. It departs from existing texts on development communication that focus essentially on theories of development. It draws on existing theoretical assumptions about technology and development to demonstrate pragmatically what people in developing countries are doing with technologies to improve their socioeconomic conditions. The relationship between theory and practice that is largely missing in existing texts is given special but critical attention. Rather than restricting the discussion to the analysis of theoretical models of development, new perspectives are explored through social, political, economic, cultural and structural issues that inform why some people in some countries use technologies the way they do. Of course, theory is important. It serves as an organising framework for disseminating ideas. It enables a researcher, for example, to organise and emphasise certain facts. As Sahay and Walsham (1995, p. 112) argue, a good theory supports 'the refinement and testing of models and frameworks'. Additionally, they state that 'a good theory allows the researcher to inform practice in a meaningful manner... Theories also serve socio-political needs related to legitimacy and recognition of an academic discipline.'

It is important for us to understand what people do with technology in different contexts in different societies. This is the 'practice' part of this book. A key question examined here is: what are people in developing countries *doing* with new technologies, and how are they using the technologies? (See Couldry, 2004). This is one innovative feature of this book that sits at the intersection of theory and practice. There is a mutually beneficial relationship between theory and practice. In general, theories are proposed to understand human behaviour. Various theories provide an organising framework for understanding the themes discussed in the chapters. Couldry (2004, p. 120) argued that 'in formulating a new paradigm of media research, we should open our lens even wider to take in the whole range of practices in which media consumption and media-related talk is embedded, including practices of avoiding or selecting out, media inputs'.

In his discussion of the sociology of practice, Couldry (2004, p. 121) asked two important questions that are focused on media: 'what types of things do people do in relation to media? And what types of things do people say in relation to media?' Although this book looks at various uses of technologies in different contexts in developing societies, Couldry's questions are relevant because they help us to examine not only what people *do* with new technologies but also what people say about technologies in their everyday life. The significance of practice, according to Couldry (2004, p. 125), is that it seeks to 'ask open questions about what people are doing and how they categorise what they are doing'. Here, we seek to understand how people perceive and use new technologies in their everyday lives because, as Couldry (2004, p. 129) further states, 'we need the perspective of practice to help us address how media are embedded in the interlocking fabric of social and cultural life'. Elsewhere, Christensen and Røpke (2010, p. 234) state that 'ICTs have become integrated into a wide range of practices of everyday life.' Nevertheless, the practice approach discussed in the chapters also explores the conditions of the marginalised, those who are silenced in society and are therefore unable to use or appropriate new communication technologies.

Outline of the chapters

The debate on the interlocking relationship between new technologies and the socioeconomic development of Africa and other developing countries is examined in Chapter 2. While research evidence shows a positive relationship between uptake of new technologies and economic growth of developing countries, that evidence is disputed by some scholars who caution against undue optimism. The growing debate in the literature has triggered the question: is the presence of new technologies evidence of socioeconomic progress in countries that adopt new technologies? Or, does failure by a country to adopt technology imply lack of economic progress by the country? The chapter examines methodically the debate in the literature on new technologies and economic growth, including how the adoption and use of technology is contributing to the growth of Africa and other developing regions of the world. While adoption of new technologies is contributing to the development of Africa and other regions, the technologies have also exacerbated existing infrastructural, structural, economic, social, political and cultural obstacles that constrain Africans and people in other developing regions from harnessing new technologies in productive ways. Another problem that hinders wider constructive use of technology is the absence of an enabling environment that promotes awareness, understanding and acceptance of the values of new technologies.

Also explored are the various ways that scholars have conceived the term 'development'. Two important questions are posed to map scholarly views on the concept of development. The questions are: What does it mean for a country to be developed? What conditions should be in place and at what level before a country can be adjudged to be developed? Nobel laureate Amartya Sen (1999) conceives development partly as a measure of the level of freedom that individuals enjoy in their society. He describes development as a process of increasing the freedoms that individuals enjoy. In his view, freedom is fundamental to the achievement of human objectives. According to Sen, 'Development requires the removal of major sources of unfreedom: poverty as well as tyranny, poor economic opportunities as well as systematic social deprivation, neglect of public facilities as well as intolerance or overactivity of repressive states' (1999, p. 3).

Chapter 2 also analyses theories that inform the relationship between technology adoption and socioeconomic growth. The theories include but are not limited to the diffusion of innovations model that shows how new technologies or ideas are introduced, adopted and diffused in human society. Another perspective is the endogenous growth theory, which looks at how technology and human capital drive economic growth. Other topics examined include digital divide and digital poverty, how technology is empowering disadvantaged women in Africa and other developing regions, and Internet penetration and use in Africa.

Chapter 3 analyses the history of public service broadcasting (PSB), which has been dominated by critical questions about its remit, the best funding mechanism to sustain the model of broadcasting, the essential elements that distinguish PSB from commercial channels, its role in democratic societies and its relevance in the age of new technologies in which information is openly available on the Internet. The emergence of the Internet has exacerbated rather than eased the debate. Concerns have persisted also because of the central role that PSB is believed to play in facilitating deliberative democracy, free expression of diverse views and equal access to information, and as a medium for cultural expression and language preservation. PSB is premised on the right to freedom of expression. The chapter looks at PSB in Africa and other developing and developed countries, in particular the challenges that confront PSB owing to technological transformations, and how it serves as a vehicle for economic development and preservation of lesser used languages. Also examined are critical questions about the best funding model for PSB that will guarantee independence for the broadcaster and therefore freeing it from political interference and the influence of advertisers and other market forces.

New technologies have raised further concerns about the lack of global recognition for Indigenous knowledge systems and the rights of Indigenous people to their intellectual property. This is the focus of Chapter 4. In it, Greaves (1996, pp. 25–26) makes the powerful argument that

> While we assiduously protect rights to valuable knowledge among ourselves, indigenous people have never been accorded similar rights over their cultural knowledge. Existing Western intellectual property laws support, promote, and excuse the wholesale, uninvited appropriation of whatever indigenous item strikes our fancy or promises profit, with no obligation or expectation to allow the originators of the knowledge a say or a share in the proceeds.

Critical to any discussion on the intellectual property rights of Indigenous people is the question of ownership and preservation of

Indigenous knowledge, art, craft and traditional practices, as well as respect for the cultural expressions of the people. Indigenous people are concerned that new technologies have presented them with a dilemma. While technologies have increased the profile and prominence of Indigenous people across the globe, the same technologies have also encouraged the widespread unauthorised sale and criminal duplication and reproduction of Indigenous cultural expressions. Indigenous people hold the view that new technologies have not only denied them their right to express themselves but also undermined their rights to protect their traditional practices, their land, art, craft, sacred sites and other cultural expressions, including rights to ownership of their intellectual property. Technologies are seen to have threatened and indeed undermined the right of Indigenous people to protect their private and sacred knowledge from unauthorised publication on the Internet. Also examined in the chapter are other ways that globalisation and technological changes have created problems for Indigenous people, including how their intellectual property rights are being violated and abused.

Indigenous people are concerned not only about the non-recognition and lack of protection for their intellectual property rights in relation to arts and copyright, but also that other areas of their cultural heritage and intellectual property rights such as language, dance, song, story, sacred sites and objects have not been recognised and, therefore, have not been protected. Part of the reason why existing intellectual property laws are believed to be inappropriate and ineffective in protecting Indigenous cultural expressions is that cultural creations are owned and managed by Indigenous communities rather than by individuals.

In different societies, new technologies serve different important roles. Chapter 5 examines the specific ways in which African youth use new technologies to empower themselves, to engage in participatory communication in the public sphere, to contribute to public discourse and civic deliberation, and to hold political leaders to account. The chapter draws on the theoretical frameworks of uses and gratifications, Jürgen Habermas's theory of the public sphere, and the media richness theory to show how African youth use new technologies to express themselves, as well as to contribute to political and social debates in their societies. These issues are important in the digital era in which new technologies empower citizens by giving voice to the voiceless. However, the extent to which new technologies are used by African youth to express their views and to participate in the public sphere has drawn little attention from researchers and communication scholars. Research into how African youth are harnessing new technologies is critical to the development of knowledge and official policy for social change in the continent. The youth constitute an important segment of African society because of their ability to engineer social change.

Chapter 6 looks closely at the various ways that new technologies are affecting journalistic practices in Africa and other developing regions. In the digital era, Singer (2006) argues that the free, participatory and democratic appeal of online media has encouraged all types of news, resulting in different kinds of news reporters and different genres of news. One effect of this transformation in technology is that our understanding and perceptions of journalists as gatekeepers who provide audiences with news and information are being challenged by the active involvement of civil society in news reporting and production. Before the emergence of new technologies, news was collected and distributed by professional journalists. Now, the outlets for news gathering, production and reporting have broadened to include citizens with computer access, digital cameras, mobile phones and other electronic devices. Access to new technologies has empowered citizens to produce news as professional journalists do.

In Africa, the involvement of citizens in the news process is growing. The chapter analyses new forms of citizen journalism, not only from western scholarship but also from non-western contexts, as shown in research conducted in Africa. The point is made that new technologies have not reduced or eliminated the threats to the lives and freedom of expression of professional and citizen journalists in Africa. If anything, new technologies pose new threats and challenges to professional and citizen journalists. The concept of network-convergent journalism is analysed, including how it is promoting greater interaction between professional journalists and citizens. Other issues discussed include the role of social media in engineering political change in Africa and other parts of the world, the strengths and drawbacks of social media use, online discussion forums and their important role in Africa, as well as specific instances of citizen journalism practices in Kenya and Nigeria.

Chapter 7 examines efforts by researchers in the health sector, medical doctors, governments, NGOs, aid agencies, communication scholars and civil society groups to investigate and understand the main causes of the HIV/AIDS virus, how it is spread, the factors that slow or hasten the spread of the virus, the existing course of treatment for the virus, strategies used to achieve attitude and behaviour change in various countries and the future outlook for developing a vaccine for the virus. Research shows that in the campaign to stop further spread of the virus, cultural practices and belief systems act as a major impediment. Public information campaigns to achieve attitude and behaviour change have moved from the use of the mass media to the use of social media and other digital technologies to reach the youth, to create awareness and to sensitise the public to the disease. Regardless of its shortcomings, entertainment-education is seen as a tested and valuable strategy that is used in the campaign to achieve HIV/AIDS prevention.

Chapter 8 looks critically at the challenges of conducting ethnographic research in natural settings and in the online world of research participants, particularly research relating to technology adoption and use. Ethnography is a qualitative research paradigm that is widely applied in studies in which the researcher may not know much about the social groups or communities that are being investigated. Therefore, ethnography looks at how individuals or groups make sense of the world in which they inhabit. In their attempt to understand the multiple realities that exist in various societies, ethnographers do not start their research with fixed or prearranged propositions to be tested and confirmed or refuted.

Ethnographic researchers start from the premise that human lives are socially and culturally constructed and that social meanings cannot be predicted and measured with statistical instruments that are commonly used in positivist research. Rather than undertake research on the assumption that there is one reality out there to be discovered and described, ethnographers proceed cautiously on the assumption that there are multiple realities in human societies and those realities cannot be quantified and measured through strict scientific procedures. Against this background, the chapter discusses the advantages and drawbacks of ethnographic research, and examines closely the different methods of data collection in traditional ethnographic research, as well as ethical issues in traditional ethnography. Owing to the growing engagement of people in online activities, the chapter analyses ethnography in online environments, including the different methods of conducting online interviews and online observations, as well as the ethical challenges that confront online ethnographers.

Chapter 9, the final chapter, analyses mobile phone use in Africa and other parts of the developing world. There is no question that mobile phones are transforming the mode of communication in Africa, including how African citizens interact among themselves, how they do business, how they work and how they entertain themselves. Mobile phones have also reduced or removed the physical distance between people who reside in rural and remote communities and those who live in cities. The chapter argues that mobile phones have been successfully harnessed by African citizens because the technology has many communication benefits and has therefore filled a niche in the lives of ordinary people.

This chapter presents a general introduction of the eclectic topics covered in the book. It contributes to theoretical and practical understanding of the factors that drive adoption and use of new technologies in different contexts in Africa and other societies. It analyses social, political, cultural, structural, infrastructural, economic and global influences that affect technology adoption. While some people assume incorrectly that new technologies have spread across all countries at an equal rate, the reality is that some people in some countries, particularly people in remote and rural locations in developing countries, still lack access to technology. Access to technology, however, is only one part of the problem. If people have access to technology but lack the knowledge and skills necessary to use it in meaningful ways, they cannot make valuable use of the technologies that are within their reach. As Delgado-P (2002) stated with regard to the situation in Indigenous communities, 'indigenous worlds are today still divided between the cybernetically informed and the non-informed. There are those that would like to plug in PCs but can't; there are those who have computers but are getting a headache from them.' What this highlights is the digital divide that exists in many parts of the world in different forms, namely those who have access to technology and those who lack access, those who have knowledge of technologies and those who don't, as well as those who have the skills to use the technologies and those who don't. While it is true that new technologies are having impacts on people in different parts of Africa and the developing world in various ways, there are still impediments to people's ability to acquire or access technologies.

2
New Technologies and the Socioeconomic Development of Africa

Introduction

There is a growing belief that new information and communication technologies (ICTs) play an important role in the economic growth of nations. However, the extent to which new technologies accelerate the socioeconomic development of developing countries has been debated vigorously in the development literature. While some scholars see a direct relationship between the uptake of new technologies and enhancement of economic development, other scholars express doubts. This has prompted the question: do new technologies trigger economic development? Do countries that fail to introduce and adopt new technologies lag behind the rest of the world?

The question of the relationship between new technologies and economic growth has received significant attention in the literature. Madon (2000) believes that new technologies can aid various aspects of development. Still, the nature of the relationship between new technologies and socioeconomic development is contested by scholars. This chapter examines critically scholarly arguments about new technologies and economic growth, including the extent to which communication technologies contribute to the socioeconomic development of Africa and other developing regions.

Ideological schools

There are at least two dominant schools of thought that contest the impact of new technologies on Africa's socioeconomic development. These are the optimists (regarded as technological determinists) and the pessimists (referred to as the naysayers). Technological determinists perceive new technologies as the solutions to Africa's economic problems. Africa's transition to socioeconomic development, they argue, would be smoother and more rapid if it harnessed the full benefits of communication technologies. The pessimists advance equally strong arguments, such as the notion that there is no direct link between the uptake of technologies and Africa's economic development. They contend that Africa is under pressure to introduce and adopt new technologies because it will serve the interests of western communication hardware and software producers who are keen to market their products in Africa. There are also those who hold the middle ground that suggests that technologies are neither helpful nor harmful to developing countries. Regardless of the divergent views, 'The challenge is for African governments, private businesses, community groups and individuals to find practical ways to unlock the keys that prevent the continent from accessing the full benefits of new technology...' (Obijiofor, 2009a, p. 33).

Relationship between technology and economic growth

As far back as 2000, Castells had argued that countries that neglected the valuable benefits that accrue from introduction and adoption of new technologies would have only themselves to blame, as they would be marginalised in the global economy (Castells, 2000). Similarly, Mansell and Wehn (1998) state that, although developing countries may not have the capacity to develop or produce technology, their ability to adopt and modify technology will be essential to the development of information societies. Parmentier and Huyer (2008, p. 14) suggest that while the benefits of new technologies will elude countries that lack the technological means, facilities or the economic foundation to adopt them, the most urgent concern for those developing countries aspiring to achieve the Millennium Development Goals (MDGs) is the skilful use of existing technologies.

The World Summit on the Information Society (WSIS) states in its Declaration of Principles in 2003 that the transfer of technology and investment in ICTs constitute effective vehicles for attainment of sustainable information society by developing nations. Specifically, Principle 51 of the WSIS Declaration of Principles states categorically that

> The usage and deployment of ICTs should seek to create benefits in all aspects of our daily life. ICT applications are potentially important in government operations and services, health care and health information, education and training, employment, job creation, business,

agriculture, transport, protection of environment and management of natural resources, disaster prevention, and culture, and to promote eradication of poverty and other agreed development goals. ICTs should also contribute to sustainable production and consumption patterns and reduce traditional barriers, providing an opportunity for all to access local and global markets in a more equitable manner. Applications should be user-friendly, accessible to all, affordable, adapted to local needs in languages and cultures, and support sustainable development. To this effect, local authorities should play a major role in the provision of ICT services for the benefit of their populations.

(WSIS, 2003, Principle 51)

This principle is based on a number of assumptions. It assumes that ICT acquisition and use would benefit human society regardless of structural and social barriers that may prevent people from productively harnessing technologies. It also assumes (without clarifying what they might be) that 'traditional barriers' must be removed before ICTs can contribute to sustainable production and consumption. To promote capacity building and worldwide participation in the information society, Principle 33 encourages partnership between developed and developing countries, including countries whose economies are in transition. This principle ignores the historical economic and power relationship between developed and developing countries, between colonial powers and the colonised people that contributed immensely to the underdevelopment and exploitation of developing countries.

Perhaps more relevant in terms of the objectives of the WSIS Declaration of Principles is Principle 43, which highlights clearly the need to integrate ICT efforts into national and regional development programmes. Essentially, if countries make no deliberate and concerted efforts to integrate ICT policies into their national development programmes, they can expect the benefits of ICT adoption to elude them. This point seemed to be reinforced in a statement by the United Nations Conference on Trade and Development (UNCTAD) that said: 'Since new and emerging technologies increasingly affect the volume, composition and direction of world trade, countries that are unable to gain access to these new technologies, and successfully absorb them, will find themselves progressively disengaged from the global economy' (cited in Juma and Clark, 2002, p. 2). This and similar messages from international intergovernmental organisations and United Nations agencies have attracted the attention of African countries that believe that introduction and adoption of new technologies will enable them to leapfrog other stages of development. As Juma and Clark (2002, p. 3) noted,

> The application of these ideas to the developing countries took a number of different forms, including the mistaken belief that the mere transfer of technology defined in a narrow sense would enable developing countries to leap across the centuries and repeat the industrial revolution. It was with this false hope that the United Nations Conference on the Application of Science and Technology for the Benefit of Less Developed Areas was held in Geneva in 1963. It was believed then that the developing countries could benefit from the experiences of the industrialised countries and that there were no vested interests to undermine the success of such countries in assimilating imported technology.

These assumptions were strengthened by the belief that there existed a direct relationship between technology adoption in developed countries and the end of economic deprivation. Technology uptake was therefore perceived as a solution to poverty (Juma and Clark, 2002). These assumptions and other principles contained in the WSIS Declaration of Principles in 2003, in effect, acknowledged the significant and beneficial impact that new technologies will have on developing countries in terms of the effect on the socioeconomic conditions of the people, healthcare, employment opportunities, educational development, agricultural production, business growth, management of the environment and alleviation of poverty, as well as improvements in transport and infrastructure.

Regardless of these positive views about the role of technologies in society, Rodriguez and Wilson (2000, p. 3) offer a contrary view, suggesting that 'Although these new technologies appear to be improving economic performance and welfare among the user populations, the link between ICTs and society-wide economic progress has been more elusive.' May (2012) cautions that a one-size-fits-all adoption of ICTs to solve all problems in human society could in fact widen the existing knowledge gap between urban and rural areas, and also exacerbate the gulf between the rich and the poor. Balnaves and Caputi (1997) advocate emphasis on quality of life rather than on technology. In their view, 'The concept of the information age, predicated upon technology and the media, deals with the transformation of society. However, without improvements in quality of life there would seem to be little point in adopting online multimedia services' (Balnaves and Caputi, 1997, cited in Selwyn, 2003, p. 108). In his contribution to the debate, Selwyn (2003, p. 109) asks an important question: 'If one of the perceived benefits of using ICT is to "increase a sense of community", "trust", and "interaction" between people – why would people already established and "strong" in these areas necessarily turn to ICT over and above their already successful sources of community and interaction?' He cautions that researchers and other scholars who address the question of technology and society must shun the attempt to assume that 'technology is always (a) available and (b) a "good" thing' (Selwyn, 2003, p. 112).

Despite these doubts, some scholars believe that a strong link exists between ICT adoption and poverty reduction (Flor, 2001; Marker, McNamara and Wallace, 2001). In the development and ICT literature, there is a strong view that new technologies are synonymous with economic growth and that developing countries must not miss the great opportunity to use the technologies to address the multifarious socioeconomic and political problems that confront them. The longer developing countries delay the introduction and use of technologies, the wider will the gap between the information rich and information poor grow. As Marker et al. (2001, p. 4) argued categorically, 'Properly deployed, ICTs have enormous potential as tools to increase information flows and empower poor people.' Nevertheless, doubts exist. For instance, Avgerou (2010) argues that despite claims that new technologies can improve the socioeconomic conditions of people in developing countries, it is often the case that the development potential of new technologies is overstated. While Röller and Waverman (2001) demonstrate a link between economic growth and diffusion of new technologies, Gillwald (2010) argues, however, that the evidence requires further clarification with regard to the nature of the causal relationship. On that basis, she asks: 'Does ICT penetration improve economic growth, or does economic growth drive ICT penetration?' (Gillwald, 2010, p. 81). It has been pointed out that access to information through new technologies must be seen as 'a question not only of connectivity, but also of other deprivations that influence the capability of individuals and communities to access and use these new tools' (May, 2012, p. 35). This is a valid point because many people in developing countries, particularly those who reside in remote and rural locations, lack access to new technologies.

In their analysis of the relationship between poverty and general lack of access to information technology, Marker et al. (2001, p. 7) state:

> Poverty has multiple and complex causes. The poor are not just deprived of basic resources. They lack access to information that is vital to their lives and livelihoods: information about market prices for the goods they produce, about health, about the structure and services of public institutions; about their rights. They lack political visibility and voice in the institutions and power relations that shape their lives. They lack access to knowledge, education and skills development that could improve their livelihoods. They often lack access to markets and institutions, both governmental and societal, that could provide them with needed resources and services. They lack access to, and information about, income earning opportunities.

Regardless of the diverse views in the literature, Sein and Harindranath (2004) point out that there is lack of clarity on the role that ICTs play in national development. In other words, knowledge of how technologies influence national development is still missing. What do we really mean when we use the term 'development'?

Different views about development

The concept of development is equally contested. What does it mean for a country to be developed? What conditions should be in place and at what level before a country can be adjudged to be developed? There are diverse readings of the term 'development'. Definitions of development differ according to historical and other conditions (Andrade and Urquhart, 2010). For example, the concept has moved on from its original connection with economic growth and modernisation as conceptualised by the west to another view that associates it with 'health, education and quality of life that recognises cultural differences' (Andrade and Urquhart, 2010, pp. 353–354). There is also the notion of development that relates to the Human Development Index. This indicator includes the following elements: income, life expectancy and level of education. Nobel laureate Amartya Sen (1999) conceptualises development as a measure of the level of freedom that individuals enjoy in their society. He perceives development as a process of increasing the freedoms that people relish. Freedom therefore is seen as key to achievement of human objectives. According to Sen, 'Development requires the removal of major sources of unfreedom: poverty as well as tyranny, poor economic opportunities as well as systematic social deprivation, neglect of public facilities as well as intolerance or overactivity of repressive states' (1999, p. 3).

Apart from freedom, another key concept in Sen's analysis is the term 'capability approach'. He believes the chief aim of human development should be 'our capability to lead the kind of lives we have reason to value' (Sen, 1999, p. 285) instead of focusing on gross domestic product and other western indices of development. In his thesis on development, Sen identified five freedoms that determine the extent to which individuals can be seen to be developed. These are: political freedoms that include freedom of expression and the liberty to examine and question people in positions of authority; economic facilities that include possibilities for increase in people's income; social opportunities that include access to education and health services and opportunities for involvement in other social activities; transparency guarantees that highlight openness and accountability by government officials, thus underlining the extent to which the people have faith in the government; and protective security that relates to the safety of the weak and defenceless members of society.

Barder (2012) agrees with Sen. In his view, 'development must be judged by its impact on people, not only by changes in their income but more generally in terms of their choices, capabilities and freedoms; and we should be concerned about the distribution of these improvements, not just the simple average for a society' (Barder, 2012).

Sen's work on development has been criticised by some scholars. In his critique, O'Hearn (2009) states that one weakness in Sen's analysis is the absence of a theory that addresses global capitalism, such as inequalities in trade, unfair division of labour at the international level, the application of global authority and the activities of global finance organisations.O'Hearn argues that 'Sen has either not read or simply decided to ignore the role of the West and global processes in causing famine....'

Theoretical frameworks

A number of theories underpin the important role that new technologies play in socioeconomic development and in the campaign to alleviate poverty. One of the theories is the endogenous growth theory (also known as new-growth theory). The theory states that technology and human capital drive economic growth and facilitate the process of development of a country. 'Logically, workers who are better-educated, better-fed, healthier and technologically capable can produce more than those who are illiterate, hungry, unhealthy and unskilled' (Hosman and Fife, 2008, p. 55). Other scholars (e.g., Hudson, 2006, 1978) have also highlighted the value of telecommunications technology to developing countries.

Reinforcing their argument that new technologies contribute to socioeconomic development, Hosman and Fife (2008, p. 56) identify various ways through which ICT use can empower communities in developing countries:

> In the field of ICT, broadband connectivity can enable local small business entrepreneurship, provide crop pricing information in advance of sales, increase knowledge of successful farming techniques and of labour opportunities and going wage-rates, and allow for the institution of tele-education and tele-health.

This is consistent with the World Bank's and the African Development Bank's (ADB) view about the revolutionary impact that new communication technologies are having on Africa. According to the World Bank and the ADB, 'The effect of ICTs on the African economy is impressive, but it is the way they are changing the everyday lives of Africans that is genuinely transformational' (The World Bank and African Development Bank, 2012, p. 13). These two global financial institutions speak with high optimism about the value of new technologies to Africa:

> ICTs now offer major opportunities to advance human development – from providing basic access to education or health information to making cash payments and stimulating citizen involvement in the democratic process. Phones, computers and websites are powerful tools but it is individuals, communities and firms that are driving change. Mobile phones and the internet are helping to release the dynamism of African society. State-owned monopoly telephone companies were, for too long, a barrier to African ingenuity – due to waiting lists, high prices and unreliable services – but now a thriving local ICT sector is part of the solution, not the problem. In many of Africa's largest cities, smartphones can now be obtained for under US$100.
>
> (World Bank and African Development Bank, 2012, p. 13)

This is an exceptionally optimistic assessment of the impact of ICTs on Africa. The idea that smartphones can be bought at a cost lower than

US$100 seems to suggest uncritically that many people in Africa can afford the money. Yet it is common knowledge that US$100 can achieve a lot in Africa. It can feed a family of four in a rural village for more than one month. It can pay the annual school fees of a secondary school student. The money can go a long way in Africa. Many people do not earn that much on a monthly or six-monthly basis, if the local exchange rate is taken into consideration.

The World Bank and the ADB note that although new technologies are having a significant impact on Africa in various ways, there are some challenges and drawbacks. As they point out, 'This growing social and economic dependence on ICTs brings new challenges, not least the need for infrastructure to become more robust and resilient, and for services to become more reliable. Issues of cyber-security and data protection will also come to the fore as security and trust become increasingly important' (p. 13). Similarly, preliminary research on ICT adoption in Africa and the Asia-Pacific regions found serious barriers that hinder use of new technologies in educational and socioeconomic development. Some of the impediments include lack of infrastructure support, lack of access to new technologies and lack of opportunities for training and skills development, as well as rigid social systems that determine who has access to new technologies and who is denied access (Obijiofor, Inayatullah and Stevenson, 2000).

Another theoretical framework is diffusion of innovations that contributes to our understanding of how new technologies (including new ideas) are introduced, adopted and diffused in human society and the contexts in which the diffusion takes place. One of the contextual factors is the role of culture in the adoption of new technologies. Yet another theoretical framework that applies to the introduction and use of new technologies is the Actor Network Theory (ANT). The theory aims to show the relationship between society and technology or, as some scholars (Andrade and Urquhart, 2010) have mentioned, the relationship between human and non-human elements. As they argue, 'ANT makes it possible to frame the analysis of the interplay between technology and society in the middle ground amid two conflicting approaches:

(1) technological determinism; and
(2) social determinism' (Andrade and Urquhart, 2010, p. 356).

Still another theoretical perspective is social embeddedness, which 'takes the view that the development and use of ICT artifacts in developing countries concern the construction of new techno-organizational arrangements in the local context of a developing country' (Avgerou, 2010, p. 4). The theory brings into research focus issues associated with meaning – 'the meaning of the developmental capacity of ICT within the context of an innovation effort – and associates people's actions with the frameworks of interpretation sustained by the cultures of their context' (Avgerou, 2010, pp. 11–12).

The question has been asked: 'What can information and communication technologies (ICTs) do for the world's 900 million extremely poor people who live in rural areas?' (Gillman, Pinzon and Samii, 2003). The authors note there was agreement at the WSIS side event that technology was a plausible tool but not a solution. This is based on the understanding that development is not all about technology or information but has everything to do with empowering people economically, socially and politically (Gillman et al., 2003). They make the point that when we talk about new technologies, the accent must be on communication rather than technology. This is because communication entails participation in knowledge sharing, as well as deference toward diversity and cultural differences.

Michael Spence (2010) argues from a growth and development viewpoint that ICTs have created many opportunities such as avenues for safe and secure savings, more channels of relevant information relating to weather, market prices and market conditions, and opportunities to get credit, banking and payment services. On this basis, he argues that 'The rapid deployment of ICT will provide additional tools to facilitate knowledge transfer and its productive deployment . . . will make it more efficient, more inclusive, and less costly' (Spence, 2010, p. 6).

New technologies as facilitators of Africa's development

Across the world, global attention has been focused on Africa and special economic initiatives have been mapped out by international finance organisations, regional economic communities and intergovernmental agencies to assist Africa. Underpinning the global emergency assistance package to Africa is the notion that introduction and adoption of new technologies will help the region to overcome most of its socioeconomic problems and enable the continent to reap the benefits associated with new technologies. As far back as 2002, the heads of state of the Group of Eight industrialised countries approved 'the program and implementation plan for the New Partnership for Africa's Development (NEPAD)' (Okpaku, 2003, p. 23). The NEPAD programme was later adopted in July 2002 by the Summit of the Organisation of African Unity (OAU, now known as African Union, AU). According to Okpaku (2003), the NEPAD programme was focused on information and communication technology for development. Similarly, the G8 Action Plan for Africa pledged to encourage the use of ICT for development of Africa. More significantly, the G8 member countries pledged to provide support to assist Africa to boost its ability to develop the capacity to harness new technologies (Okpaku, 2003). Specifically, Article 5.5 of the G8 Action Plan for Africa pledged to support plans by Africa to harness ICT to address health and education problems. It also pledged to support Africa to increase access to ICT and to use new technologies to address governance, and to facilitate the development of appropriate strategies that will aid greater 'efficiency, effectiveness, transparency and accountability of government' (Okpaku, 2003, p. 25).

In the context of Africa, Emeagwali (2007) is adamant that a positive relationship exists between new technologies and economic growth. He states that 'Africa's inability to realise its potential and embrace technology has left it at the mercy of the West.' For its part, the African Information Society Initiative (AISI) perceives new technologies as valuable tools that will transform African economies. AISI argues that ICTs will help Africa to leap through the challenges that confront the continent as it struggles to achieve economic growth and development (May, 2012). As a reflection of the prevailing sentiments, many African countries have begun to invest heavily in ICT infrastructure acquisition and development.

Wilson and Wong (2003, p. 156) express optimism about the influence that new technologies can have on economic growth. They state that 'Africa's future growth and the well-being of its people will hinge in part on its capacity to make these resources widely available.' They make the point, as other scholars have done, about the many possibilities that new technologies have for Africa. Two key reasons are offered for the widespread adoption and acceptance of new technologies by Africans, Asians and South Americans. The first, they argued, is the inability of the old telecommunications systems to produce dependable, candid and extensive networks for information transmission. In the mid-1990s, about 1.2 million telecommunications customers in sub-Saharan Africa waited for approximately five and half years for telephone line connection. The weak and poor quality of telecommunications services thus created a large population of discontented people. The second factor that accounted for the widespread uptake of new technologies was the economic globalisation that increased worldwide competition. Against this background, they state that

> One of the first questions a potential investor asks of African and other governments around the world is whether the country has a modern and effective telecommunications system. Telecommunications systems have become a requirement for attracting direct foreign investment. Inexpensive, reliable, and ready access to information and communication is no longer a luxury for the few; it is a necessity for the many.
>
> (Wilson and Wong, 2003, pp. 156–157)

Former United Nations Secretary-General Kofi Annan also canvassed the great potential of new technologies to enhance economic growth and development in human society, particularly in developing countries. Noting that new technologies can assist humanity to turn this possibility into substantial opportunities, Annan (2003, p. xiv) argues that nowhere is the need for new technologies more acute than in Africa. He says pointedly that 'ICT is a chance for Africa. It is not, of course, a magic formula that is going to solve all the problems. But it is a powerful tool for economic growth and poverty eradication, which can facilitate the integration of African countries into the global market' (Annan, 2003, p. xiv). He warned that reducing the digital divide in Africa and other parts of the world would require leadership and willingness by leaders, the public and private sectors to commit to resources. In his view, 'investments will still be necessary, not only to ensure that people have the technical skills and the literacy level needed to use information technology facilities and service them, but also to create content that reflects the interests of that part of the world' (Annan, 2003, p. xiv).

There are nevertheless views that caution against excessive optimism about the ability of new technologies to transform Africa instantly. A paper prepared for the NEPAD Ministerial Conference on Science and Technology for Development (Chetty, n.d.) makes the argument that, while empirical evidence shows that new technologies are an influential force in Africa's move toward socioeconomic development (such as the link between ICT access and gross domestic product per capita), there is inadequate evidence to explain the type of relationship. The paper states that although new technologies can serve as a trigger for economic growth, technologies should not be seen as a solution for problems in developing countries. 'ICTs are merely tools; and no single technology in isolation can solve the problem of poverty which has multiple causes and is complex and multidimensional' (Chetty, n.d., p. 1).

Fuchs (2008, p. 304) notes that developing countries are operating in the international community from a position of disadvantage, as these countries are excluded from wealth and they are also unable to harness new technologies. He cites two gripping statistics to illustrate how the developed countries have ensured the underdevelopment of developing countries. In 1999, for example, $56 billion in foreign aid came from the west to the developing countries. However, the receiving countries paid more than double that amount just to service their debt to the west. Specifically, developing countries paid back $136 billion to service their debt to western countries (Fuchs, 2008). He notes further that although Africa comprised 14 per cent of the global population as at 2005, only 1.7 per cent of the African population are categorised as global Internet users (Fuchs, 2008). While there is a powerful message in his figures, it must be noted they are somewhat dated. More recent figures about Internet users and penetration in Africa are presented in this chapter in the section entitled 'Status of new technologies in Africa'.

In what ways can new technologies facilitate the socioeconomic development of Africa? Gumuchio-Dagron (2003) ridicules the view that ICTs will propel developing countries to attain socioeconomic development on the same scale as developed countries. He says that it is presumptuous to argue that making computers and Internet connectivity available to the poor in developing countries will eliminate poverty. In his view, 'Development is much more complex than planting the seeds of ICTs in poor rural areas or marginalized urban neighbourhoods... ICTs are no magic solution for anything...' (Gumuchio-Dagron, 2003, p. 27). He argues that 'The development of local content is the single most important non-negotiable condition for the development of ICTs for social change and material progress in urban and rural communities' (Gumuchio-Dagron, 2003, p. 34).

In a similar tone, Figueres (2003) notes that despite advantages that new technologies may have conferred on humanity, there are many people who lack access to the technologies. In fact, the Internet Live Stats (n.d. – http://www.internetlivestats.com/internet-users/) reports that 'Around 40% of the world population has an internet connection today... In 1995, it was less than 1%' (Internet Live Stats, n.d.). This leaves a large number of people in Africa and other parts of the world without access to the Internet.

Citing the benefits of new technologies such as job creation, business expansion and improvements in the lives of people, Figueres (2003,

p. ix) cautions that the effects of the spread of new technologies cannot be regarded as all positive. He states that a majority of the human population, particularly those who live in abject poverty, have been passed over by the technological revolution. He warns that developing countries, in particular the rural population, are at risk of lagging further behind in the age of new technologies. Consequently, the gap between the technology 'haves' and the 'have-nots' has widened owing to the ability of the new technologies to empower those who have access to them, as well as those who are able to harness technological resources. He states:

> Nowhere is this digital divide more pronounced than in countries of the African continent. Africa is the most unconnected, in an increasingly connected world. Yet, given the broad spectrum of development challenges, including fighting diseases, famine and poverty while striving for socio-economic, technological and industrial development, and the promotion of its vast material and intellectual resource and cultural heritage for global competitiveness, ICTs offer a remarkable opportunity and set of tools for achieving substantive progress.
>
> (Figueres, 2003, pp. ix–x)

Wilson and Wong (2003) argue that while Africa is harnessing new technologies and reaping some benefits, the technologies present Africa with some challenges such as weak institutions, enduring poverty, lack of foresight by political leaders, fragile institutions and policies that do not reflect the realities on the ground.

Fuchs (2008) recommends various ways through which the situation in developing countries could be improved. The first step would involve far-reaching redistribution of wealth across the world. This will involve a rise in human aid to people in those countries, an increase in income earned by the poor and cancellation of debts owed by developing countries to rich countries. Additionally, efforts must be made to adapt technologies to the needs of people in developing countries, including integration of traditional knowledge into technologies. Fuchs posed an important question: 'Can solutions to the problems of developing countries be provided by Western technologies that are applied in Third World countries?' (2008, p. 304). He said recognition of local and national ideas must be taken seriously as western initiatives are often seen as a form of imperialism that is highly resisted in developing countries. 'Western habits, colonialism, and post-colonial practices are part of the causes of the problems that Third World countries are facing today'

(Fuchs, 2008, p. 304). These are valuable ideas but we must be mindful that every country has its development strategies that may not align with the approaches outlined by other countries. This makes it difficult to prescribe a global panacea for development problems.

While some scholars have questioned the ability of ICTs to assist the socioeconomic development of Africa and other developing regions, Hosman and Fife (2008) perceive ICTs as tools that facilitate development because economic development relates to technological change in one way or another. As they point out, 'To claim that development without technology is possible is to turn a blind eye to reality' (Hosman and Fife, 2008, p. 53). They acknowledge that ICT projects cannot be successful unless locally appropriate technology is integrated into the projects. 'When projects are well thought out, technologically appropriate, and designed with long-term sustainability and the empowerment of the localities in mind, they can bring about real socio-economic benefit in the basic needs areas...' (Hosman and Fife, 2008, p. 54).

Research has examined the extent of the accessibility and use of new technologies in Africa (e.g., Obijiofor, 2009a; Obijiofor et al., 2000). The knowledge derived from this research is important not only because it contributes to understanding of the situation in the continent but also because it will help to close the existing gap between the information rich and poor, the literate and illiterate, and the 'haves' and 'have-nots'. When African leaders understand clearly the nature of the relationship between new technologies and economic growth, they will be able to construct valuable policies that will assist citizens to reap the benefits associated with technology adoption.

Challenges posed by new technologies

The debate over the contributions of new technologies to Africa's development has raised important questions about the challenges that confront the continent. New technologies are often associated with improved efficiencies, faster ways of doing business and reduced stress at work. The challenges that confront Africa as it tries to catch up with the rest of the world include initiating a realistic science and technology policy, developing and implementing a policy on computer appreciation from primary school to university level, provision of computers to educational institutions to enhance the quality of teaching and learning and research, and removing technical, infrastructural and socioeconomic obstacles that prevent Africans from accessing and using new technologies. As noted in the ICT literature, it is not the mere presence of technology that drives educational and social development but the use which people make of the technology (Kwansah-Aidoo and Obijiofor, 2006). In the electronic age, it is important to encourage school children to learn to use computers to advance their knowledge, to do assignments at school, to improve reading, writing and arithmetic skills, and to communicate with their peers. Even as children are introduced to new technology, it is equally important to teach children that it is inappropriate to access unsuitable content on the web, such as pornography.

However, in Africa there exists a gap between policy and practice. In Nigeria, for example, the science and technology policy encourages acquisition of knowledge of computer skills. Unfortunately, many young people who attended and graduated from computer training institutes and colleges lack access to computers. A majority of these graduates have no personal computers. They have only limited access to computers and the Internet through cybercafés. Owing to these circumstances, they have no prospects of securing jobs in an industry in which they will be able to put their skills into practical use. These graduates constitute a wasted generation. If the country has a pragmatic and effective science and technology policy, these young graduates should not be wandering the streets, looking for something to engage their attention and skills. It is not enough to train the youth to develop computer knowledge and skills. Government and the private sector must assist them to find meaningful ways of putting their skills into practice. This is one way to reduce the digital divide among the youth, that is, the gap between the technology 'haves' and the technology 'have-nots'.

In their investigation of the impact of new technologies on sub-Saharan Africa, Adam and Wood (1999) argue that the possible impact of ICT is dependent on existing and future technologies. A number of factors will inform the impact of ICTs on the region. The factors include accessibility of new technologies 'to a wide range of users' and their applicability to local conditions (Adam and Wood, 1999, p. 312). 'This requires the development and introduction of sound policies that enable growth. In addition, there needs to be a willingness and the ability to tailor ICT to national requirements' (Adam and Wood, 1999, p. 312). Some of the constraints identified include undependable telecommunications and power supplies, weak connectivity, poor maintenance culture, and restricted access in rural and remote areas (Adam and Wood, 1999). In related research, Conradie, Morris and Jacobs (2003) state that Internet use in South Africa is affected by geographic location (urban–rural digital divide) and other demographic factors such as level of education, income and social status. They point out that 'Rural areas in the country are unfortunately not only lagging behind with regard to Internet access, but also with regard to those very factors (such as literacy, computer skills and high income rates) that could possibly contribute to the bridging of the urban-rural digital divide' (Conradie et al., 2003, p. 199). Similar sentiments were expressed by Alozie, Akpan-Obong and Foster (2011) who note that, despite Internet connectivity that occurred early in Africa, the growth has been slow. One of the reasons was that 'While cellular phones are deemed indispensable by many Africans, the computer remains mostly disconnected from the masses as fewer than five in 100 Africans own a computer and fewer have private access to the Internet' (Alozie et al., 2011, p. 753).

In terms of the rapid diffusion of mobile phones in Africa, four reasons have been identified. The first is that mobile telephone service is relatively inexpensive. The second is the user-friendly nature of the technology that makes it possible for many illiterate people in the continent to use the mobile phone. A third is the immediate access the technology offers to users. The fourth is that mobile telephone technology is able to overcome the infrastructural obstacles that undermined the growth and development of the landline telephone system. It is these features that have ensured that mobile phones have 'given voice to the voiceless and created socio-political awareness and agitation among people who would otherwise have been indifferent' (Alozie et al., 2011, p. 761). Beyond facilitating socioeconomic development, Mudhai (2004) states that the introduction of new technologies has increased media freedom in Africa through the interactive features of online editions of newspapers that allow news consumers to 'comment, give feedback and vote on controversial issues' (Mudhai, 2004, p. 326). However, despite this development, freedom of the press is still threatened by autocratic African leaders.

Despite available evidence of the positive role of new technologies in facilitating development, questions persist about the exact form of the relationship. A pilot study that investigated the impact of new technologies on the socioeconomic and educational development of Africa and the Asia-Pacific regions found that developing countries in the regions are under pressure. They realise their future generations will be condemned to a life of poverty and will lag behind if they are not introduced to the new technologies or if they do not use the technologies (Obijiofor et al., 2000). It is perhaps this understanding that sustains the prevailing view that 'if one just purchases a few computers and modems, a post-industrial society can magically result', as a way to leapfrog into the future (Obijiofor et al., 2000, pp. 59–60). While there are sentiments such as these that circulate within Africa and other parts of the world, they are essentially too optimistic and idealistic, and do not reflect the reality on the ground. However, Guermazi and Satola (2005, p. 23) argue that

> For ICTs to deliver on their promise of economic and social development, it is critical that countries adopt enabling legal and regulatory environments that support e-development... this enabling environment was recognized in the Declaration and Action Plan of the first phase of the World Summit on the Information Society (WSIS), which emphasized that a trustworthy, transparent, and non-discriminatory environment was essential for the use and growth of ICTs in the developing world.

Telecommunications and socioeconomic growth

A number of scholars have identified the value of telecommunications to the socioeconomic growth and development of Africa and other regions (Agbobli, 2008; Chavula, 2013; Hudson, 2006, 1978; LaFraniere, 2005; Mirandilla, 2007; Morris and Stavrou, 1993; Neto, Kenny, Janakiram and Watt, 2005; Pitroda, 1993; Soriano, 2007; Tarawe and Harris, 2007). Chavula (2013) argues that the contributions of telecommunications to economic growth are unquestionable. In his view,

> Telecommunications investments lead to increases in the demand for goods and services and the economic return on these investments are envisaged to be far much greater than the return on investment alone... These investments are envisaged to increase in Africa, especially due to the untapped large market potential... Telecommunications also facilitate information flow and enhance communication between buyers and sellers, rural and urban areas and within the different sectors....
>
> (Chavula, 2013, p. 7)

Using rural areas of Africa as an example, Chavula draws on research by Aker and Mbiti (2010) (cited in Chapter 9) to outline various ways that mobile phone technology has had significant impacts on Africa because they enable farmers to compare the market prices of the goods they produce while fish farmers are in a position to sell their fish and avoid wastage by identifying their customers (Chavula, 2013, p. 12). Farmers can also share news of natural disasters. Additionally, in the health sector, mobile phones enable health workers to remind HIV-AIDS patients to take their medication. Similarly, unemployed people can find job opportunities through mobile phones and people can find easy ways to transfer money through mobile banking facilities. Through mobile phones, 'people learn how to read, write and send text messages; and election campaigns are monitored to prevent cheating' (Chavula, 2013, p. 12).

Other scholars have highlighted the importance of telecommunications to socioeconomic development at small and large-scale levels. In a number of surveys conducted in black townships of South Africa, Morris and Stavrou (1993, p. 531) argued that 'increased access to telephones in underdeveloped areas leads to improved levels in the quality of life of those communities'. They insist that 'not only can the successful transmission of information via an effective telecommunications network significantly improve the quality of life for people at the micro or community level, but it can also stimulate and facilitate the macro development process generally' (Morris and Stavrou, 1993, p. 531). Similarly, Pitroda (1993, p. 79) argues that 'When telecommunications comes to the Third World, it brings with it new economic activity, new higher-paying jobs for parents, and new technologies that reduce the utility of unskilled child labor.' Citing India as a case in point, Pitroda (1993) notes that many villages bear witness to the stirring impact that telecommunications have had on industrial growth, job opportunities and the people's quality of life. Similarly, Hudson (2006) identified a direct link between telecommunications infrastructure and socioeconomic development, such as facilitating distance education and promoting telemedicine that links patients to doctors in specialist medical facilities. Henten, Falch and Anyimadu (2004, p. 3) also underscore the gains that are associated with use of the Internet and email technologies:

World Wide Web and e-mail provide new opportunities for low cost communication and dissemination of information, and thereby promotion of economic and cultural development. Tele-medicine can extend the outreach of public health services, tele-learning and online extension services can support farmers and increase agricultural production, and producers have better access to market information and marketing.

There is no doubt that access to mobile phones and other technologies by rural people in Africa has helped to transform their lives in various ways. Art and craft manufacturers, for example, can extend the reach of their products to global audiences through marketing their products on the Internet and other social media. This will help to internationalise and transform the scope of the local business from a community-oriented business to a business that attracts buyers from across the world. The manufacturers can remain in their rural settings and still take and receive orders for their products. Business growth will impact not only on profits but also on opportunities for jobs. Local tourist groups and other businesses can benefit by advertising and popularising their businesses on the Internet. However, business growth and development on the Internet will require education (literacy), as well as technical skills and knowledge of how to operate on the Internet. Despite the positive reports, Chavula (2013) cautions that mobile phones alone cannot serve as the sole engine that propels the economic development of Africa. More research evidence and impact assessments of mobile phones are needed to understand how mobile telephony affects economic growth and development in Africa.

Nevertheless, developing African countries can harness Internet resources and reap the benefits that accrue from that activity by engaging in more investments, as 'huge investments are a prerequisite to building effective communication networks' (Oyelaran-Oyeyinka and Lal, 2003, p. 34). One view advocates that private investments in telecommunications, economic policies that trigger investments in the telecommunications sector, and an expansion in the density of personal computers will accelerate Africa's growth and development (Oyelaran-Oyeyinka and Lal, 2003). They also encourage more access to computer technology, which they perceive as 'a necessary condition for Internet access' (2003, p. 33). The drawbacks of lack of access to computers have been highlighted by Rodriguez and Wilson (2000, p. 33) thus:

> The reason that computers raise inequality appears to be two-fold. First, workers with greater levels of education are precisely the workers who are best able to use information technology. Therefore the introduction of information technology widens the gap in opportunities: it allows college graduates to earn higher wages while it reduces demand for – and the wages of – unskilled workers with a high school diploma or less. Second, the introduction of a new technology allows firms to substitute machines for people. The people who are displaced by machines create a new mass of unemployed that depresses existing wages.

There are other ways that new technologies have been deployed to enhance the socioeconomic conditions of people in various countries.

One widely cited example is the CELAC project (www.celac.or.ug) in Uganda. It is a project in which mobile phones and the Internet are deployed to improve knowledge sharing by local farmers. Another example from Africa is the Acacia Initiative in Senegal, a project established by the International Development Research Centre (IDRC) of Canada. The project has resulted in the setting up of a number of telecentres in Senegal (Agboboli, 2008). The Acacia project also includes the 'Village Land Management and Rehabilitation Project' that aimed to make ICTs accessible to less privileged people (Sissouma, 2000). In the Philippines, Mirandilla (2007, p. 1) reports on how telecentres in a remote location of the country assisted the people to gain 'access to information on health and sanitation..., and open up employment opportunities for disadvantaged sectors such as out-of-school youth'. The e-Bario project in Malaysia that began more than ten years ago is another example. According to Tarawe and Harris (2007, p. 1), the project was set up to provide 'modern Information and Communication Technologies (ICTs) to a remote and isolated village in the Kelabit Highlands of northern Sarawak, one of the Malaysian states on the island of Borneo'. Investments in new technologies are therefore seen to speed up economic development.

Scepticism among scholars with regard to new technologies and their impact on economic growth has not deterred African governments from seeking to exploit the economic, social, political and educational benefits associated with uptake of new technologies. President Paul Kagame of Rwanda sees in the new technologies a wide range of benefits. In his words, 'Success in promoting democracy, human development, socio-economic development, international cooperation, trade and commerce, require access to information and our ability to use it effectively' (Kagame, cited in Wilson and Wong, 2003, p. 157). Kwansah-Aidoo and Obijiofor (2006, p. 359) point out that 'various African governments have recognised the strong link between new technologies and socioeconomic development and are proceeding to put in place measures aimed at harnessing and maximising their perceived benefits'. This is evident, for example, in Uganda's National Information and Communication Technology Policy Framework that 'recognises that ICTs have a big role to play in stimulation of national development, in particular modernization and globalization of the economy' (Mwesige, 2004, p. 88).

The Ugandan government pledged in July 2002 that it would remove the duties imposed on imported computers as an incentive that aimed 'to promote the development of information technology' (cited in

Mwesige, 2004, p. 89). This resolution followed Ghana's decision in the mid-1990s to cancel the tariffs that were enforced on computers imported into the country. Ghana's decision was meant to promote public access to computers and to motivate secondary school students to show more understanding of the benefits of computer literacy. As Kwansah-Aidoo and Obijiofor (2006) note, the decisions by Ghana and Uganda should be seen as recognition that new technologies stimulate economic growth and development. Beyond the impact of technologies on the socioeconomic development of Africa, scholars have also examined how social media are contributing to a climate of political change in Africa.

Role of social media in political change

While social media have been identified as tools used by civil society to engineer massive demonstrations and political change in some African and Asian countries, opinions are divided among scholars about the role that social media played in 2011 in the revolution in Egypt that led to the overthrow of President Hosni Mubarak. While some people believe that social media and mobile phones helped to stir and mobilise the masses for the demonstrations, others argue that, on the contrary, other new technologies were used by the Egyptian government to repress mass participation in the uprising (Loudon and Mazumdar, 2013). These views project technology in two opposing ways: as an enabler of deliberative democracy and civil protests, and also as a tool used by the state to repress free expression of views by civil society. On the one hand, civil society groups perceive new technologies and in particular social media as great assets that empower the powerless to express their views and to participate in the process of governance. Authoritarian governments, however, perceive the new technologies as tools that enable anarchists and anti-government protesters to destabilise society (see also Ott and Rosser, 2000).

Ott and Rosser (2000) discuss various ways through which the Internet has been beneficial to African citizens. These include serving as a forum used by citizens to frustrate government attempts to stifle information about human rights abuses the government does not want to be revealed in the public sphere, as well as alternative channels used by citizens to publish information on the Internet and thereby evade government censorship and control of mainstream media. 'By contributing to free speech and the free flow of information, electronic communication has clearly exhibited the potential to augment the power of the

African citizen vis-a-vis the state, with beneficial effects for liberalization and democratization initiatives' (Ott and Rosser, 2000, p. 139). Additionally, they note, 'The electronic media has given a larger percentage of constituents than ever before the ability easily and quickly to transmit their opinions on public policy issues to their representatives' (2000, p. 140).

Essentially, new technologies help to empower ordinary citizens to participate more directly in the political system, thus enhancing the important role that citizens can play in policymaking. However, even as scholars celebrate the liberating effect of new technologies, it should be pointed out that access to the Internet and other new technologies is still restricted to many people in Africa, particularly those who reside in remote and rural areas. Another constraint that must be identified is the impact of illiteracy on the ability of ordinary African citizens to participate in deliberative democracy and to freely use the Internet. Other difficulties include unreliable power supply, high cost of Internet access, poverty and poor infrastructure. As Ott and Rosser (2000, p. 149) argue, 'Considering the persistently high illiteracy rates in Africa, it is unlikely that a significant percentage of Africans will be able to use the Internet as an interactive communication tool in the near future.'

Status of new technologies in Africa

The number of people with access to the Internet in Africa is most certainly on the rise. As of 31 December 2013, there were an estimated 240,146,482 Internet users in Africa. The estimated number of Internet users in the world at the same period stood at 2,802,478,934. The top three African countries with the largest number of Internet users as of 31 December 2013 were Nigeria (67,319,186 Internet users), Egypt with 43,065,211 Internet users and South Africa with 23,655,690 Internet users (Internet World Stats, n.d.).

The Internet penetration rate in Africa stands at 21.3 per cent as of 31 December 2013 compared to a world average of 39.0 per cent at the same time, while the rest of the world stands at 42.3 per cent (Internet World Stats, n.d.). In Africa, Morocco has the highest penetration rate of 56 per cent based on an estimated population of 32,987,206 for mid-year 2014. It is followed by Seychelles with a penetration rate of 50.4 per cent based on an estimated population of 91,650, and Egypt with a penetration rate of 49.6 per cent based on an estimated population of 86,895,099 for mid-year 2014. All figures were reported by the Internet World Stats (n.d.).

The figures differ from the numbers provided by the Internet Live Stats, which estimates a total of 268,209,162 Africans who use the Internet as at 1 July 2014. This number places Africa fourth in the world in terms of number of people who use the Internet (see Internet Live Stats, n.d.).

Regardless of the disparities, the figures show a marked improvement on the situation 13 years earlier. For example, Jensen (2002) estimated that, as of 2001, there were between five million and eight million African Internet users out of an estimated African population of 816 million people. When compared with the data presented above, it becomes clear that Africa has made significant improvements in terms of use of the Internet and penetration by the Internet.

To the questions 'What explains different levels of diffusion? Why do different African countries and regions have such different ICT profiles?' Wilson and Wong (2003, p. 163) answer that the 'differences reflect differences in levels of economic performance and economic structure both within Africa and globally'. They state that many countries mapped out and adhered to similar ICT policies in four main ways. The policies were designed after the end of the Second World War to advance each country's national interests and to enable it to reap the global benefits of ICT. The four ways through which countries promoted their ICT policies were 'public over private, domestic over foreign, monopoly over competition, and central control over de-centralized distribution' (Wilson and Wong, 2003, p. 165).

In terms of mobile phone diffusion, about 65 per cent of families in 23 countries in Africa's sub-Sahara region owned at least one mobile phone in 2013. This gives a mean growth rate of 27 per cent from 2008 (Tortora, 2014). However, in Zimbabwe, for example, 'growth has far outpaced the average, rising from 26% of households in 2008 to 80% in 2013, and 9% annually' (Tortora, 2014). Mauritania leads African countries in terms of percentage of households with at least one mobile phone in 2013. In Mauritania 96 per cent of households have at least one mobile phone, followed by Botswana (87 per cent) and Senegal (82 per cent), with Ghana and Zambia on 81 per cent each (Tortora, 2014). Sub-Saharan Africa thus stands as the second-largest mobile phone market and indeed the fastest growing region.

What Africans are doing with the Internet

Beyond the performances recorded by Africa, the question must be asked: what are Africans doing with the Internet and other new technologies? Research shows that many people in Africa use the Internet mostly for email communication, at least at the micro level. For example, Mwesige (2004, p. 96) found in his study that 98 per cent of the people in Uganda admitted they used Internet cafés for email communication. However, 61 per cent of his respondents said they used the Internet for surfing the web. Kwansah-Aidoo and Obijiofor (2006) found in their study of Internet use by Ghanaian university students that a majority used the Internet for email purposes. In Senegal, Robins (2002, p. 243) found that journalism students who frequented an Internet café in the capital city of Dakar were busy 'writing email to one another and checking out entertainment sites'. What these findings show is that the use of the Internet is restricted mostly to email communication. This implies that 'The vast potential of the Internet for research and education, as well as for commerce, would be lost to this majority' (Sonaike, 2004, p. 43). For higher education institutions in Africa such as universities, the figures are even more telling.

In a study of 200 teachers in ten universities in Kenya and Nigeria, Oyelaran-Oyeyinka and Adeya (2004) reported that over 85 per cent of Kenyan university teachers identified email as their principal reason for using the Internet while slightly more than 79 per cent identified research as their foremost objective for using the Internet. The findings for Nigeria are not markedly different. Over 50 per cent of Nigerian university teachers said email was their major reason for using the Internet, while a little over 57 per cent said they used the Internet for purposes of research. Only a few of the respondents in both Nigeria and Kenya said they used the Internet for electronic commerce (e-commerce). Based on these findings, Oyelaran-Oyeyinka and Adeya (2004) highlighted the under-utilisation of the Internet by Africans for financial or commercial purposes. On this basis, they argue:

> The low intensity of Internet use for e-commerce is symptomatic of the deeper problems of the underdeveloped finance sector. The reasons include lack of credit cards to poor financial resources. The lack of credit facilities compounds the problems, since it is a necessary component for online shopping. Obtaining an international credit card from African financial institutions requires proof of a healthy bank balance and above average income. This locks out most lecturers/researchers and limits their involvement in e-commerce.
>
> (Oyelaran-Oyeyinka and Adeya, 2004, pp. 75–76)

Questions about access to technologies

Access to the Internet has been a recurring topic of concern among scholars. For example, Ho, Baber and Khondker (2002, p. 129) note that 'Questions about the information and organizational capacities of the Net will also have to address the reach of the Net to various popula-tions.' This is an issue that should concern ICT policy makers in Africa. As Obijiofor et al. (2000) found out, without access to the Internet, a majority of the African population will further lag behind. Although it is more than 13 years since Ott and Rosser published their work, the situation in Africa has improved considerably relative to what it was at the beginning of the first decade of the 21st century. Despite the nega-tive assessment, Ott and Rosser believe the Internet has the possibility to influence economic growth and political development in Africa, and thus enhance Africa's place in the global economic and political system.

General economic climate and infrastructural problems have been identified as factors that inform the inability of Africans to use the Inter-net. Other problems include poor network services provided by Internet service providers, poverty, illiteracy, erratic supply of electricity and high cost of accessing the Internet. Henten et al. (2004, p. 1) identify other problems that are associated with the scarcity of telecommunications technologies in Africa:

> most African countries suffer from a severe under-supply of tele-phone lines. In 2001 the penetration of phone lines in Africa was at meagre 2.6 lines per 100 inhabitants. This is, indeed, a substan-tial improvement compared to the 1.7 lines per 100 inhabitants in 1994 . . . In most of these countries, the overwhelming majority of the lines are located in the capital, and most rural areas are still without any provision of telecom facilities at all.

The figures cited here are somewhat dated, as they are 13 years old. Also, they may not provide an accurate account of telephone pen-etration rates in Africa. However, there is a link between quality of telecommunications services and access to the Internet, even at a time when Wi-Fi Internet services are becoming common in capital cities. This view is consistent with evidence in the literature in which it was acknowledged that 'Lack of appropriate telecommunication infrastruc-ture on the African continent has contributed much to limiting the rate and quality of growth of Internet technology in African coun-tries and may derail the few gains made in development during the

1990s' (Sonaike, 2004, p. 42). Mwesige (2004, p. 87) makes a similar point, noting that 'the biggest challenge to Internet penetration in Uganda, as in the rest of sub-Saharan Africa, is the very low level of telecommunications infrastructure, which is crucial to connectivity'.

Technology and empowerment of women

Access to new technologies is helping to break down the gender divide and disadvantages that women in various parts of the developing world suffer. In a study of the use of new technologies by women in two Indian districts of Kanpur and Lucknow, Sharma, Sharma and Subhedar (2007) found that community projects open opportunities for women to be able to direct and use technology. On the basis of their findings, they argue that 'Designing community-based projects that will improve the lives of disadvantaged women needs to be a priority' (Sharma et al., 2007, p. 16). Their research data helped to answer important questions they asked about whether ICTs can improve the capacity of women in the informal sector to enhance their earnings, whether ICTs can improve the capacity of women involved in embroidery business to increase their incomes, and whether ICTs can help to improve the capacity of women to achieve sustainable livelihoods.

Davis (2007) investigated the benefits and limitations of ICT use by illiterate women in two rural locations in Morocco where the women sell on the Internet the rugs they knit. She found the constraints the women faced included illiteracy, lack of Internet skills and absence of Internet connectivity in the village. Some of the advantages they enjoyed were enhanced sales facilitated by the global marketing of the rugs and consequently greater profits made possible by the elimination of the intermediaries. These benefits have empowered the women and enabled them to provide financial support to their families and to pay for their children's education.

The important role that ICTs could play in empowering women was recognised in the MDGs in which gender equality was identified as a major objective. The WSIS held in Geneva, Switzerland, in 2003 gave further impetus to this goal. With specific reference to the experience in Asia, Nancy Spence (2010) outlines examples of the various ways that ICTs enable women to overcome the digital divide, including instances of how ICTs have helped women to change the way they conduct business.

With reference to Africa, Nancy Spence (2010) also shows how ICTs serve as tools for empowerment and liberation of African women. She identifies a mix of factors that constrain African women from benefiting from the services offered by new technologies. Drawing on evidence in the literature, she observes that factors such as literacy and education, geographic location of ICTs, cost, available time and language, as well as social and cultural norms, limit African women's ability to access new technologies (Nancy Spence, 2010, p. 70). On account of these, she states that 'The priorities of intervention, in addition to equal use of ICTs by women and men, must also focus on the participation of women in decision making, the fight against illiteracy, and the removal of constraints related to the triple role of women' (Nancy Spence, 2010, p. 70). This is consistent with the view in the literature that suggests that the ways in which new technologies are used by men and women reflect the sociocultural and economic conditions within which the technologies are used. For example, lower levels of education and literacy by women constitute one of the factors that contribute to the gender digital divide (Geldof, 2011).

In her study of the relationship between gender and ICTs with regard to low-literate youth in Ethiopia and Malawi, Geldof (2011) found that the relationship was socially constructed and was not embedded in the design of the technology. On this basis, she concludes that 'changing an ICT design is not enough to change the gender digital divide; the gendered context of use also needs to change to provide an environment in which women have equal opportunities to use ICTs' (Geldof, 2011, p. 78). The following section analyses a related problem: digital divide and digital poverty.

Digital divide, digital poverty

There is a vast literature on the digital divide that exists between developed and developing countries and also among people within each country. Various concepts have been used to describe the economic and information inequalities that exist. Generally, the disparities that exist between those who have access and those who lack access to new technologies is widely described as the 'digital divide'. However, May (2012, p. 36) distinguishes between digital divide and 'digital poverty'. Digital poverty, according to him, includes various dimensions such as the demand aspect that reflects situations in which people cannot afford an ICT service, the capability element that reflects a situation in which people lack the skills to use the ICT service, and the supply factor that suggests a lack of infrastructure to deliver the ICT service (May, 2012). Barrantes (2007, p. 33) states that digital poverty 'tries to find the minimum ICT use and consumption levels, as well as the income levels of the population necessary to demand ICT products'.

Global attention to poverty and other inequalities is growing. For developing countries, the pressure to achieve the MDGs by 2015 has received further impetus as the deadline approaches. The eight MDGs include eradication of extreme poverty and hunger, attainment of universal primary education, support for gender equality and empowerment of women, reduction of child mortality, improvement in maternal health, halting the spread of HIV-AIDS, malaria and other ailments, promoting environmental sustainability and achieving global partnership for development (United Nations Millennium Development Goals, n.d.; Mutula, 2008). It is in the context of the efforts to achieve the MDGs that we can understand attempts by African leaders to close the digital divide that exists among African countries and within each country. Eliminating the digital divide cannot be achieved successfully without tackling other economic, social, political and structural problems that hinder economic growth and development. There is a need to address the digital divide in an all-inclusive way that takes into consideration inequalities such as lack of access to new technologies, as well as lack of the requisite skills and knowledge to use technologies.

Mutula (2008, p. 475) is not optimistic that the digital divide that exists between Africa and the west will be closed any time soon because 'economic gaps have never been effectively narrowed between developed and developing countries despite protracted interventions by multilateral financial institutions such as the World Bank and the IMF'. Despite his negative outlook, Africa has not been discouraged. A range of initiatives designed to reduce or overcome the digital divide are being implemented in various parts of the continent. The programmes include efforts by the AISI to construct an African information superhighway that will use ICTs to hasten Africa's socioeconomic growth and development.

There is also the New Partnership for Africa's Development (NEPAD), which aims to use ICTs to facilitate collaboration within and between African countries at various levels, such as an education project in which schools were equipped with computers, Internet access and connectivity, and a telehealth service. As a demonstration of Africa's determination to rid the continent of the digital divide, the establishment of the African Regional Bureau must be noted (Mutula, 2008). The bureau was the brainchild of the African regional conference on the WSIS that was hosted in Mali in 2002. Mutula (2008, p. 478) notes the bureau was tasked with 'developing a set of principles and recommendations for developing a common African vision for an information society' that will guarantee every African citizen access to information, which is seen as a fundamental human right. These and other initiatives, including regional efforts by the Economic Community of West African States (ECOWAS), the East African Community (EAC) and the Southern African Development Community (SADC), to mention a few, are anchored in the belief that ICTs are the tools that will help Africa to achieve economic growth and to eliminate obstacles that exacerbate the digital divide.

The global response to the digital divide is an acknowledgement of the threat it poses to stable development, as well as widening the disparities in communities, societies and countries. Fonseca (2010, p. 25) argues that efforts to bridge the digital divide 'tend to focus on the acquisition of computers, information, and Internet skills, and in most cases, basic knowledge about technology in job-related contexts'. With reference to acquisition and distribution of computers, one example that comes to mind is Nicholas Negroponte's 'One Laptop per Child' initiative. The initiative's mission statement says:

> We aim to provide each child with a rugged, low-cost, low-power, connected laptop. To this end, we have designed hardware, content and software for collaborative, joyful, and self-empowered learning. With access to this type of tool, children are engaged in their own education, and learn, share, and create together. They become connected to each other, to the world and to a brighter future.
>
> (One Laptop per Child – http://one.laptop.org/about/mission)

Spence and Smith (2010) identify five different ways that ICTs are affecting development and assisting in poverty reduction. In terms of connectivity and universal access, they note that while there has been a worldwide increase in the use of ICTs, their use remains very low in Africa even though their rate of growth is quite high there. For example, with regard to mobile phone diffusion in Africa, they argue that 'income-poor people spend surprisingly large fractions of disposable income on mobile phone use, including calls, messages and other innovative techniques to communicate cheaply or for free (e.g., beeping and "missed call" messages). Research shows that poor people, like others, highly value communication for social, economic, and other benefits' (Spence and Smith, 2010, p. 12). The authors caution that, regardless of the increasing use of mobile phones, there are still many challenges ahead as many poor people are yet to achieve broadband connection.

With regard to services and benefits associated with ICTs, Spence and Smith point out some economic and social services that are facilitated by ICTs such as mobile 'banking, remittance transfer, micro finance, and insurance'. Others include principal producers having direct contact with markets, 'reduced distribution margins, and buyer oligopoly'; casual workers securing employment through the phone; the ability to deal with security, handling childcare and other domestic services; and public services such as telehealth, distance education and other electronic government services (Spence and Smith, 2010, p. 12).

In terms of open access, it has been pointed out that ICTs have facilitated 'open source software, open government, open educational resources, open standards, and open access to journals, books, and media', thus 'making it possible to communicate, organize, produce, and consume more widely and collaboratively' (Spence and Smith, 2010, p. 13).

Community-based development initiatives

Community-driven development schemes tend to develop more quickly and those communities tend to adopt a distinctively different and more successful development pathway (Breytenbach, de Villiers and Jordaan, 2013, p. 138). What this suggests is that development programmes managed by members of a local community for the community's benefit are inclined to develop more rapidly than development programmes managed by external or outside forces. In their study of technology driven community development projects in South Africa, Breytenbach et al. (2013) suggest that local resources and local motivation should drive successful ICT development projects.

> For a project to run sustainably on local resources only, enough community members must buy into the potential development as proposed by the project. Community members become involved only when they witness achievements and measurable benefits directly or indirectly related to the project or when they are given public recognition for their participation.
>
> (Breytenbach et al., 2013, p. 148)

Conclusion

This chapter analysed theoretical and practical arguments on the relationships between new technology adoption and Africa's socioeconomic development. It identified scholarly arguments that show a positive relationship between adoption of new technologies and the economic growth of Africa. Similarly, the chapter synthesised arguments by scholars who do not agree that a positive relationship exists between uptake of new technologies and development. Other issues examined in this chapter include factors that contribute to the digital divide and digital poverty; how access to new technologies empowers women and helps them to break free from the cycle of poverty; how Africans are engaging with the Internet and other digital technologies; the role of social media in facilitating political change in Africa; and the challenges that new technologies pose to Africa. One dominant view in the literature is that lack of access to new technologies constitutes the greatest barrier to adoption and use of new technologies in Africa. Access to new technologies is critical because it determines the ability of citizens to respond to efforts by governments, civil society organisations and international aid agencies to put in place programmes and policies to promote greater diffusion of technology to the people.

Even when people have access to technology, research shows there is an under-utilisation of technologies such as the Internet and email. Low utilisation of technologies adversely affects various sectors of the national economy in many African countries. Email is but one of the ways through which African citizens use the Internet. However, when African youth use the Internet essentially for email communication, they miss out on a range of other valuable services the Internet provides. Finally, there is need for the development of a policy framework that will inform and drive diffusion of new technologies in Africa. In this regard, both the government and the private sector must contribute to promote wider appreciation and adoption of new technologies by the citizens. The government and the private sector must assist people to overcome all the obstacles that hinder them from accessing and using new technologies to improve their socioeconomic conditions. Chief among the problems are the cost of the technologies which relates to grinding poverty among the population, poor infrastructure that is unable to support service delivery, illiteracy, erratic supply of electricity, and lack of computer knowledge and skills.

3
Public Service Broadcasting for Economic Growth and Language Development

Introduction

The history of public service broadcasting (PSB) has been dominated by critical questions about its remit, the best funding mechanism to sustain the broadcasting system, the defining elements that distinguish PSB from commercial channels, what its role should be in democratic societies, and latterly its relevance in the age of new technologies in which information is openly available on the Internet. The emergence of the World Wide Web has not eased the debate. Concerns have persisted because of the central role that PSB is believed to play in facilitating deliberative democracy, free expression of diverse views and equal access to information, and in serving as a vehicle for cultural expression and language preservation.

PSB is premised on the right to freedom of expression. The right to freedom of expression is clearly expressed in Article 19 of the United Nations Universal Declaration of Human Rights, which states that

> Everyone has the right to freedom of opinion and expression; this right includes freedom to hold opinions without interference and to seek, receive and impart information and ideas through any media and regardless of frontiers.
>
> (Article 19, 2006, p. 15)

The right to seek and receive information is associated with the right of the public to access information through any media platform, including public service broadcasters. The right to impart information and ideas 'relates to the right of broadcasters to communicate without interference, but also of the right of the broader public to have access to the broadcast media' (Article 19, 2006, p. 15). It has been pointed out that 'Public service broadcasters are not driven by the profit motive and should have as a specific part of their remit to meet the information and entertainment needs of various minority or neglected groups: national or linguistic minorities, old and young people, people with disabilities and so on' (Article 19, 2006, p. 19). Price and Raboy (2001, p. 182) emphasise that '[i]n new democracies of Africa, Asia and central and Eastern Europe the public broadcasting model is [being] seriously examined as an alternative to its strictly commercial counterpart'.

In its various forms, PSB caters for the different needs of audience members. Burns (2008, p. 868) states that the notion of PSB 'maintains that there is a "public", or even "publics", to be served, and that this public(s) shares a national identity'. She argues that the way in which the PSB idea was achieved 'varied according to the broadcaster in question, to its place in its particular governmental ecology, and to its particular interpretation(s) of the Public Service Broadcasting idea...' (Burns, 2008, p. 872).

Definitions of public service broadcasting

A number of questions have been asked in relation to public service broadcasting, for example: what is PSB and how does it differ from mainstream system of broadcasting? What role does a public service broadcaster perform in contemporary society? In the digital era, how has PSB confronted the challenges of online broadcasting? As PSB plays different roles in different societies, there is no universally acceptable definition of the concept. Tungwarara (2013, p. viii) defines PSB as 'a broadcaster that serves the public as a whole and is accountable to the public as a whole'. Drawing on Blumler (1993), Fourie (2004) states that PSB is expected to provide citizens with quality programming that will:

- provide them with information that will allow them to participate fully in their societies
- foster their development, curiosity and education
- tap the best of a nation's cultural resources in literature, art, drama, science, history and so on
- express national and regional cultural identity.

(Fourie, 2004, p. 5)

PSB is built on fundamental principles such as access to all citizens, multiplicity of programmes, editorial independence, free expression of ideas and freedom from political interference (Gray, 2013). The Council of Europe's Independent Television Commission identified in 2004 some elements that distinguish public service broadcasters from commercial broadcasters. These are universal coverage, restricted advertising, universal access, independence and neutrality that promote diversity of views, and a variety of quality programmes that caters for different interests and recognises cultural and linguistic diversity, including the interests of minority groups and the poor (Article 19, 2006).

In general, PSB is identified by its characteristics. These elements were also identified in 1986 in the most widely cited features of PSB outlined by the Broadcasting Research Unit. Features of PSB include: programmes must be available to a wide audience; programmes must provide for all tastes and interests; programmes must recognise and provide for minority groups and less privileged people; there must be appreciation of national identity and a feeling of community; broadcasters must be detached from government officials, as well as from other economic, business and political interests; broadcasting must be funded through a variety of sources and users; broadcasting should encourage competition for quality programming rather than competition for number of viewers or listeners; and broadcasting policy should unshackle rather than constrain programme producers (Broadcasting Research Unit, 1986). Despite the long list of the underlying objectives of PSB, Ruth Tomaselli (1989, p. 31) contends that 'Public broadcasting as we know it internationally exists nowhere in its pure state.'

There are at least four types of PSB that reflect different political, economic, social and cultural systems, interests and funding models. The first of these four systems is the state broadcaster, which is controlled by the state and advances the interests of the state. This broadcaster is funded through public money. The second is the government broadcaster, which is controlled by the government and advances the interests of the executive arm of government. This broadcasting system is funded in part through public revenue. The third is the public broadcaster, which is owned by the public and responsible to the public. This broadcasting system is funded in part through public money. The fourth is the public service broadcaster with a clear and detailed remit requiring it to broadcast in the public interest (Article 19, 2006). A public service broadcaster could also be privately owned. However, a public service broadcaster must have specified roles and responsibilities (Article 19, 2006).

Smith (1998) says the diverse forms of PSB across cultures could be attributed to differences in political plans, the size of each country, the country's closeness to other forms of broadcasting systems and the desire for national harmony. He states that

> For Canada national broadcasting was a chance to resolve a troubled national unity; but for Lebanon to attempt a single national system in radio would have put paid to any chance of unity. For Nigeria a national system could only exist in the English language, while all its indigenous peoples have to be reached through a multitude of stations using scores of tribal languages. In both the Soviet Union and in India regionalism of broadcasting was the ideal method, for they could tailor the signals to fit the geographic contours of their internal national and language groups, under supervision of central government. But to reach the Lappish people as a group a broadcast signal has to cross the boundaries of three Scandinavian countries.
>
> (Smith, 1998, p. 40)

While the elements outlined specifically for PSB might appear all-inclusive, they raise questions about concepts such as 'vested interests', 'national identity and a sense of community', 'universal access' and 'universal appeal'. Using the concept of 'vested interests' as an example, Banda (2007) states that 'Public broadcasters may have "vested interests" of their own. "Vested interests" may also manifest themselves in the way the executive officers of public broadcasting institutions are appointed' (2007, p. 162). He argues that the standards stipulated by the Broadcasting Research Unit for PSB did not quite fit post-colonial Africa because post-colonial media in Africa did not tolerate expressions of 'national and regional cultural diversity' in a system in which the emphasis was on broadcasting as a symbol of national unity rather than diversity (Banda, 2007, p. 162).

Article 19 identified three categories of broadcasting that include public broadcasters set up by legislation and funded partly through public money. This is regarded as the most dominant form of broadcasting in Africa. Another category comprises private broadcasters that are operated and managed by profit-oriented commercial organisations. They make their money mostly through advertising revenue. The third category is community broadcasters that operate within specific communities. They are controlled by the communities in which they operate (Article 19, 2006). These conceptualisations raise a number of questions about PSB in Africa.

What is the place of PSB in Africa and how does it contribute to socioeconomic development? Is there any broadcasting system in Africa that could be strictly categorised as a public service broadcaster? While public broadcasting systems are common in Africa, they do not operate as public service broadcasters that serve the public interest. Rather, they function as government or state broadcasting organisations (Article 19, 2006). In fact, Gray (2013) argues that 'South Africa is the only African country that can boast a true PSB. The rest are more or less state run.'

Public service broadcasting in Africa

Although many African countries claim their broadcasting systems perform public service roles, the existing broadcasting systems in the continent are clearly different. Attempts have been made in some African countries to transform state broadcasting institutions into some kind of PSB system. For example, Banda (2006) notes the Zambian parliament's decision in 2002 to pass the Zambia National Broadcasting Corporation (ZNBC) (Amendment) Act to facilitate the transformation of the state broadcasting corporation into a public service broadcaster. Similarly, the South African Broadcasting Corporation (SABC) was transformed from its hitherto apartheid-era state-owned and controlled broadcasting institution into a model public service broadcaster in Africa. Still, arguments persist about whether it is possible to have a public service broadcaster that is state-owned or whether a public service broadcaster can be free from state ownership and control. While some scholars argue that state ownership of PSB should not imply state control of the broadcaster, others insist that state ownership is necessary in developing countries for a public service broadcaster to perform its nation-building role or to assist in national socioeconomic development (Banda, 2006).

Across Africa, there are different regulatory frameworks under which public service broadcasters operate. Three major types include: first, self-regulation, such as the SABC and Ghana's National Media Commission (NMC); second, a system in which the broadcaster reports directly to the state, such as the ZNBC that reports to the Ministry of Information and Broadcasting Services (MIBS) and the Kenya Broadcasting Corporation (KBC) that is administered by a board of directors (although the head is chosen by the President while other members are appointed by the minister for broadcasting); and third, a system in which the public service broadcaster reports to and is controlled by media authorities (Banda, 2006). An example of this is Uganda, where the public service broadcaster is regulated by the Broadcasting Council that also regulates the Uganda Broadcasting Corporation (UBC) (Banda, 2006).

PSB systems are perceived in different ways in different African countries because of the different roles they play and the services they provide. In South Africa, as Fourie (2003) observes, development and nation-building underpin the central role of PSB. However, in Malawi, the role of PSB differs because it is expected to project the country 'to the World and to observe the principles and norms of a democratic society' (cited in Banda, 2007, p. 161). In Ghana, the aim is to use PSB to forge national identity (cited in Banda, 2007).

As seen in the definitions above, the key elements that define PSB also constitute some of the problems that threaten the viability of the broadcaster. These include independence of the broadcaster from economic, business and political forces; a variety of funding sources that do not tie the broadcaster to any particular interest group; universal access and diversity of programmes; ethnic and racial diversity; promotion of lesser used languages; and limited or no advertising. These are difficult objectives that also pose challenges to the principles of PSBs. For example, how could a public broadcaster in a multicultural country meet its mandate to reflect the diversity of languages in its programming? How could a public service broadcaster satisfy the broad interests of diverse ethnic and racial groups in society? Some of these issues are examined in this chapter. Examples are taken chiefly from Canada, South Africa, Australia and some other African and European countries, to illustrate how public service broadcasters are fulfilling their mandates or are constrained by their public service obligations.

Independence of the public broadcaster

One defining element of PSB is independence in terms of funding sources, enabling legislation, freedom from government control or interference by market forces, independence in the appointment of board members and public accountability, usually through parliament. The law that establishes PSB must guarantee its independence (Article 19, 2006, p. 38). For many years, PSB has faced challenges such as inadequate funding, government control and interference, censorship and other forms of political pressure. Independence is at the heart of a reliable and credible public service broadcaster. As a former Director-General of the British Broadcasting Corporation (BBC), Greg Dyke, argued,

> PSB has to be independent of government, ask questions and not be bullied by government. Governments seem to believe they own

PSB, and PSB needs to rethink what their role is, affected now by ideological changes like technical development and changing audiences with a declining older audience and a younger audience, the digital generation more used to social media.

(cited in Gray, 2013)

The problems confronting PSB have generated predictions of its demise. For example, Curran, Elstein and Gitlin (2002, cited in Fourie, 2003, pp. 148–149) summed up the situation of PSB thus:

Public service broadcasting is in the dock. What justifies it now? Originally defended as a way of dealing with the limits of 1920s technology, it now operates in a world where there is no technical limit on the number of broadcasting channels, and where technology offers the prospects of ever greater choice and freedom of expression. Once defended on the ground that it alone provides programme diversity, it now confronts expanding choice through the market's niche channels. Once supported in the name of programme quality, it now struggles to define just what quality is. Once defended as a way to umpire pluralistic debate, it stands accused of cosiness with government and corporate centres of power.

Debate over funding mechanisms

One dilemma that challenges the effectiveness of PSB whether in South Africa, Australia, Canada or indeed in other countries across the world is lack of sufficient funds that will allow the broadcasters to meet their public service obligations. There are three major channels through which Canada's public service broadcaster, the Canadian Broadcasting Corporation (CBC), generates funds for its programmes. These are parliamentary appropriations, advertising and other miscellaneous sources. In South Africa, the mandate of the SABC allows it to generate funds through advertisements, subscription, sponsorship and licence fees. Teer-Tomaselli (1998, p. 149) says that, in light of these sources of funding, the SABC could be described as a public service broadcaster that 'operates in a commercial environment, under commercial constraints'.

There are reasons to worry about how advertising and other market forces might destroy the independence of the SABC and the CBC, including the quality of their programmes, as both public broadcasters raise revenue through some form of advertising. There is growing concern about commercialisation of media and its impact on quality journalism (McManus, 2009; Obijiofor and Hanusch, 2011, pp. 154–176; Picard, 2004). Commercialisation, even in a disguised form, has its consequences for public service broadcasters. There is concern that a public service broadcaster that generates revenue through advertising could expose itself to market forces, dilute the quality of its programmes and therefore abdicate its public service obligations. Although commercialisation of media has drawn adverse comments from media audiences, there are no easy solutions. Public service broadcasters are yet to find a mix of acceptable funding mechanisms that will guarantee full independence for the broadcasting system.

As evidence of the strict funding conditions under which Australia's public service broadcasters operate, the Australian Federal Minister of Communication, Malcolm Turnbull, announced in November 2014 that the government will cut the ABC budget by $254 million over the next five years. The minister said the ABC would receive $5.2 billion in funding over that time which amounts to a cut of 4.6 per cent. He said the country's second public service broadcaster, the Special Broadcasting Service (SBS), would have its budget reduced by $25.2 million or 1.7 per cent over the same period (http://www.abc.net.au/news/2014-11-19/abc-funding-cuts-announced-by-malcolm-turnbull/5902774).

Since the emergence of PSB, there has been sustained debate about how to fund the broadcasting system and still maintain its independence from political interference, government officials and market forces. In their widely cited book, Price and Raboy (2001, p. 8) acknowledge the complexity of the problem.

> Issues of financing public service broadcasting are – quite obviously – key to its success and its pattern of performance in a society. Globally, there has been a search for the magic way to provide financing that has aspects that are almost always impossible, in combination, to achieve. The ideal financing has these qualities: (a) it is guaranteed for many years so that politicians cannot interfere; (b) it is sufficient to achieve the multiple tasks the public service broadcaster must perform; and (c) it allows some opportunity for accountability.

Although a variety of funding sources are used to support PSB, three main sources of funding have been identified. Similar to the funding models in South Africa and Canada discussed in the preceding paragraphs, the funding sources are parliamentary subventions, licence fees paid by television set owners and advertising revenue. Other minor sources include sale of music videos, books and so on (e.g., the ABC shop that sells products such as music DVDs, books, magazines, toys and clothing).

With regard to African countries, several funding models have been cited (Banda, 2006). These include the licence fee which features in countries such as Ghana (GBC) and Zambia (ZNBC), including the South African model discussed above. The licence fee is problematic for a number of reasons. It is difficult to collect the fee either because many set owners do not pay (as in South Africa) or the method of payment is unsystematic. This makes it difficult to track those who paid and those who did not pay. The licence fee therefore serves as an insignificant source of revenue for public service broadcasters in Africa. Another source of funding is direct state subvention. This is problematic also because it tends to dilute the independence of the broadcaster, as it leaves the organisation vulnerable to political influences and interference by government officials. A third mechanism is a mixed formula in which public service broadcasters draw revenues from commercial activities (such as advertising) and sponsorship by private organisations (Banda, 2006). Commercial broadcasters criticise this practice on the basis that public service broadcasters should not compete for advertising revenue with commercial broadcasters as it would go against the core value of the PSB as an independent broadcaster. This funding formula is more evident in South Africa (SABC), Ghana (Ghana Broadcasting Corporation – GBC), Zambia (ZNBC), Malawi (Malawi Broadcasting Corporation – MBC) and Radio Maputo, to mention a few (Banda, 2006). The fourth funding formula is what has been termed 'Deficit financing from government, with an over-reliance on advertising revenue' (Banda, 2006, p. 7). This is more evident in the SABC and the ZNBC models.

Advertising as a source of revenue for the public service broadcaster has been criticised by interest groups across the world who advocate for a strong and independent public service broadcaster free from commercial interests and the influence of economic forces. Another source of revenue, one that is considered minor, is the sale of non-essential material such as music (Banda, 2006). As Heath (2001) advocates, 'What are needed are steady, reliable sources of revenue that do not depend upon the whims of politicians, agendas of NGOs, or imperatives of the marketplace.' In Ghana, the Ghana Broadcasting Corporation is funded through parliamentary allocations, spot advertisements, licence fees, sponsorships and other means. Sponsorships have come from local arms of multinational companies that operate in Ghana such as Unilever, Daiwood, Fan Milk and Samsung (Heath, 2001).

To sustain PSB in Ghana, Heath (2001) calls for dependable sources of funding free from political influences, economic forces or the personal interests of private sponsors. Alternative sources of revenue to fund PSB in Ghana could be from 'corporate income taxes currently levied on commercial radio and television enterprises' but this would only be possible if the Ghana Broadcasting Corporation became independent and when it halted all commercial activities. Additionally, Heath suggests the Ghanaian legislature could set up an independent audiovisual production company that could lease its equipment to private and public production organisations. The money earned from this business would be used to fund a restructured Ghana Broadcasting Corporation. 'Such a centre would make local production more cost effective, encourage Ghanaian talent and diversity of cultural expression, and resolve the contradictions inherent in a public service broadcasting system driven by commercial imperatives' (Heath, 2001).

Fourie (2003) recommends that the funding of PSB in Africa or elsewhere should be guided by five key principles. First, funding must be realistic and sufficient to enable the public service broadcaster to undertake the tasks assigned to it by legislation. As he argued, asking the SABC to broadcast in 11 official languages in a situation in which the broadcaster is constrained by inadequate funds is a meaningless assignment. Second, funding must be substantive to enable the public service broadcaster to compete with commercial broadcasters and to fulfil its mission. It is not a good idea to cut the funding of a public service broadcaster on the grounds that it is performing below its mandate or public expectations. What should be considered is the role of the public service broadcaster in facilitating deliberative democracy, in encouraging popular participation, in fostering political debate and in serving as a vehicle for cultural expression. Third, funding must be provided to enable the public service broadcaster to produce quality programmes that distinguish it from commercial broadcasters. Fourth, funding must be provided to ensure the independence and accountability of the public service broadcaster. As Fourie (2003) notes, the funding mechanism will affect public perceptions of the independence of the public service broadcaster from political interference.

Whatever funding mechanism is adopted, it must guarantee some form of stability and predictability of funds available for multiple years. In this context, licence fee funding is regarded as more stable and predictable, as long as it is free from political interference and as long as it can keep up to speed with the cost of the broadcaster's services (Fourie, 2003; Price and Raboy, 2001).

Faced with dwindling finances and growing unwillingness on the part of governments and other agencies to increase funds, public service broadcasters have been compelled to explore alternative sources of funding in order to be less reliant on government revenues and other external funding sources. This is critical. As many scholars have noted, for PSB to be credible and relevant, it must be independent of all political, economic and cultural influences (Banda, 2007; Broadcasting Research Unit, 1986; Fourie, 2003; Price and Raboy, 2001). In regions where PSB is funded through licence fees and parliamentary appropriations/subventions (such as the European Union), parliaments are beginning to question the existing funding arrangements, as debate grows about the relevance of PSB in the age of new technologies which has seen the emergence of multiple news channels and diverse choices for citizens (Heath, 2001).

Across the world, globalisation, competition and technological changes are transforming PSB. These and other developments have affected the way audiences, governments and funding agencies perceive PSB.

New challenges for public service broadcasting

Has the advent of new technologies signalled new roles for PSB, and therefore the need to reposition the broadcaster for new challenges in a digital era? The key task is to reposition PSB to reflect the realities of the 21st century broadcasting environment and to make it more relevant and responsive to the needs of society. It has been argued that the gradual demise of the PSB system started with the adoption of the United States' dual model of broadcasting in which the commercial and public service media operate in the same market but with a less dominant role assigned to public service media (Fourie, 2003). However, there are drawbacks to the market-oriented system. In this system, broadcasting is expected to educate, inform and entertain viewers. This implies a shift in emphasis to commercial interests which seek to provide the audience with what they want. This change in direction was facilitated and indeed accelerated by technological transformations that introduced convergence of media, digitisation and different delivery systems. While, for example, deregulation of the broadcasting sector gave rise to widening of choices of platforms available to media consumers, it has also spawned growing competition at national and international levels, as well as the quest for advertising revenue and new funding mechanisms (Fourie, 2003).

One consequence of greater competition and commercialisation is the focus on entertainment-driven and sometimes low quality programming. This has compelled broadcasters to seek alternative sources of funding, and to go online. With specific reference to Australia's public service broadcaster (the ABC), Burns (2008) states that in the early 1990s, there was optimism that the Internet could be used to deal with some of the public broadcaster's enduring problems such as 'services to youth and rural users, centralized operations, and listener/viewer feedback' (2008, p. 876). This was because 'the Internet offered possibilities to better achieve the Public Service Broadcasting goals of "universal" access and education, and to encourage contributions from the public' (Burns, 2008, p. 879).

PSB has been criticised for attempting to unify two different and contrasting broadcasting systems by shifting its focus from its traditional role as a facilitator of deliberative democracy and an avenue for cultural expression, by competing with commercial broadcasters in order to access new sources of funding beyond advertising and subscription, and by adopting new technologies to reach more viewers and listeners (Fourie, 2003, p. 151). Similarly, the notion that public service broadcasters are best placed to promote an inclusive public sphere is being challenged by the emergence of a diversity of news channels in which viewers are presented with 24-hour news and entertainment.

In the existing broadcasting environment marked by funding problems, technological developments, multiple channels of news, convergence of media and greater audience choices, Steemers (2002) and Fourie (2003) note that public service broadcasters face a major predicament. They can either sustain their public service obligations by serving as vehicles for cultural expression, equal access, balanced reporting and democratisation of information or they can abandon these roles by responding to the challenges of broadcasting in the age of new technologies and greater competition in the market. The dilemma facing public service broadcasters is thus clear. On the one hand, they can adhere to their public service obligations. On the other hand, if they fail to rise to technological and competitive challenges, they will abdicate their public service obligations and face the possibility of losing their audiences in the process. There are no easy solutions to these challenges.

PSB has been identified as an important institution of society that assists in language development and cultural preservation. In many countries, in particular multicultural societies, the important role that public service broadcasters play as a vehicle for cultural preservation and the promotion of minority or lesser used languages has been emphasised.

Language development and preservation

Language has been described as a source of identity, power and ideology (Wilkinson and Chen, 2001). Fishman (1972) points out that the use of a language or speech in a society greatly influences the acceptance of that language or speech. Thus, a minority language is often perceived as a form of inferiority on the part of the speakers of that language. This is an important subject that deserves systematic analysis. Language use in media is very important because it determines who has access to media and the right to receive information. Language use in the media is also informed by the need to 'protect and promote diversity and ensure the representation of existing pluralities within society' (McGonagle, Noll and Price, 2003, p. 3). PSB is regarded as one of the important channels through which minority languages can be promoted and developed, to prevent their extinction. McGonagle (2004) outlines a number of reasons why language use in broadcasting should be taken seriously. First, language can be an instrument for 'unity and division' in society. Second, language can serve as a tool for strengthening a sense of national identity. Third, language is tied to cultural matters such as 'language and education; language and the media, and language and participation in public life generally' (McGonagle, 2004, p. 2). These relationships, he argues, can lead to greater unity or division in society.

At least two international treaties support the right of minorities to express themselves through their language, culture and religion. Specifically, the International Covenant on Civil and Political Rights (ICCPR) adopted by the United Nations Human Rights Office of the High Commissioner for Human Rights and the International Covenant on Economic, Social and Cultural Rights (ICESCR) and a United Nations General Assembly Declaration on the Rights of Persons Belonging to National or Ethnic, Religious or Linguistic Minorities support the rights of minorities to use their languages. For example, the ICCPR (1976) stated in Article 27 that 'In those States in which ethnic, religious or linguistic minorities exist, persons belonging to such minorities shall not be denied the right, in community with the other members of their group, to enjoy their own culture, to profess and practise their own religion, or to use their own language' (United Nations Human Rights Office of the High Commissioner for Human Rights, 1976). Similarly, Article 2.1 of the United Nations General Assembly Declaration on the Rights of Persons Belonging to National or Ethnic, Religious or Linguistic Minorities (1992) states clearly that 'Persons belonging to national or ethnic, religious and linguistic minorities ... have the right to enjoy their own culture, to profess and practise their own religion, and to use their own language, in private and in public, freely and without interference or any form of discrimination.'

The document – *Guidelines on the Use of Minority Languages in the Broadcast Media* – produced by the Organisation for Security and Cooperation in Europe (OSCE) High Commissioner on National Minorities (HCNM) – examines the extent to which international human rights law allows states to legislate on the use of language in broadcasting. The general principles of the guidelines address issues such as freedom of expression, cultural and linguistic diversity and protection of identity, as well as equality and non-discrimination. The document states, in the section on protection of identity, that 'All persons, including persons belonging to national minorities, have the right to maintain and develop their identity, including through the use of their language(s), in and through the broadcast media' (Organisation for Security and Cooperation in Europe High Commissioner on National Minorities 2003, 2010, p. 7). In paragraph 5 of Section II, which addresses policy matters, the document enjoins states to 'develop policy to address the use of minority languages in the broadcast media' (2010, p. 8). Not only does the document mention broadcast media as a channel for language and cultural expression by people who belong to national minorities, it specifically mentions the use of PSB to serve the interests of persons belonging to national minorities (see paragraph 7).

In specific reference to the promotion of minority languages, the OSCE High Commissioner on National Minorities calls on states to 'support broadcasting in minority languages... through provision of access to broadcasting, subsidies and capacity building for minority language broadcasting' (see paragraph 14, p. 10). With regard to funding, the High Commissioner mentions that states should 'consider providing financial support for minority language broadcasting... through direct grants, favourable financing/tax regimes, and exemption from certain fees payable on award or alteration of a license' (2010, p. 12).

The Council of Europe adopted its Charter on Regional or Minority Languages in Strasbourg in 1992 in which it defined minority languages (in Part 1a) as

languages that are:

(i)   traditionally used within a given territory of a State by nationals of that State who form a group numerically smaller than the rest of the State's population; and

(ii) different from the official language(s) of that State;

it does not include either dialects of the official language(s) of the State or the languages of migrants.

(Council of Europe, 1992)

McGonagle et al. (2003) note that the European Court of Human Rights has clarified language use in broadcasting. In their study of minority-language related broadcasting and legislation in the OSCE, they suggest that 'Language regulation should consider the function of the PSB, the general availability of material in a variety of the relevant languages, and the sense of satisfaction among the communities affected' (2003, p. 7). They refer to a ruling by the European Commission on Human Rights which implies that 'Regulations requiring the sole use of the State language at the national level may not be acceptable, even where minority language programming is available at regional level' (McGonagle et al., 2003, p. 7). In their study, the researchers point out that 'A local station broadcasting in a minority language, but whose airtime is devoted mainly to music, might not be considered to fill adequately the news and educational needs of a local minority-language speaking population' (McGonagle et al., 2003, p. 7). They also note how the emergence of new technologies such as the Internet has, in some OSCE states, disrupted the traditional balance in language use that was created during the era of radio and television.

A reduction in state regulation caused by new technologies (such as new media) poses clear challenges to pre-existing broadcasting regulations and policies. McGonagle et al. (2003) found that a range of languages often exist side by side in a state (such as Canada, Finland, Ireland and Switzerland) and differing levels of official recognition are accorded to the languages. Similarly, while some European states identify a national language, they also have provisions for the protection or development of what they refer to as 'other languages' (McGonagle et al., 2003, p. 9). While the study looked at the various uses of PSB and private broadcasting in serving language communities, the researchers found that different states apply different rules. For example, while some member countries of the OSCE address the problem from the principle of egalitarianism or fairness, other states consider the important subject of the civil rights of language communities or minorities.

In looking at the role of PSB in promoting minority or lesser used languages, McGonagle et al. (2003) take, as their point of reference, the six features of broadcasting identified by Barendt (1993). The features include: wider accessibility; recognition of culture and national identity; autonomy from state and commercial interests; neutrality of programmes; diversity of programmes; and significant financing through a charge levied on users (Barendt, 1993, cited in McGonagle et al., 2003).

With reference to Africa, Heath (2001) points out that radio broadcasting was hampered not only by unclear signals and poor reception but also by the use of the language of the colonial rulers, which in most cases posed difficulties for audiences. She states that

> Typically, African broadcasters have employed the language of the former colonial power, which had been adopted as an official language, plus a number of African languages. For example, in Zambia time was allocated to seven African languages in proportion to the size of language community in the nation ... The Voice of Kenya (now the Kenya Broadcasting Corporation) transmitted two services to the entire nation: the General Service used English; the National Service used Swahili.
>
> (Heath, 2001)

Similarly, there were radio services in which programmes were broadcast in different languages. Radio Ghana 1 – a non-commercial service – broadcast in six local languages, namely Akan, Dagbani, Ewe, Ga, Nzema and Hausa, as well as English. Heath notes that this radio service did not serve the people effectively and could not be viewed as a vehicle for socioeconomic development because fewer than two hours each day were allocated to any one language while various language communities were disregarded (Heath, 2001). She observes that, at the time, broadcasting policy in Ghana stipulated that 80 per cent of the programmes should be broadcast in local languages. Despite this policy requirement, the percentage of local language use in broadcasting in Ghana varies from station to station. While some stations use local languages in their programmes, in other stations local language use is almost nil. For example, the language used by the great majority of the Indigenous people who inhabit the Greater Accra area of Ghana (the Ga language) was missing from radio broadcasts in 1998 except for one programme that was broadcast in a commercial station (Groove FM). However, there has been a significant improvement in the use of major Ghanaian languages in programmes broadcast in GBC stations (Heath, 2001).

In terms of using PSB for promoting minority or lesser used languages, the literature shows that different countries have different policy frameworks. While some countries have a clear policy that mandates the use of PSB to promote minority languages, other countries have no such policy. By its charter, the SABC is required to map policies that will enable it to address matters relating to news and editorial, programming, local content, education, universal service and access, language and religion (SABC Charter, http://www.sabc.co.za/wps/portal/ SABC/SABCCHARTER). Section 8c of the SABC charter outlines clearly the organisation's language requirement. That section states that

(8) The Corporation must develop a Code of Practice that ensures that the services and the personnel comply with-
    (c) the constitutional requirement of equitable treatment of all official languages.
(SABC Charter, http://www.sabc.co.za/wps/portal/
SABC/SABCCHARTER)

Clearly, the promotion of language is recognised in the SABC charter. There are sound reasons for this. During the apartheid era, people who spoke minority languages in South Africa were discriminated against. That was the time when English and Afrikaans were the two officially recognised languages of the country. Finlayson and Madiba (2002, p. 44) explain that during the period of apartheid, 'the indigenous languages were only important in so far as they served as tools for the division of the African people into a large number of conflicting and competing so-called ethnic groups'.

In South Africa, there is a constitutional policy that requires the SABC to promote the country's major languages by broadcasting in 11 officially recognised languages. This mandate is supported by two major legal frameworks – constitutional recognition of 11 official languages and the SABC charter that mandates the broadcaster to reflect all 11 official languages in its programming in an even-handed manner. This places South Africa one step ahead of other countries, particularly countries with diverse ethnic and language groups. The recognition of 11 official languages in South Africa is founded on the argument that the recognised languages are widely spoken by a large majority of South African people. It is a valid point but minority languages should not be allowed to wither simply because they are spoken by minority members of the population.

Minority languages must be protected and preserved through official policy and other mechanisms that encourage their wider use. Language is a symbol of a people's identity and no language deserves to be allowed to vanish. When a language goes into extinction, a people's identity also goes with it. Some problems have arisen from the

SABC's mandate to broadcast in multiple languages. The recognition of 11 official languages in the South African constitution seems to have underestimated the importance and relevance of more than 24 languages that are spoken in the country. The South African constitution is mute on the status of these 'unrecognised' and 'unofficial' languages. Additionally, when a language is not recognised officially in a country's constitution, does that imply that the language and the people who speak the language should be disregarded? If a language does not enjoy the status of official recognition, should it be allowed to disappear?

There are challenges that confront the SABC as it strives to meet its mandate in terms of broadcasting in 11 official languages. Slabbert, van der Berg and Finlayson (2007) outline some of the problems the SABC will face in trying to meet its language mandate. The first challenge relates to equitable allocation of time and resources to programming. Funding is the key problem. Without adequate funding, it will be extremely difficult for the SABC to produce and broadcast programmes in 11 official languages equally. For example, how would news and current affairs, as well as entertainment and documentary programmes, be produced and presented in 11 languages and in an unprejudiced way? Another problem concerns how the SABC will manage, in the limited time available, to broadcast programmes in all 11 official languages. In broadcasting, time is a finite resource. Other limitations include the differences and similarities among the 11 official languages. For example, some language groups are bigger or smaller than others. Also, some languages are 'more marginalised than others (Xitsonga, Tshivenda, siSwati and isiNdebele) and the additional responsibility this places on institutions such as the SABC to address this marginalisation' (Slabbert et al., 2007, p. 339). It has also been argued that the recognition of 11 official languages in South Africa 'further entrenches the responsibilities of broadcasters both in terms of advancing linguistic democracy and in terms of safeguarding the rights of those whose languages have been disregarded in the past' (Maingard, 1997, p. 262).

Of all these challenges, funding is the most critical. Without adequate funds, the SABC will find it difficult to operate and meet its obligations to broadcast in 11 official languages in an equitable manner. This means the SABC and parliament must work out various independent sources of funding that will allow the public broadcaster to fulfil its social and constitutional obligations. The challenge is not easy because some countries have tried a number of funding strategies. Advertising, for example, is not an easy option because it will destroy the independence of the public broadcaster and expose the broadcaster to the influence of market forces.

Despite these difficulties, Slabbert et al. (2007) show through their study that soap operas produced and presented in multiple languages can assist in the development of multilingual broadcasting on television. They demonstrate in their study of three soap operas produced and broadcast in multiple languages on SABC that knowledge of minority languages can indeed be improved and widened through television programmes. They report that

> in a multicultural and multilingual context, multilingual soap operas that mirror the realities of language use can be powerful and commercially successful vehicles for the promotion of diversity and multilingualism. However, the successful local multilingual soap operas would probably not have been produced without the South African Constitution's position on languages and the resulting language mandates of the SABC.
>
> (Slabbert et al., 2007, p. 354)

The SABC has also used other strategies to promote multilingualism in broadcasting. One instance is that

> often several presenters will anchor a single news programme or quiz show, each presenter speaking a different language (and thus representing and speaking to a different language constituency in South Africa); sometimes individual hosts will switch between two or three languages, often within the same sentence. Popular soap operas represent perhaps the apogee of this trend: different characters may speak different languages, individual characters may switch languages depending on whom they are addressing, or sometimes within sentences spoken to a single addressee, and dialogue is often subtitled into an additional language.
>
> (Barnard, 2006, p. 49)

Slabbert et al. state that 'What the South African broadcasting scenario has amply illustrated is that a public broadcaster's language mandate acts as a facilitating instrument to uncover the commercial viability of multilingualism' (2007, p. 355). While this might be the case, it is clear that the attainment of multilingualism on television programming was influenced by the general appeal of the soap operas. An unpopular programme that did not appeal to viewers would not have attracted the mass audience. Clearly, beyond soap operas, there are other avenues for language promotion and development on television. Opportunities exist in news and current affairs that are televised in local languages. Similarly, religious services could be broadcast in local languages given the important role that religion plays in the lives of African people. Local languages could also be promoted through children's programmes, sports and other forms of entertainment.

South Africa needs a public service broadcaster that will broadcast in the languages that are spoken by the people, the languages that will unify the people and sensitise the population to the need to engage in the socioeconomic development of the country (Fourie, 2003). Nevertheless, the requirement that a public service broadcaster should fulfil the language, educational and entertainment desires of diverse ethnic groups could impose financial burdens on the broadcaster. Teer-Tomaselli (1998, pp. 156–157) notes that 'Catering for the information and entertainment needs of small pockets of distinct language speakers is costly, with a very low marginal rate of return on the numbers of viewers and listeners reached. This is particularly true of television, where original programming is very expensive.'

Since 1994, South Africa has set out a range of objectives to be achieved through broadcasting, but the level of funding has always been an issue. The SABC was obligated to tackle problems of national development such as inequity in distribution of infrastructure; disparity in allocation of resources; imbalance in broadcasting programmes in areas such as language, culture and education; absence of diversity in programming and choice of programmes; and limited coverage and access (Fourie, 2003). PSB in South Africa is clearly expected to engage in 'the task of nation building and to construct a vibrant and democratic dispensation fostering national and cultural identity, equality and respect for the fundamental rights of all South Africans as enshrined in the new constitution' (cited in Fourie, 2003, p. 153). Despite the problems that confront the SABC, opinions are divided about the extent to which the broadcaster is fulfilling its public service obligations. Some audience members hold the view that news lacks depth and context, as well as a diversity of views. In terms of using the SABC TV to develop languages, some African- and Afrikaans-language speaking people have expressed disappointment that the SABC is not doing enough to promote their languages, as outlined in the SABC mandate (Fourie, 2003).

There is no question that the SABC is operating in a difficult broadcasting environment in which it has been constrained by lack of funds and by political interference. As discussed in this chapter, one of the challenges that threaten the relevance of the SABC relates to its mandate and constitutional requirement to broadcast programmes in 11 official languages. What the mandate did not address is how broadcasting in 11 official languages will be funded. Thus, the ability of the SABC to fulfil its obligations is further limited by inadequate funding. Who will bear the cost of broadcasting in 11 official languages? This is the question that is yet to be answered under the current mandate of the SABC. It is a huge challenge to broadcast in diverse languages in an environment in which funding sources are drying up.

Fourie (2003) points out that less than 3 per cent of the SABC funding is derived from government subventions. A large part of the public service broadcaster's revenue is obtained through advertising and commercial sponsorships. Licence fees earn R355 million. In the SABC's estimation, about 1.8 million households did not pay television licence fees in the 2001/2002 financial year. That is certainly a large number of people who evaded their duty to pay their television licence fees. This level of breach will certainly undermine the financial independence and ability of the SABC to operate effectively. SABC's position is made even more difficult by the growing number of competitors and the task of broadcasting in the era of new technologies. As Fourie (2003, p. 155) explains,

> After being the monopoly broadcaster for more than four decades, the SABC now has to compete with 14 private radio stations, 1 free-to-air private national terrestrial television channel, e-tv, and MultiChoice, provider of the subscription television channel M-Net and the DStv (Digital Service TV) satellite bouquet with more than 50 channels including BBC World, CNN, Sky News, National Geographic, Discovery Channel, MTV, various sport channels (SuperSport), various niche channels, and various community channels including a successful channel for the Afrikaans-speaking population, namely kykNET.

This is not to forget the numerous community radio stations that are scattered around South Africa. Yet there is a strong need for an effective public service broadcaster in South Africa. In a country in which nearly half of the population is impoverished and many people are plagued by health problems such as HIV-AIDS, the importance of a strong public service broadcaster cannot be overemphasised (Fourie, 2003). Such a public service broadcaster will help to create public awareness of the country's problems and challenges, especially ways to overcome the problems.

In Canada, the major public broadcaster is the CBC. The country's Broadcasting Act of 1991 mandates the CBC and other public broadcasters to transmit programmes in English and French, including Indigenous languages. The CBC also manages another service that broadcasts to people in the far north in their native languages. As well as the CBC and other public broadcasters, the Aboriginal People's Television Network (APTN) also broadcasts programmes in Indigenous languages. The APTN, which was launched on 1 September 1999, broadcast 56 per cent of its programmes in English, while 16 per cent of the programmes were broadcast in French and 28 per cent in about 15 Aboriginal languages that include Inuktitut, Cree, Inuinaqtuun, Ojibway, Inuvialuktun, Mohawk, Dene, Gwich'in, Miqma'aq, Slavey, Dogrib, Chipweyan, Tlingit and Mechif (Aboriginal Peoples Television Network, 2005). By broadcasting in these languages, the APTN is promoting language diversity in Canada. Nevertheless, the percentage of time the APTN dedicates to broadcasting in Indigenous languages must be seen as insufficient, given that 56 per cent of its programmes are broadcast in English. The APTN should ensure that a greater percentage of its programmes are broadcast in Indigenous languages.

In the electronic era, there are a number of factors that have transformed public broadcasters across the world.

Forces that drive broadcasting reforms

There are at least three forces that are driving reforms and restructuring of PSB systems in many parts of the world. The first is technological transformations that have challenged the traditional view that PSB is the only media that can guarantee universal access to citizens. In light of the development of the World Wide Web and diverse sources on the Internet, the argument that PSBs are the only guarantors of universal access to information is no longer tenable.

The second element related to technological changes is growing competition. Competition from other traditional and non-traditional news sources has whittled down the audiences that patronise PSB. In order to retain their dwindling audience share, public service broadcasters have been forced to compete with other media by producing and broadcasting entertainment-oriented programmes that have drawn criticisms from the public owing to concerns about their perceived poor quality. The third force driving the debate for a review of PSB roles and responsibilities is dwindling funds and the quest to devise sustainable funding mechanisms to ensure that public service broadcasters remain in business.

Advocates of PSB argue forcefully that diversity of viewpoints and plurality of media will be sustained in an environment in which PSB is properly financed and supported. In the spirit of democracy, it is argued that only PSB can cater for the needs of minority groups and less privileged members of society, thereby facilitating a deliberative democracy that promotes robust discussion of issues in a public sphere in which people enjoy universal access to information.

Unfortunately for Africa, PSB is seen largely as a 'distant ideal, not a working reality' (Raboy, 1995, p. 78). Banda (2006, p. 8) argues that PSB in Africa is largely an undeveloped sector and even in countries 'where PSB seems to be stronger, such as Ghana and South Africa, the commercial imperatives seem to be driving the sector'. Drawing on studies of African broadcasting systems, Heath (2001) contends that 'no African system has achieved public service standards of independence, impartiality, universal access, or special consideration for minorities'. The broadcasting systems that are more common in Africa are those that serve national or state interests (Heath, 2001).

This gloomy assessment does not take into account the fact that many state broadcasters in Africa regard themselves as an offshoot of the PSB services that were inherited from their former colonial rulers. It has been argued that accounts of the media in Africa are usually tied to Africa's colonial history. Golding (1977), for example, argues that descriptions of the media in any developing country that make no reference to an international context of dependence are incomplete. He illustrates how colonial ties were sustained in the broadcasting sector through staff training, programming and education. For instance, until a few decades ago, Nigeria's radio broadcasting followed, essentially, the BBC model in which staff undertake short training courses in London (Golding, 1977).

A survey of the status of public broadcasting in 11 African countries found, among other things, that: broadcast media is mostly accessible to a greater proportion of the African population; no other media can satisfy the information needs of African people in terms of news, education and entertainment, in the absence of a public broadcaster; commercial broadcasters are profit-driven and serve the economic interests of their owners rather than the overall interest of the public; although community broadcasters are accepted within the communities in which they operate, they have a limited influence on the general public; and the Internet represents an additional source of information but is only accessible to a minority elite (Bussiek, 2013). The survey found that, although all national broadcasters in the 11 countries studied claim to be 'public broadcasters', this is far from accurate as they are state-controlled institutions. Additionally, the study found that many African governments want to retain their ownership and control over state broadcasters but they also continue to reduce the funds provided to the broadcasting organisations. Inadequate funds have compelled the broadcasters to transform into state-controlled commercial broadcasters and subsequently forced them to compete with commercial broadcasters in a competitive environment. This situation has resulted in state-controlled broadcasters accumulating huge debts and becoming bankrupt.

For public service broadcasters in Africa to achieve their mission, governments must provide adequate funds or find alternative funding mechanisms that will not render the broadcasters vulnerable to the influence of political leaders and economic forces. The success of public service broadcasters in Africa will be determined by the extent to which they are independent of government officials and market forces, and the extent to which they are provided with adequate funds to enable them to carry out their public service goals.

Following years of state control of the broadcast media in Africa, the situation is changing as PSB is seen to drive a culture of democracy and freedom of expression. It was assumed that an independent and free public service broadcaster that is free from government control and interference could advance democracy in African countries. This growing sentiment was supported by pro-democracy rallies and developments that toppled authoritarian regimes in Eastern Europe such as the collapse of Nicolae Ceausescu's government in Romania in 1989, the fall of President Ferdinand Marcos of the Philippines in 1986, as well as the dismantling of the Berlin Wall in East Germany in 1989.

Across Africa in the late 1980s and early 1990s, efforts to transform state-controlled broadcasting institutions into PSB systems were slowed or halted by economic constraints, political instability, internecine civil strife and lack of political will to implement the new idea (Heath, 2001; Zaffiro, 2000). Surprisingly, Fourie (2004) has called for a shift in focus from the traditional understanding of PSB as an institution to consider 'public service broadcasting as a genre offered by all role players in the broadcasting sector' (Fourie, 2004, p. 1). He argues that broadcasting, in particular radio broadcasting, can help to make people aware of their needs, to rally them to a particular cause and to help them appreciate the values of national development.

The environment for PSB has been transformed by globalisation, which was also facilitated by technological changes that spawned the move toward digitisation, convergence of media and the emergence of diverse channels of news delivery. These, in turn, resulted in deregulation of the public service broadcast market, leading to increases in competition in local, national and international markets, the development of multiple choices for consumers and the struggle for advertising income as alternative sources of funding (Fourie, 2004). These developments seem to be based on the presumption that market forces are the best mechanisms to promote democracy. The market approach has its shortcomings, one of which is that it treats audiences as commodities to be marketed or sold to advertisers. Rather than aim to satisfy audience needs, the market approach seeks to maximise audience figures in order to satisfy commercial interests. According to Fourie (2004, p. 5), 'This has led to increased commercialisation, popularisation, repetition, less depth and less diversity in programming despite the rise of so-called niche channels.' The aim of the market approach is not to satisfy the welfare of audience members but to satisfy commercial interests. In fact, the market approach sees communication as business.

One of the changes that has taken place in PSB is the move toward digitisation and Internet broadcasting.

Broadcasting on the Internet

The Internet has increasingly become an established outlet for distribution of broadcasting services. The convergence of the Internet and broadcasting services therefore strengthens the case for the use of the Internet for PSB. The Internet can be used to deliver various television services on the web. For example, rather than posing a threat to the survival of minority languages, the Internet can in fact enable speakers of minority languages to achieve complete control over representations of themselves, as well as the language they choose to communicate in the public domain. The Internet should be seen as a site where significant and meaningful cross-cultural communication and language learning can take place. It is also a place for dissemination of information controlled by minority groups to the wider public. Additionally, the web can be used to store huge files of language resources and to preserve those languages that are threatened. Thus, one area where digital technology could prove to be of major benefit to speakers of minority languages is the preservation of their languages.

There are various ways that web-based broadcasting will be valuable to citizens. Internet-based television broadcasting will expand opportunities available to audiences to access television programmes and to learn minority languages. On-demand viewing of television programmes broadcast via the Internet will eliminate problems associated with access (Middleton, 2010, p. 166).

One of the defining characteristics of the Internet is its resistance to outside interference. The very nature of the technology means that it is exceptionally difficult to regulate the content of the Internet. The only real way of doing so is by methods that would be utterly counterproductive in their heavy-handedness. Those governments that have successfully censored the Internet have done so by one of a variety of means: by demolishing the technical equipment; by using discreet technology to scrutinise sites visited by citizens; and by stringent monitoring of Internet Service Providers (Article 19, 2006). The popularity of the Internet is derived from the freedom it grants to users and the promotion of interactivity. On the Internet, people can access information when they want and they can also respond directly to the provider of the information. This is one way the Internet promotes interaction between users and content producers.

Canada's public service broadcaster – the CBC – is regarded as one of the broadcasters that pioneered broadcasting on the web. The development of its website (www.CBC.ca) in 1995 has been described as a major shift in the organisation's move toward the expansion of its coverage to include 'a national and international profile for Canadian news and media content' (O'Neill and Murphy, 2012, p. 163). Another public broadcaster that is widely credited with having led the way to Internet broadcasting is the BBC. With regard to Canada, O'Neill and Murphy (2012) state that one of the reasons why the CBC showed interest in the Internet much earlier than other broadcasters was to ensure that Canadian content was widely available to Canadian audiences. The challenges that confronted the CBC as a result of cuts in funding and other modifications in the management and organisation of the broadcast industry in the country compelled it to think of a new scheme to survive the challenges of broadcasting in the digital age. This reconsideration was necessary as it allowed the CBC to engage in web-based content delivery (O'Neill and Murphy, 2012). The broadcast industry regulator – the Canada Radio-television and Telecommunications Commission (CRTC) – helped the CBC to move into digital broadcasting when it freed 'new media broadcasting' and the Internet in the country from regulation (O'Neill and Murphy, 2012, p. 165). According to the researchers,

> The Commission argued that the circumstances that led to regulation of Canadian content in traditional broadcasting did not exist in the internet environment at the time and that market forces were

providing a sufficient Canadian presence on the internet supported by a strong demand for Canadian new media content.

(O'Neill and Murphy, 2012, pp. 165–166)

This decision by the CBC in 1999 clearly distinguished between broadcasting provided through 'terrestrial, cable and satellite and those services delivered by the internet, releasing the latter from any form of regulatory control...' (O'Neill and Murphy, 2012, p. 166). CBC's first move into digital broadcasting was done through the broadcaster's radio arm. Citing Patrick, Black and Whalen (1996), O'Neill and Murphy state that a test in 1993 'encoded episodes of CBC programs as audio files which were then offered for download via FTP, Gopher and the World Wide Web' (O'Neill and Murphy, 2012, p. 167). The experimental broadcast was so widely received it persuaded CBC radio management to start 'radio.cbc.ca' in December 1994 (2012, p. 167).

One line of reasoning that backed broadening the public service responsibility to include the Internet was that it was intended to ensure that the public service broadcaster was able to broadcast across a range of new media outlets and to sustain a prestigious profile on the Internet. In its (CBC) transition to Internet broadcasting, the BBC was cited as a model to which the CBC should aspire because of the BBC's track record in digital broadcasting and its international profile as an exemplary public service broadcaster. The additional responsibility that came with the CBC broadcasting on the Internet was not only the extension of its programmes to a global audience but also the financial implications of doing so. As O'Neill and Murphy point out, 'the CBC had to either self-finance or cross-subsidize from other activities' (2012, p. 170). Nevertheless, the CBC's move into digital broadcasting has had significant implications for the public service broadcaster.

It made the CBC the number one media/broadcasting company online in Canada, a position it does not maintain in the offline world. It brought the CBC to younger audiences – its online service has the highest proportion of 18–34 year olds of all CBC services. It also succeeded in extending audiences for CBC content in new timeslots where traditional media has had relatively little success.

(O'Neill and Murphy, 2012, p. 171)

In Australia, Burns (2012, p. 52) notes that 'when web-based news services were being introduced in Australia in the early nineties, the ABC was the only truly multiplatform media operation in Australia, and it adapted quickly to online'. How did that happen? In the move toward web-based broadcasting, the radio arm of the national broadcaster, the ABC, enjoyed several advantages and privileges over other forms of media such as print and television. According to Burns (2012, p. 52),

> Whereas newspapers and television networks, accustomed to a daily deadline, had to change their production methods to meet the 24 hour schedule of the web, the ABC had the experience of hourly radio bulletins to which it was able to add its televisual experience and its local and overseas reporters. It thus entered the web world with several advantages over many other media organisations.

The situation is that, as of November 2006,

> the ABC offered four national radio networks and 60 local stations, three Internet-based music services, ABCTV via analogue or digital; one digital TV station; 2.3 million web pages across 12 subject gateways, an international radio service, an international television service and 41 ABC shops and 90 ABC centres. It operates alongside the other Public Service Broadcaster, the SBS, in a broadcast system that includes commercial free-to-air radio and television stations, as well as community broadcasting and pay TV.
>
> (Burns, 2008, p. 872)

Conclusion

This chapter examined PSB as an important institution that serves different purposes in different societies. One of the underlying reasons for the establishment of PSB systems in different countries is the expectation that they should cater for the diverse needs of audiences. For this and other reasons, PSB enjoys popular support because of the principles on which it is based. Despite the admirable characteristics of PSB, questions are being raised about its relevance in a digital age in which information is mostly accessible through the Internet and other new media. In many developing countries in Africa, South America, Asia and the Middle East, PSB is regarded as an important instrument for nation-building and a tool for the development of a strong and deliberative democracy. PSB is generally used for nation-building in developing countries because the mass media are regarded, correctly or incorrectly, as facilitators of social change and development.

Different countries have different policy frameworks for the promotion of minority or lesser used languages through PSB. South Africa serves as an example of a country in which the constitution requires the SABC – the public broadcaster – to reflect and promote 11 official languages in its programmes. In Africa, while debate continues over the value of a state broadcaster serving as a PSB system, some countries have tried to fashion their broadcasting systems according to the PSB model. There are different frameworks under which public service broadcasters operate. These include the self-regulated system of broadcasting, a system in which the broadcaster is seen as an institution of the state and therefore responsible to the state, and a system in which the public service broadcaster is controlled by media authorities.

One crucial element of PSB is the requirement that it be independent in funding, and free from political interference and the influence of market forces. This requirement is seen as an ideal because of the difficulty that public service broadcasters have in generating funds independently of government subventions, parliamentary allocations and advertising.

The emergence of new technologies has produced new roles for the PSB, particularly the need for public service broadcasters to reflect the realities of the 21st century and to make broadcasting more pertinent and alert to the needs of audience members. Globalisation and technological changes that facilitated media convergence and digitisation have resulted in a deregulated market that has spawned greater competition and multiple platforms of news production and delivery to consumers. These transformations have made people question whether the remit for PSB is still relevant in the modern world.

Growing competition and the fascination for raising revenue through advertising have compelled public service broadcasters to aim for entertainment-driven content that does not guarantee high quality programmes. The challenge for public service broadcasters is to uphold their public service mandates or to relinquish their roles in order to compete for audiences with commercial broadcasters in the new environment.

In multicultural and multilingual countries, PSB has played a crucial role as a vehicle for the promotion and preservation of minority languages that are facing extinction. Language maintenance is crucial because it is a symbol of national and ethnic identity. Language is also a unifying force, particularly in multicultural societies.

The future of PSB will depend to a great extent on how it generates revenue and still retains its independence from government and economic influences. Public service broadcasters that rely on advertising as a source of revenue will undermine their independence and also their ability to produce quality programmes. Other factors that will challenge the effectiveness of PSB are globalisation, technological transformations and competition for revenue and audiences from commercial broadcasters. Some renowned public service broadcasters such as the CBC in Canada and the BBC in the UK have moved into Internet broadcasting for a number of reasons, such as to resist interference in editorial contents by outside forces, to expand programme reach and coverage areas, and to cut costs. Essentially, the move toward broadcasting on the web was a response by public service broadcasters to threats posed by new technologies to their existence and relevance.

4

Indigenous Knowledge and Intellectual Property Rights in a New Age

Introduction

Concerns have persisted about the state of Indigenous knowledge and intellectual property rights of Indigenous people in the digital age. Central to the debate is the ownership and preservation of Indigenous knowledge, art, craft and traditional practices, as well as respect for the cultural expressions of Indigenous people. In the age of new technologies, there are reasons why Indigenous people should be concerned about the extent to which information and communication technologies allow them to express themselves without undermining their rights to protect their land rights, art, craft, sacred sites and other traditional cultural practices, including their rights to ownership of their intellectual property. Essentially, globalisation has thrown up a challenge to Indigenous people. On one hand, globalisation has facilitated transformations in technology, aviation, telephony and the World Wide Web that have not only brought together Indigenous people across the world but have also increased the profile and prominence of Indigenous people.

However, globalisation has also made it easier for the world to exploit and misappropriate Indigenous knowledge and cultural expressions without the consent of the people. Daes (2004) notes that 'globalization is creating two potentially opposing forces: the global marketing of goods and the global marketing of ideas. Indigenous peoples are rich in ideas and stories; it has always been their principal form of capital.' However, globalisation has also come with some ironies. It has placed Indigenous people in a Catch-22 situation in which it is difficult to take the good aspects of globalisation without also accepting the culturally harmful aspects. Globalisation, as Daes points out, has presented Indigenous people with a dilemma:

> It is creating a global market for dissemination of fresh ideas and new voices, while making it easier for one voice to drown out all the others. It is providing each of us with finger-tip access to the whole range of human cultural diversity while, at the same time, it is dissolving all cultures into a single supermarket with standard brands. It is making it possible for even the smallest society to earn a livelihood by selling its ideas, rather than selling its lands or forests. But it is also threatening the confidentiality of Indigenous peoples' most private and sacred knowledge.
>
> (Daes, 2004)

With or without globalisation, there are concerns over the widespread unauthorised sale and criminal duplication and reproduction of Indigenous cultural expressions. For example, Greaves (1996, p. 25) notes the devaluing of Indigenous knowledge and the disappearance of their cultural expressions. He states that

> The very cultural heritage that gives indigenous peoples their identity, now far more than in the past, is under real or potential assault from those who would gather it up, strip away its honored meanings, convert it to a product, and sell it. Each time that happens the cultural heritage itself dies a little, and with it its people.
>
> (Greaves, 1996, p. 25)

Before discussing the various concerns that Indigenous people have about lack of international recognition for, and protection of, their knowledge and intellectual property rights, it is important to understand the various ways that scholars have conceptualised Indigenous knowledge and intellectual property rights.

Conceptualisations of Indigenous knowledge

There are two descriptions of Indigenous knowledge that are explored in the literature (Brush, 1996). One definition sees it as 'the systematic information that remains in the informal sector, usually unwritten and preserved in oral tradition rather than texts' (Brush, 1996, p. 4). A narrower definition makes reference to the 'knowledge systems of Indigenous people and minority cultures' (1996, p. 4). Indigenous knowledge is therefore steeped in the cultural traditions of Indigenous people. Mugabe (2007) states that Indigenous knowledge is synonymous with traditional knowledge but traditional knowledge does not quite fit into Indigenous knowledge. He defines traditional knowledge as 'the totality of all knowledge and practices, whether explicit or implicit, used in the management of socioeconomic and ecological facets of life. This knowledge is established on past experiences and observation' (Mugabe, 2007, p. 99). Moahi (2007, p. 72) clarifies the point by identifying the unique elements that underpin Indigenous knowledge (IK):

(a)   Any one single individual does not own IK because it is a product of the culture tradition and way of life of a community. It is thus community owned;

(b)   It is usually passed orally from generation to generation, it is not codified or documented anywhere except in the minds of the community and the community's knowledge custodians, such as chiefs, traditional doctors, etc.;

(c)   It has a potential (and has in many cases) to provide economic returns either to the community that owns it, or to the individuals who may have taken it away from the community for meagre economic gain, or through some other fraudulent means. It is thus a very valuable resource, and this has prompted more debate on the intellectual property rights of IK.

One concern over the ability of Indigenous people to protect and preserve their intellectual property rights is that IK is hardly documented. This means that valuable knowledge could disappear as the elders and custodians of such knowledge pass away (Moahi, 2007, p. 73). The best way to preserve knowledge is to document it; however, documentation implies the knowledge would have to be copyrighted. This therefore raises the question about the copyright owner of the documented knowledge. Moahi raises critical questions about the dilemma over who owns the copyright: 'is it the community from which it was obtained or is it the individual or organisation that took the responsibility to document the knowledge?' (Moahi, 2007, p. 73). He argues that, naturally, the Indigenous community should own the copyright to the documented knowledge, although this has always been contested and remains unresolved.

Existing intellectual property laws are seen as inadequate in helping to protect and preserve the rights of Indigenous people to their intellectual property. A typical and most frequently cited example of bias is the law that grants copyright to individual creators of knowledge but ignores the fact that IK is not individually owned in Indigenous communities. The limitations of copyright laws with regard to IK and protection of intellectual property rights of Indigenous people have been identified by scholars such as Morolong (2007) and Kiggundu (2007). There are various sound reasons why the intellectual property rights of Indigenous people should be recognised, protected and preserved in international law. Some of the arguments are that Indigenous people should have the right to own and manage IK; they must have the right to stop or manage the commercial use of their knowledge; they must also be granted the right to profit from commercial use of their knowledge; they should have the right to be recognised and credited with the knowledge; and they must have the right to stop any disparaging, insulting or deceptive use of their knowledge (anonymous, cited in Moahi, 2007).

Mugabe (2007) states that despite the controversy over how to protect and preserve the cultural expressions of Indigenous people in existing intellectual property laws, it could still be argued that the property rights of Indigenous people are already covered in the Universal Declaration of Human Rights and the International Covenant on Economic, Social and Cultural Rights (ICESCR). Mugabe cites, for example, Article 1 of the ICESCR which 'establishes the right of self-determination, including the right to dispose of natural wealth and resources. This implies the right to protect and conserve resources, including intellectual property' (Posey, 1994, cited in Mugabe, 2007, p. 111).

Technological transformations have made more complicated the rights Indigenous people have to their intellectual property. This concern has been expressed by many scholars such as Moahi (2007), Daes (2004) and Davis (n.d.). Citing the literature, Moahi (2007) notes that the digital age has modified the economics of information transmission, as it is now easy to reproduce or duplicate copies of other people's intellectual works. 'In the digital world, opportunities for theft are much greater than they were before' (Moahi, 2007, p. 70).

Challenges of globalisation and technological changes

While the Internet has promoted the democratisation of information, Indigenous people are concerned about how they can protect and keep their sacred knowledge out of the public sphere that the Internet represents. As Daes (2004) states, 'Anyone who has been following the legal battle over free distribution of recorded music over the Internet – the Napster case – is aware that globalization of communication has made it far easier than ever for Indigenous peoples' sacred and special knowledge to be appropriated illicitly.' Therein lies the predicament that confronts Indigenous people over how to protect their intellectual property in the age of new technologies that make it possible for anyone to access the intellectual property of Indigenous people that is posted on the Internet.

Daes (2004) raises a critical question that underpins the debate over the protection of intellectual property rights of Indigenous people: 'If an element of a knowledge is sacred or confidential, how can disclosing it worldwide protect it?' It is this point that Tafler (2000) highlights in an example of how new media, such as the CD-ROM, can threaten Indigenous cultures. Drawing on an example from the Australian Aboriginal communities in the Pilbara and at Yuendumu, he notes:

> CD-ROMs pose an added risk to the preservation of Indigenous culture. Within the community, traditional owners have final say over content. Constant negotiations determine viewing practices, in particular over who may or may not have the right to view images of the dead. For a society that not only values knowledge but also articulates procedures that ensure that an acquired wisdom frames its transmission, the distribution of recorded devices means that a privileged part of their culture travels beyond the boundaries of community control. The interactive system must incorporate a means of protecting that knowledge, controlling its negotiation, preserving property and custodial rights over secret information. Some of the facilitators/developers shun CD-ROM technology as a means of preserving and protecting, of conveying culture. They consider CD-ROMs a by-product of game and entertainment technology, a Whitefella toy, a cheap way to record culture and in the process make it open to exploitative manipulation.
>
> (Tafler, 2000, p. 36)

Tafler (2000) notes how electronic media, telephones, computers, digital cameras, satellite technologies and new media are having a profound impact on property rights, family relationships and the reconfiguration of power relationships in Indigenous communities. 'For indigenous communities, global networks mean the disruption of traditional networks, connections and cycles that have endured for centuries' (Tafler, 2000, p. 27).

Inadequacies of existing intellectual property rights laws

One obstacle that Indigenous peoples face when they notice a breach of their traditional knowledge is that 'they cannot secure or afford adequate legal representation in national courts – particularly if their dispute crosses national borders' (Daes, 2004). Additionally, while about 95 per cent of Indigenous people reside in developing countries, national laws passed by these countries are regarded as inadequate to halt the illegal use of copyright material relating to IK by researchers and companies in developed countries (Daes, 2004). The problem has been described thus: 'The real issue is not the problem of defining Indigenous cultural and intellectual property, nor of agreeing that the heritage of Indigenous peoples, should in principle, be protected by law, like other property. The real issue is *enforcement*, where disputes routinely cross international frontiers…' (Daes, 2004).

It is perhaps for this reason that Indigenous peoples have continued to argue that the existing intellectual property systems offer them little protection for their intellectual knowledge and cultural expressions. Indigenous peoples' intellectual property rights are being violated and abused in various ways such as art works being stolen, and 'Indigenous peoples' biological resources, knowledge and human genetic materials being assembled and patented without due recognition being given or benefits distributed to the Indigenous peoples concerned' (Davis, n.d.).

Attempts by states and intergovernmental agencies to define Indigenous people's rights and responsibilities with regard to their heritage seem to work against the tenets of Indigenous self-determination (Daes, 2004). As Indigenous people claim ownership of their intellectual and cultural heritage, it follows that efforts to classify into a set of laws or rules Indigenous peoples' intellectual property rights will be inconsistent with Indigenous peoples' right to self-determination. It is perhaps for these reasons that Indigenous leaders assert that current intellectual property rights legislations do not grant them and their people sufficient acknowledgment of their rights, including the rights to preserve their cultural products and expressions (Davis, n.d.). Existing intellectual property rights are perceived as a danger to Indigenous peoples' right to self-determination and cultural preservation. When reference is made to Indigenous peoples' intellectual property rights, it often includes rights to land, cultural heritage and environment, as well as cultural expressions.

Rights to recognise and protect Indigenous cultural knowledge can also be widened to include the environment and its preservation. In this regard, reference is made to the 1992 United Nations Conference on Environment and Development (UNCED), in particular Agenda 21, which relates to the Convention on Biological Diversity that required member countries to preserve and safeguard Indigenous peoples' knowledge, discoveries and traditional practices that relate to the preservation of biological diversity (Davis, n.d.). In the Rio Declaration on Environment and Development at the UNCED held in Rio de Janeiro (3–14 June 1992), it was also acknowledged that Indigenous people will play an important role in sustainable management and development of their environment owing to their valuable knowledge and traditions. Principle 22 in particular states that

> Indigenous people and their communities and other local communities have a vital role in environmental management and development because of their knowledge and traditional practices. States should recognize and duly support their identity, culture and interests and enable their effective participation in the achievement of sustainable development.
>
> (United Nations Environment Programme, Rio Declaration on Environment and Development, 1992)

Posey (1994, p. 120) notes that it is the first time that 'indigenous and local communities embodying traditional lifestyles are expressly mentioned in the Convention and their invaluable contribution to biological diversity conservation recognized'. Despite this recognition, advocates of Indigenous rights to knowledge and intellectual property argue that few attempts have been made to recognise and protect the intellectual property rights of Indigenous people. Drawing on Morphy (1984, p. 28), Tafler (2000, p. 33) identifies three types of rights that Aboriginal people have or acquire with regard to sacred law. These are 'rights of ownership (clan), managerial rights (cuts across clan), rights as guardians (clan)'. He points out that, in instances in which ownership dictates the rights of access and includes an obligation to protect a restricted knowledge, the society determines who has the right to know, to speak and to speak for another person in transmitting information (Tafler, 2000). It is this system of rights that Michaels (1984) ascribed to some kind of political economy of communication in Indigenous societies.

> In societies without print, where the word is inseparable from the author of the word, information can take on special values. Where material production is not emphasized, the ownership and exchange of information can become elaborated through economic systems where knowledge is wealth of a particular sort. To assure the maintenance of this economy, conventions arise and may be invoked with

force of law regarding who may know and who may say. So even though somebody tells me something of significance, my right to tell another is not assured.

(Michaels, 1984, p. 52, cited in Tafler, 2000, p. 33)

Concerns about non-recognition of areas of cultural expression

Indigenous people are not only concerned about the non-recognition and lack of protection of their intellectual property rights in relation to arts and copyright, they are also concerned that other areas of their cultural heritage and intellectual property rights such as language, dance, song, story, sacred sites and objects have not been recognised and therefore have not been protected. In fact, there are growing concerns on the part of Indigenous people that their intellectual property rights will never be recognised and protected by the international community. Posey (1994, p. 121) states that 'Indigenous groups doubt that existing international and national laws will adequately recognize and protect their knowledge, innovations and practices.' There is no doubt, he argues, that existing intellectual property rights were designed to safeguard individual, technological and industrial creations, and not designed 'to protect the collective, trans-historical and intangible qualities of indigenous cultures' (Posey, 1994, p. 122).

Indigenous people see intellectual property laws as alien legislation that has been imposed on their communities to strip them of their rights to ownership of their knowledge and intellectual property. Even the 1948 Universal Declaration of Human Rights, which is often cited as evidence that the intellectual property rights of Indigenous people are recognised in international law, is dismissed on the basis that collective rights that apply in Indigenous communities are antithetical to intellectual property rights that are designed to protect individual creative works, not works owned by Indigenous communities (Mugabe, 2007).

Part of the reason why existing intellectual property laws are inappropriate and ineffective in protecting Indigenous cultural expressions is that cultural creations are owned and managed by Indigenous communities rather than by individuals. Therefore, 'if an individual wishes to perform, transmit, or make manifest an aspect of culture – such as a design or motif – he or she will require the authority, consent or permission of others who may have rights and interests in the particular design or motif' (Davis, n.d.). However, intellectual property rights, as perceived and defined in the western legal framework, relate to copyright, patents, trademarks, designs and trade secret laws, as well as infringement of confidentiality. As Davis (n.d.) states, western understanding of intellectual property rights is founded on the notion that works that are created, as well as ideas and innovations or discoveries that are articulated through various ways can be possessed, and that every individual has clear and unique property rights to their works and products. Article 2(viii) of the 1967 Convention Establishing the World Intellectual Property Organisation (WIPO) defines 'intellectual property' to include rights that relate to:

- 'literary, artistic and scientific works,
- performances of performing artists, phonograms, and broadcasts,
- inventions in all fields of human endeavor,
- scientific discoveries,
- industrial designs,
- trademarks, service marks, and commercial names and designations,
- protection against unfair competition,
- and all other rights resulting from intellectual activity in the industrial, scientific, literary or artistic fields'.

(Convention Establishing the World Intellectual
Property Organization, 1967)

This definition, however, is informed by the western legal framework that differs markedly from the way intellectual property rights are conceptualised and understood in Indigenous societies. Indigenous people view western legal interpretations of intellectual property as narrow. Indigenous people not only seek protection for created or invented products but also believe they have the right to protect the processes that lead to the creation of their cultural products. They believe their culture also incorporates the knowledge, creativity and traditions that contribute to the creation of the cultural products and expressions (Davis, n.d.). Cultural identity and community practices are therefore central to Indigenous peoples' demand for recognition and protection of their intellectual property rights. Indigenous people see cultural heritage as a part of their intellectual property rights. Cultural heritage thus includes and is not limited to issues such as music, dance, songs, traditional rites, cultural possessions, artistic designs and environmental knowledge.

Although new technologies have democratised communication across the globe, especially for people who have access to the technologies, the impact on copyright laws has been largely negative. As Mazonde (2007,

p. 2) argues, the Internet has aided copyright infringements. While this might be the case, it is also incorrect to suggest that the Internet has caused the violation of copyright laws. It is not the technology that has breached the copyright laws but people who use the technology to engage in illegal activities. People use technologies in appropriate and inappropriate ways. It is therefore not the technological artefact that should be held responsible when people use the technology to commit crimes or to engage in legally inappropriate activities.

Protection of Indigenous knowledge in Africa

Regardless of how people use technology, it has been suggested that the need to protect the intellectual property rights of Indigenous people should be placed on the same priority scale as efforts to protect Indigenous cultures. With specific reference to Africa, Masoga (2007) identifies the value of protecting and using IK for the benefit of humanity:

> it is essential to protect and effectively utilize indigenous knowledge that represents a major dimension of the continent's culture, and to share this knowledge for the benefit of humankind. The New Partnership for Africa's Development will give special attention to the protection and nurturing of indigenous knowledge, which includes tradition-based literacy, artistic and scientific works, inventions, scientific discoveries, designs, marks, names and symbols, undisclosed information and all other tradition-based innovations....
>
> (Masoga, 2007, p. 3)

This places a burden on the leaders of NEPAD (the New Partnership for Africa's Development) to act to protect IK in Africa through ratification of proper laws. The protection and promotion of Africa's IK is particularly urgent, not only to demonstrate the relevance of other existing worldviews other than the dominant western perspectives but also to showcase Africa's contributions to the world in terms of intellectual knowledge systems. Africa and other developing regions of the world have IK systems that are unique and central to their socioeconomic development. In the 21st century, the world cannot continue to rely on western-dominated theories of knowledge when there are important and appropriate non-western knowledge systems that are beneficial to humanity. As Thomas and Nyamnjoh (2007, p. 12) point out, 'There are communities around the world who have always had a different relationship to knowledge from the dominant norm. Their knowledge has been critical to their physical, cultural and ontological survival.' This view is supported in the literature.

The critique of dominant western worldviews suggests that, although we live in a multicultural and postmodern world, Eurocentrism 'still permeates every field of study and every sphere of life' (Miike, 2006, p. 5). Miike put forward an important question: 'How can scholars pursue truly non-Western ideas when their ways of knowing are so inflected by the Western worldview?' (2006, p. 9). Gordon (2007) states that when scholars borrow from the heavily skewed western systems of knowledge, they forgo alternative worldviews. Satoshi (2007) says that it is these dominant theoretical perspectives that have been upheld, adopted uncritically by scholars and applied extensively in western and non-western societies. Following the line of argument made by Thomas and Nyamnjoh (2007), Miike (2010) advocates Asiacentric and Afrocentric views because they are more accommodating and reflect diverse worldviews. For example, the Asiacentric idea, he argues,

> demands that (1) Asian people or texts are viewed as subjects and agents in their narratives, that (2) Asian interests, values, and ideals are prioritized in the discourse on Asians and their experiences, and that (3) an Asian person, document, or phenomenon is located in the context of her/his or its own history and heritage.
>
> (Miike, 2010, p. 4)

He notes that the value of Afrocentric and Asiacentric viewpoints is that they are not universalist in nature; they do not perceive their 'cultural worldview as the only universal frame of reference and impose it on all human beings. They do not deny the value of other cultural perspectives on Africans and Asians' (Miike, 2010, p. 4).

Challenges that confront Africa in the information society

Chikonzo (2006) outlines the challenges that confront Africa in the attempt to harness new technologies for purposes of gathering, protecting and distributing IK on the continent. The challenges include the absence of an enabling environment to facilitate widespread use of technologies, prohibitive costs of Internet connectivity and services, exorbitant costs of computer hardware and software, low level budgets for development of the information and communication technology sector, absence of training relating to information and communication technologies to help Africans to develop necessary skills and knowledge, and general lack of other technological resources. Most of these problems are already well known to policymakers in government departments. To overcome these obstacles, African countries must commit to the development of an effective ICT sector. They must also provide adequate funds to facilitate the transformation to an information society that they pledged at the inauguration of the NEPAD. All these must be accompanied by the presence of a strong science and technology development policy that should drive Africa's move toward the growth of an information society.

Commercialisation of intellectual property

The commercialisation of intellectual property of Indigenous people has raised concerns not only among Indigenous people but also in civil society, international organisations such as the WIPO, and United Nations agencies. Concerns over the commercialisation of Indigenous cultural expressions and resources such as songs, dances, music, weaves, art and craft, and other artefacts are based on the degradation or adulteration that strips them of their cultural value and relevance. It is worth noting that Indigenous people who are denied rights to their intellectual property are neither compensated nor recognised. In fact, dispossession of Indigenous people of their intellectual property rights carries with it denial of their identities and traditional knowledge systems (Thomas and Nyamnjoh, 2007). In the digital era in which global capitalism is projected as the norm, IK is 'displaced from the hitherto protected, narrow boundaries and confines of the clan, tribe, village, community and is being redesigned and reconfigured in response to the asking and dictate of global capital' (Thomas and Nyamnjoh, 2007, p. 14).

Bias in intellectual property laws

One of the biases identified in the existing intellectual property laws is that they are designed to benefit western cultural practices and understandings of intellectual property such as privileging individual ownership over community ownership. In essence, intellectual property laws tend to respond to western views about what constitutes ownership of intellectual property, especially when dealing with copyright or folklore (see, for example, Daes, 2004; Davis, n.d.; Kiggundu, 2007). Kiggundu (2007) states that intellectual property law as it currently exists was designed by westerners not only to advance their cultural interests but also to protect their values. He perceives a conspiracy that occurred as far back as colonial times, when the colonial powers took their intellectual property laws to the colonised countries with the purpose of exploiting the colonies. This resulted in exploitation of the resources and cultural expressions of Indigenous people. Consequently, the colonial intellectual property law paid no attention to the cultural values of Indigenous people. According to Kiggundu (2007, p. 27), 'During the colonial era, the colonial powers plundered indigenous knowledge in their colonies and repatriated as much of it as they could back to the developed countries. They repatriated artefacts, paintings, mummies, jewellery, ancient literature and historical documents, plants, animals and entire manufacturing processes.' Against this background, he suggests that developing countries should place more emphasis on the preservation of their IK.

In terms of cultural heritage of Indigenous people, folklore is believed to be an important aspect of this. Folklore incorporates but is not limited to elements such as belief systems, myths, folk tales, proverbs, metaphors, dances, songs, art and craft forms, traditional medicines, tools, architecture and agricultural practices, as well as traditional and cultural practices that are owned and transmitted from one generation to another. Arguments for the protection of folklore are based on the view that folkloric works that belong to Indigenous people and developing countries are increasingly adulterated and damaged in the process of trying to modify them to suit western cultural needs (Morolong, 2007). For example, Janke (2003) points to how cultural performances such as music, dances and songs that originate from Indigenous communities are recorded, replicated and marketed on the Internet. Morolong (2007) and Kutty (2002) believe the rampant abuse and mutilation of Indigenous cultural expressions such as folklore has been facilitated by the Internet and other new technologies. For example, 'it is now possible to download traditional music from free music archives onto one's home computer and have it stored as digital information that can be transferred into other sound files (that is new compositions) where it can be manipulated in whatever manner one sees fit' (Morolong, 2007, p. 50). Other views suggest that the folklore of Indigenous people and developing countries should be protected and recognised like other intellectual property rights.

Problems of classifying folklore within intellectual property laws

As discussed earlier, one of the problems of classifying Indigenous folklore within the existing intellectual property laws is that some creations of cultural expressions are owned by communities rather than by individuals. In other words, there is no exclusive individual right to intellectual property that applies in Indigenous communities. As Morolong (2007, p. 52) underlined the point, 'Members of the cultural communities would not be able to create new works based on cultural heritage if private property rights are established over it.' Several limitations of copyright law that undermine efforts to protect and preserve expressions of folklore have been identified.

The first problem is that the copyright law requires that the work be original. This requirement means that expressions of folklore that are produced in an Indigenous community are disqualified from copyright protection. Another problem is that copyright law recognises the owner or author of a work but this does not apply to expressions of folklore that originate from, and are owned by, Indigenous communities. Moreover, the expressions of folklore are passed on from one generation to another. In essence, folkloric works are outcomes of community efforts, not the result of an individual's creativity. So, no individual can claim sole authorship or ownership of folklore produced in an Indigenous community because the work must have been passed on from one generation to another. This makes it problematic to associate the folkloric work with a particular individual. Even if an individual produced the work, the work will become the property of the Indigenous community as soon as the individual has passed on. Therefore, a work produced by an individual in an Indigenous community loses its right to individual ownership over the years because the original creator can no longer be identified. The third problem with copyright protection of expressions of folklore is that copyright does not last forever. It is effective and applicable over the natural life of the author or creator of the work. So, when the copyright expires, the folkloric work could be open to abuse and the owners of the work could be denied the benefits of their intellectual property. The other problem with copyright is the requirement that the work must be written and documented. Expressions of folklore such as music, dances and songs will not be able to meet this requirement (Morolong, 2007).

Morolong (2007, p. 51) states that 'intellectual property laws reflect a bias in favour of individuals who are said to own rights in the protected works. The essence of intellectual property rights is to establish private property rights in creations and innovations in order to grant control over their exploitation....' However, intellectual property in Indigenous communities is based on community ownership. This is the established and accepted practice. Moahi (2007) reinforces this point when he argues that IK constitutes a body of knowledge that belongs to groups or communities (see also Daes, 2004; Davis, n.d.; Kiggundu, 2007).

Beyond all these, Indigenous people have expressed concerns over how new technologies have diminished the role of elders as repositories of knowledge of cultural and traditional practices in their communities, including their right to ownership of their intellectual property and IK.

Impact of technology on traditional authority systems

Decades before the introduction of new technologies, Indigenous people across the world had expressed deep concerns about the lack of international recognition for their intellectual property rights, as well as their traditional knowledge systems. Their concerns were based on traditional and cultural practices in their societies, as well as the need for expressions of their identity. For example, in remote Indigenous communities of New Zealand, Canada and Australia, community elders are highly regarded. They are viewed as their communities' storehouse of knowledge, especially knowledge of traditional and cultural practices. In those communities, there are regulations that govern how traditional knowledge is acquired and owned, how the acquired knowledge is to be disseminated and to whom it should be dispensed.

In Indigenous communities, control over community knowledge, in particular knowledge of traditional ceremonies and cultural practices, represents a source of authority. The ability of community elders to manage information confers on them undisputed power which grants them the authority to speak on certain issues while community members listen (Michaels, 1994, p. 32). Respect accorded to community elders and leaders is based on their age, as well as their gender. However, new technologies, in particular the Internet, pose a major challenge to the authority of community elders and leaders, including community laws that define how knowledge is to be acquired, owned and dispensed in the communities.

New technologies challenge the traditional authority of elders in Indigenous communities because they make rules that govern traditional ownership of knowledge in their communities. For example, wide distribution of information on the Internet makes it possible for everyone to access information relating, for example, to secret ceremonies about initiation of young adults in Indigenous societies. The publication of such information on the Internet makes it extremely difficult to implement strict community rules that govern who should have access to the information. Information published on the Internet is seen to exist in the public domain and is therefore open to everyone. People who access privileged information about cultural and traditional practices in Indigenous communities become as well-informed as community elders and leaders who originally had sole access to that knowledge and information. The immediate consequence will be a decline in the ability of community elders and leaders to control knowledge of their community's traditional ceremonies and other cultural practices. They also lose the right to determine which outsiders can access community knowledge and traditional practices, and to determine the rules governing access.

The notion that community elders serve as privileged 'information elites' cannot be sustained in the Internet age in which everyone who has access to the Internet can access secret information relating to community practices and traditional ceremonies. As previously mentioned, the Internet and other new technologies have stripped community elders of their power to determine who should access secret community knowledge. Some people have suggested that community elders can still retain their power even in the age of new technologies. They can do this by issuing passwords to people who have been approved to access privileged information. However, the use of passwords will be successful only to the extent that the users do not disclose the information they accessed on the Internet or disclose their passwords to their friends, family members and associates. Once outsiders have unlawful access to the database that holds information on Indigenous community practices and ceremonies, the whole essence of elders protecting IK will be destroyed and therefore ineffective. This is how the Internet and other digital technologies diminish the authority of community elders, as they can no longer serve effectively as protectors of traditional knowledge or repositories of community knowledge.

Nevertheless, Buchtmann (2000) draws on her study of two Australian Aboriginal communities of Yuendumu (the Warlpiri people in Northern Territory) and Ernabella (the Pitjantjatjara people in northern South Australia) to argue that 'Despite the initial concerns about the impact on traditional culture and language, over the years the Warlpiri have actively adopted modern communication technology including radio broadcasts, video making and more recently on-line services' (Buchtmann, 2000, p. 60). According to her,

the Warlpiri actively embraced the new communication technology for a number of reasons. Warlpiri media has done much to preserve culture, improve information flow, support health education campaigns, increase employment opportunities and provide entertainment. It is also flexible enough to fit in with Warlpiri traditions.

(Buchtmann, 2000, p. 70)

Buchtmann's research shows the Indigenous people had no issues with adopting technology that connected meaningfully with their culture. What the research shows is that, in order for technology to be adopted, it must be perceived to be valuable to the people. It must also pose no threats to the people's cultural and traditional practices. As Buchtmann (2000, p. 67) reported, 'The Warlpiri also adopted the new technology as they were keen to maintain a powerful form of communication to promote their culture and it fitted into existing cultural patterns.'

In Indigenous communities in Australia, New Zealand and Canada, as well as in traditional societies across the world, oral communication is the predominant form of communication and plays a major role in defining the social world of community members. Therefore, in those communities that rely on oral forms of communication, traditional knowledge is conveyed from generation to generation in meticulous ways. As Buchtmann (2000, p. 60) stated in relation to the Warlpiri people of northern Australia,

all the knowledge that the Warlpiri needed for everyday living: food sources, kinship relations and technology had to be remembered and ultimately passed on to the next generation... As each Warlpiri person grew older and passed through rites of passage, such as initiation ceremonies for men and marriage and childbirth for women, they were given access to more complex traditional knowledge.

This shows how knowledge production and the right to use or own that knowledge entail a complicated system of connections that delineate who owns the knowledge and who is permitted to access that knowledge and at what time. So, in Indigenous communities, traditional knowledge arrangements and regulations that guide possession of knowledge bestow on community elders and leaders the sole right to intellectual property. That right is not available to everyone. It is a restricted right that is earned by one's age and gender, and the person's role in the community. Also, the knowledge is not freely available, as it is treated like privileged information that is not easily accessible to all classes of people. As evident in Buchtmann's research, in Indigenous communities, there are strict regulations that define who should access traditional knowledge, including how knowledge of traditional and cultural practices should be protected or preserved. Michaels (1985a, p. 58) makes the point that 'Speaking rights are highly regulated' in Australian Aboriginal communities. That is, in those communities, 'only certain people have the right to speak of or for certain things'.

Therefore, when Indigenous community leaders and elders choose particular people who should have access to traditional knowledge, they exercise their right as protectors of traditional knowledge. This intricate cultural practice, which defines regulations that govern the protection of IK and identity, differs noticeably from the open and mostly free access to information available on the Internet. Michaels (1990, cited in Buchtmann, 2000, p. 62) highlights the cultural practices that mark out who has access to information and knowledge in Aboriginal communities in Australia:

> Aboriginal modes of communication are extensions of the oral and face-to-face nature of that society. These allowed, even required, that information be owned, a kind of intellectual property at the heart of what I understand the traditional Aboriginal economy to be about. Knowledge in the form of stories and songs is the prerogative of senior men and women (elders) and the rules governing transmission are highly regulated. Violating speaking constraints and rights here is treated as theft and recognized to be highly subversive of the traditional gerontocratic social structure.

Respect for elders is highly valued in Indigenous Aboriginal communities of Canada, New Zealand and Australia. However, it is not limited to Indigenous people in these countries. Respect for elders is also a common practice in traditional African societies. For example, Jegede (1995) notes that respect for elders is a common feature of African societies. He states that in Africa, 'unquestionable deference to the elder who is seen as the repository of communal wisdom characterises the hierarchical and coherent nature of the community' (Jegede, 1995, p. 8). Bourgault (1993) also points out that respect for elders is a common feature of life in traditional oral cultures because 'older males are expected to mete kernels of wisdom in carefully inscribed formulary expressions. Their juniors are not expected to cajole and badger their elders for information. Silence and secrecy are in fact incorporated into the discourse of social domination in some societies' (Bourgault, 1993, p. 83).

Against this background, it is no surprise that new technologies have spawned research into how these technologies are impacting

Indigenous people, their traditional practices and their knowledge systems. Although the evidence is still contested, some researchers suggest that Indigenous people across the world have productively harnessed new technologies to serve their community needs (Buchtmann, 2000; Meadows, 2000; Obijiofor et al., 2001; O'Donoghue, 1998; Schaniel, 1988; Valaskakis, 1992). However, other research evidence suggests that when new technologies are introduced by improper persons in unsuitable situations, the technologies can have negative impacts on traditional cultures (Batty, 1993; Michaels, 1985b). The contradictory evidence in the literature poses the question: do new technologies (such as the Internet) allow remote Indigenous people to empower themselves without having to lose their unique cultures? While there may be evidence of the usefulness of new technologies in some Indigenous societies, questions of their appropriateness in some other remote communities remain. For instance, are the new technologies appropriate for promoting Indigenous people's culture, language and traditional practices? If they are, which specific technologies are preferred over others and for what purposes? What changes to community life do new technologies bring to remote Indigenous people?

In her research, Buchtmann (2000) provides answers to some of the questions. Ginsburg (cited in Buchtmann, 2000, p. 60) notes how the new technologies pose a major dilemma to Indigenous people: how do Indigenous people express their identity through new technologies without the new technologies threatening traditional knowledge and culture? Preservation of cultural values, languages and community identity has always been at the centre of discussion on the impact of new technologies on Indigenous communities. Australian Aboriginal leader O'Donoghue (1998) does not believe the Internet poses any threat to Aboriginal traditional practices. The Internet, she argues, will enable Indigenous people to achieve complete control over representations of themselves, as well as what they choose to release into the public domain. Roy and Alonzo (2003, p. 424) make a similar argument, pointing out that 'Digitization technologies serve to preserve images and also make them more widely available.' However, they caution that new technology could also 'serve an intrusive presence in tribal communities'. Obijiofor et al. (2001) found in their Milingimbi (Australia) pilot study that community elders were eager to learn more about the outside world through the media and to filter that knowledge to younger people, thereby reinforcing traditional social structures.

For American Indian communities, Anderson (2003, p. 452) argues that one of the most important services they [websites] can provide to tribal members is information on unemployment opportunities, both in Indian enterprises and in nearby private businesses... Community events, such as powwows and festivals, are announced on most tribal sites. This is a service both to tribal members and to tourists who would like to attend these traditional celebrations.

Arguing that 'Technology may provide native peoples with new ammunition to express and extend themselves', Roy and Raitt (2003, p. 412) acknowledge the inherent challenge that confronts Indigenous people in accessing and using new technologies: 'in many countries throughout the world, indigenous communities are not always in a position to have access to information and communication technologies (ICT) and consequently do not benefit from the resources and knowledge available' (Roy and Raitt, 2003, p. 411). This echoes the concerns expressed by O'Donnell and Delgado (1995) with regard to Indigenous peoples of Latin America and North America. They note that

> Most of the 30 million Indigenous peoples of the Americas have no direct Internet access, and this situation is not likely to change in the foreseeable future... Direct Internet access is therefore limited to people affiliated with major institutions or people who have access to a computer, modem, telephone, and the money to pay for Internet connection, telephone charges, training and support. In areas of Latin America, monthly wages for an Indigenous person can be as low as $30 US, and there may be no telephone infrastructure, even satellite telephone, for hundreds of miles.
>
> (O'Donnell and Delgado, 1995, p. 5)

Indeed, cost has been identified as a major inhibiting factor in the ability of Indigenous people in various parts of the world to access and use new technologies such as the Internet. For example, in a study conducted in New Zealand on 'Maori access to information technology', Parker (2003, p. 459) reported that 'in the year 2000 nearly 33 per cent of Maori people of working age wanted Internet access, but did not have it because of the cost'. In comparative terms, 'Maori and other New Zealanders differ in their use of Internet access at home. In early 2000 just 11 per cent of the Maori survey respondents reported home Internet access; this proportion had more than doubled by late 2001' (Parker, 2003, p. 458). The study also found that 'Maori and Pacific Island respondents had the lowest use of the Internet during 2000, with 65 and 76 per cent respectively reporting never having used the Internet' (Parker, 2003, p. 458). Despite the disappointing statistics, Kamira (2003) is hopeful that the new technologies will eventually permeate the greater population of Indigenous people.

In light of the socioeconomic conditions faced by Indigenous peoples of North and South America, including their struggles for self-determination, O'Donnell and Delgado (1995, p. 7) pose the question: 'Can the Internet help increase the strength of Indigenous nations and the power of the movement for self-determination?' The authors answer the question themselves: 'The answer rests with Indigenous peoples themselves, on how consciously and strategically they and their allies will use and modify the new communication technologies to meet their self-determination goals' (O'Donnell and Delgado, 1995, p. 7). One of the main areas where Indigenous people will benefit from digital technology is the wider representation of Indigenous cultures, history, languages and concerns. For example, McConaghy (2000, p. 49) argues that 'Indigenous representations are important in terms of correcting the images that have been constructed about Indigenous peoples and their cultural practices. They are important precisely because stereotypes and stories about Indigenous peoples have been a significant aspect of their oppression.'

There are other ways that new technologies have been used to promote the culture and traditions of Indigenous people. Using Native Americans as an example, Anderson (2003) states that, for Indigenous and non-Indigenous people, the web serves as an educational tool with regard to the promotion and understanding of their history and traditional practices. 'American Indians take great pride in their history, and many tribes use their Web site to share the story of their people' (Anderson, 2003, p. 452). He continues: 'For widely dispersed tribes, telling their stories on their Web sites may be as much for the benefit of tribal members in far-flung places as for the education of non-Indians...Web sites allow the tribes to offer language information to tribal members and to scholars of linguistics' (Anderson, 2003, p. 452). Insisting that websites are highly valuable to Native American people, Anderson (2003, p. 454) states that

> Native American tribal Web sites have the potential to be a very valuable tool for the indigenous people of North America. In addition to providing services for tribal members, they are an excellent tool for making other Americans and the world at large aware of the fascinating history of American Indians and the issues that they are facing

today. One of the challenges of living in a multicultural society is preserving one's unique cultural heritage, and Web sites can be an excellent tool for making younger generations aware of their history and traditions, so the culture remains vital and living rather than something that is merely displayed in museums..., the web is a great tool for sharing American Indian culture with the world.

(Anderson, 2003, p. 454)

Conclusion

Growing concerns about the lack of recognition for IK and intellectual property rights of Indigenous people have continued to attract scholarly attention because of the sensitivity of the issues involved. With or without international recognition, Indigenous people continue to assert their right to ownership and preservation of their traditional knowledge, creative arts, craft and cultural practices. They are also concerned about the extent to which new technologies permit them to tell their stories, to narrate their history and project their image without damaging their rights to protect knowledge of their cultural practices and their intellectual property. Globalisation has added to the dilemma that Indigenous people face because, on one hand, it has helped to bring together Indigenous people from across the globe, thus increasing their visibility to the rest of the world. On the other hand, globalisation has also made it easier for the world to access, abuse, damage and diminish Indigenous cultural expressions and symbols. Indigenous people therefore see globalisation as a double-edged tool that represents both the good and the bad.

One way through which IK and cultural practices are abused is through unauthorised publication of Indigenous cultural expressions and knowledge on the Internet. New technologies have also facilitated the illegal sale and criminal reproduction of Indigenous art, craft and designs that offer no benefits to Indigenous creators. Decades of concern about the lack of international recognition for the intellectual property rights and traditional knowledge of Indigenous people have not yielded the much-needed legal framework that will enable them to enjoy rights to their intellectual property and knowledge. Essentially, while the Internet promotes democratisation of information, it has also turned the secret knowledge of Indigenous people into open knowledge that is susceptible to abuse. This is a source of worry because Indigenous people derive their identity from their cultural heritage.

Whenever Indigenous cultural symbols and traditional knowledge are misappropriated and duplicated illegally, Indigenous people lose a part of their identity and way of life. Indigenous people continue to press for greater recognition of their rights to own their intellectual property and knowledge but they do so from a position of weakness, as existing international legislations relating, for example, to copyright ownership do not accord with communal ownership of intellectual knowledge and property that is recognised in Indigenous communities. This chapter takes the position that Indigenous people should have legal rights to their intellectual property and knowledge. No one should deny them their natural rights. The recognition and preservation of their knowledge and intellectual property rights is an obligation the world owes to Indigenous people.

Another problem that confronts Indigenous people as they seek to preserve their traditional knowledge and intellectual property is that their knowledge is largely unrecorded and undocumented and therefore likely to disappear once the custodians of that knowledge die or once they become senile. As highlighted in this chapter, knowledge preservation is best assured when it is written on paper or recorded electronically. However, even when knowledge is documented, there is also the question of the copyright owner. While international law grants copyright to an individual owner, it does not recognise undocumented knowledge owned by Indigenous communities. This is one source of anxiety for Indigenous people because, by tradition, knowledge is owned communally and no one individual can claim ownership of traditional knowledge.

Indigenous people have argued repeatedly that their right to own and manage their traditional knowledge should be recognised in law, just as legislation should grant them the right to prevent unauthorised commercial use of their traditional knowledge or their right to benefit from commercial exploitation of their knowledge and creative works.

The need to protect traditional knowledge is not restricted to Indigenous people who reside in western countries such as Australia, New Zealand and Canada. It is equally important to protect IK of African people in such areas as traditional systems of literacy, arts, creative works, designs, trademarks and other innovations that are based on tradition. It has been argued that the protection of Africa's IK will help the continent to showcase alternative worldviews that differ from the predominant western knowledge systems. However, even as Africa aims to harness new technologies for improvement of the socioeconomic conditions of the people and for preservation and dissemination of IK, there are major challenges such as the lack of an environment that encourages pervasive adoption and use of technologies, high costs of accessing the Internet, erratic supply of electricity and lack of training opportunities for the youth to develop knowledge of computer skills.

Prior to the emergence of new technologies, Indigenous elders and leaders were highly regarded as custodians of knowledge of traditional practices. Indigenous people had rules that stipulated how traditional knowledge should be obtained. The rules also applied to how that knowledge should be dispensed and to whom. Control over traditional knowledge therefore rested with elders. As custodians of community knowledge, elders had authority over who should receive information and when. However, the Internet and other digital technologies have diluted the power of elders to determine who should access traditional knowledge.

Within the literature, there are two views about how new technologies are impacting Indigenous people. One view holds that Indigenous people have productively harnessed new technologies to serve their community needs. However, another view suggests that new technologies that are introduced by inappropriate agents in improper contexts could have negative impacts on Indigenous people. Within this debate lies the need for preservation of cultural values, languages and community identity. One challenge that confronts Indigenous people is how to remove the barriers that new technologies pose to them and at the same time allow themselves to enjoy the benefits associated with use of new technologies. Another challenge could be framed this way: how could Indigenous community elders serve as custodians of cultural heritage at a time when the authority of the elders is being whittled down by the Internet and other new technologies?

5
The African Public Sphere in the Electronic Era

Introduction

In different parts of the world, new technologies serve diverse purposes for different people. They facilitate democracy; they empower the citizens by giving voice to the voiceless; they encourage civil society to contribute to the democratic process; and they assist citizens to hold public officials to account. New technologies encourage the development of a vigorous public sphere in which the citizens engage freely in participatory communication. New technologies contribute to improvements in literacy, help to alleviate poverty and serve as tools for the advancement of environmental sustainability (Iroh, 2006).

This chapter examines the extent to which African youth use new technologies to empower themselves, to engage in participatory communication to advance democracy, to contribute to public discourse and civic deliberation, and to challenge political leaders. The chapter draws on the theoretical frameworks of uses and gratifications, Jürgen Habermas's theory of the public sphere and the media richness theory to show how African youth use new technologies to express themselves in the public sphere.

The extent to which African youth use new technologies such as the Internet, mobile phones, social media, blogs and online discussion forums to express their views and participate in the political process has drawn the attention of researchers and communication scholars. Specifically, research into how new technologies are harnessed by African youth is critical to development of knowledge and official policy for social change on the continent. The youth constitute the cream of Africa's population not only because of their educational and socioeconomic status but also because of their ability to engineer social change.

Participatory communication is an important pathway for development of a strong, vibrant and dynamic public sphere that promotes democracy. Democracy propels the exchange of ideas and the development of new knowledge, and offers solutions to social and political problems. In many parts of the world, citizens utilise new technologies such as social media, online discussion forums, email, blogs, instant messaging tools and other new media in various ways. In Africa, there have been few systematic attempts to understand how the citizens use new technologies to express their views, to enhance their socioeconomic conditions and to contribute to political and social change. In various parts of the African continent, new technologies are regarded as agents of social and political change, and as essential tools for the development of a strong, healthy and collective democracy. This view is supported by the popular uprisings in 2011 that toppled governments in parts of north Africa such as Tunisia, Egypt and Libya. Chambers and Costain (2000, p. xi) maintain that 'Healthy democracies need a healthy public sphere where citizens (and elite) can exchange ideas, acquire knowledge and information, confront public problems, exercise public accountability, discuss policy options, challenge the powerful without fear of reprisals, and defend principles.'

Why African youth embrace new media

New technologies are regarded as important vehicles for participatory communication and the development of deliberative democracy in Africa. This is based on the perceived failure of the mainstream media to perform their basic roles in society. For example, Willems (2011, p. 50) perceives mainstream media in Africa as propaganda tools of the ruling authorities because of their relationship with the state, the emblem of power. Similarly, Banda (2010) sees mainstream media in Africa as vehicles for expression of official views rather than the views of the citizens. This view is constructed on the fact that the media advocate views that are at odds with their roles as public service media, conveyors of public information and facilitators of popular democracy. Therefore, when media engage in the pursuit of selfish and narrow interests and abdicate their public service roles in society, they lose credibility and respect in the eyes of the public.

Albert (2010) argues that when media intentionally include (or exclude) certain news stories designed to appeal to mass audiences because of commercial reasons, they relinquish their role as channels for the promotion of deliberative democracy. Obijiofor (2012) draws on

Banda (2010, p. 27) and McManus (2009) to explicate four reasons why mainstream media in Africa are regarded as discriminatory and biased. First, the African media are believed to give gratuitous and excessive publicity to government views rather than the opinions of ordinary citizens. Second, government officials tend to have a cosy relationship with the media which leads to the media privileging the views of government officials more regularly than the voices of ordinary people. Third, the media are accused of framing news from a rigid set of values that project the perspectives of one segment of society more than the other. Fourth, the profit motives of commercial media do not promote participatory communication or civic deliberation, and certainly do not promote democracy (Banda, 2010; McManus, 2009, cited in Obijiofor, 2012).

Nyamnjoh (2005a, p. 204) states that the shutting down of official channels of information and the constraints under which mainstream media operate in Africa have compelled African youth to adopt new media as alternative channels of information to satisfy their information needs. 'Political control, draconian press laws, selective communication and downright misinformation and disinformation by states in Africa have pushed ordinary people to seek alternative ways of satisfying their information and communication needs' (Nyamnjoh, 2005a, p. 204). This is more apparent in Ethiopia, to cite just one African example. Skjerdal (2009) notes the tight restrictions under which Ethiopian print and broadcast journalists operate. He says that Ethiopian television broadcast policy specifically directs journalists working in government-owned media to 'support the ruling party, which is elected by the interests of the public. The ruling party's policies must be reflected in each television programme' (Ethiopian Television, 2001, cited in Skjerdal, 2009, p. 24).

These forms of restrictions on the mainstream media have contributed to growing cynicism and public distrust of the media. It is therefore no surprise that mainstream media in Africa are no longer regarded as the pipelines of credible and reliable information. Evidence suggests that, in the 21st century, African youth are using new media to break free from the constraints imposed on mainstream media by government officials. The reason is obvious. New media serve multiple roles such as promoting civic deliberation and participatory communication, as well as satisfying a range of people's entertainment and news needs. Therefore, the increasing adoption of new media by African youth should be seen as their natural response to poor services provided by mainstream media, including the failure of government media to reflect the voices of ordinary citizens. As a demonstration of the extent of the disregard the African media have for ordinary people, Barber (1987, p. 3) notes that

> In Africa ordinary people tend to be invisible and inaudible...Newspapers, radio and television offer a magnified image of the class that controls them. Not only does the ruling elite make the news, it is the news – as endless verbatim reports of politicians' speeches, accounts of elite weddings and birthday parties, and the pages and pages of expensive obituaries testify.

It is for these reasons that the growth of the Internet and the widespread adoption of mobile phones have opened up new avenues for citizens to participate in news generation and distribution, particularly news about Africa (Sambrook, 2010). In Nigeria, for example, struggles for the control of natural resources and increasing public demand for environmental sustainability in the oil-rich Niger Delta region have compelled political and environmental activists to use new media to reach out to the rest of the world and to assert their right to carve out a space within the Nigerian state (Obijiofor, 2009b).

The growing popularity of new media among African youth cannot be attributed solely to technological changes or poor performance by mainstream media. The limited avenues available to citizens to express their views and to contribute to the democratic process have also spawned public interest in new media. In some African countries, official news channels have been either shut down or consistently censored by government agents who have grown increasingly intolerant of criticism (Banda, 2010; Nyamnjoh, 2005a, 2005b). Willems (2011), Nyamnjoh (2005a) and Barber (1987) recount how ordinary citizens deprived of information in various parts of Africa have adopted rumour, humour and drama to fill the information void created by government censorship of mainstream media. Barber (1987, p. 3) suggests that 'Songs, jokes, and anecdotes may be the principal channel of communication for people who are denied access to the official media.' Nyamnjoh (2005a) states that in Cameroon, excessive censorship of official sources of information, as well as poor performance by the mainstream media (e.g., undue reporting of pro-government views) have led to the emergence of rumour as a lively alternative source of information. Consequently, the appropriation of official sources of information by political authorities in Cameroon has forced the citizens to resort to rumour as an unusual channel for news and information dissemination. The use of rumour for political and social communication is therefore one of the direct consequences of the absence of credible communication channels. It is against this background that new media are being embraced by African youth. The trend is growing.

Use of new technologies by African youth

In many countries, new technologies such as social media are increasingly being used by youth as sites for social meetings and interaction. The technologies have also affected the methods through which the youth learn, communicate, collect information, collaborate with their peers and entertain themselves. These technologies have displaced traditional methods of communication, information gathering, social networking and entertainment. Omotayo (2006, p. 215) explains that 'The Internet provides scientists, lecturers and students, access to non-traditional sources of information at any point of the globe... The Internet is fast changing the methods for accessing and using information and research activities.' It is therefore important to explore the relationship between new technologies and African youth. For example, do new technologies serve as tools of political and economic empowerment or do African youth merely use them for entertainment purposes? What are the primary reasons why students, for example, use new technologies? How do students use new media technologies? What needs do students seek to gratify through the use of new technologies? Habermas (1989) argued that, in the Europe of the 17th and 18th centuries, the public sphere favoured the elite, especially men. That was then. What is the situation now? How do African youth use new media technologies for participatory communication in the public sphere?

Referring to mobile phones as an example, Last Moyo (2009b) draws on Kristóf Nyíri (2003) to make the point that, in various parts of the world,

> people use mobile phone technology to express themselves on salient issues that have to do with global justice or even local issues that affect national development. They talk, share text messages and emails to make informed choices about important issues of national concern such as elections, referendums, national and workers' strikes.
>
> (Last Moyo, 2009b, p. 146)

He says that in countries where freedom of the press has been constrained by media laws, people use mobile phones to network and mobilise for social and political causes. He points out, however, that new technologies and digital media on their own are not synonymous with participatory communication among citizens. 'Their capacity to create democratic conversations among citizens and between the rulers and the ruled, not only depends on the people's ability to use them, but also on the political, regulatory, technological and socio-cultural regimes of any given nation' (Last Moyo, 2009b, p. 146).

He illustrates how mobile phone ownership and use can contribute to deliberative democracy in Africa and other parts of the world. For example, people with mobile phones can contribute to debate on radio and television talk shows. In this context, the mobile phone serves as a tool that facilitates participation in the public sphere. Even 'texting' through mobile phones is seen as promoting interactive communication in society. Last Moyo (2009b, p. 148) notes that 'In parts of Africa, for example, "texting" has not only been used in referendums, but continues to be used to support other "guerrilla media" in the mobilization, organization and co-ordination of mass protests.'

A number of studies have established the relationship between university students and new technologies. While Jones, Johnson-Yale, Millermaier and Perez (2009) assert that students are 'heavy users of the Internet', Kubey, Lavin and Barrows (2001, p. 366) confirmed the growing popularity of the Internet among university students. Research in Africa and other developing regions of the world show that students are the main patrons of Internet services (Furuholt, Kristiansen and Wahid, 2008; Mutula, 2003; Mwesige, 2004; Odero, 2003; Omotayo, 2006; Robins, 2002; Sairosse and Mutula, 2004). Other studies found that young people are also the main users of the Internet (Adomi, Okiy and Ruteyan, 2003; Alao and Folorunsho, 2008; Aoki and Downes, 2003). In Nigeria, Alao and Folorunsho (2008) found that 'the majority of cybercafé users in the city of Ilorin were students, aged 21–25 years old, males and unmarried'. Similarly, Adomi et al. (2003) reported in their study of cybercafés in Nigeria that students were the largest client group.

In their study of the level of Internet use among undergraduate students at the Obafemi Awolowo University in Nigeria, Awoleye, Siyanbola and Oladipo (2008, p. 89) identified various ways the students perceived the Internet. The students believe the Internet 'serves as information database…, provides avenue to contact relatives and friends, widens knowledge, and gives information on education, politics and social events'. The students also believe the Internet facilitates global communication, boosts their academic performance, promotes and supports academic research, and promotes the development of online-based businesses. While these studies show that students use Internet and other technologies in various ways, what is unknown is the extent to which African youth employ the technologies as popular media to express their views, to contribute to deliberative democracy through participatory communication in the public sphere, to challenge political leaders, to campaign for social justice and to highlight cases of human rights abuses, among others.

New technologies, participatory communication and democracy

New technologies facilitate popular participation by citizens in a democracy. Additionally, new technologies promote socioeconomic development and greater citizen awareness of their obligations. Through new technologies, Africans in the diaspora participate in the public sphere in various ways, such as by contributing to debates in online discussion forums. As discussed in Chapter 2, lack of access remains one key problem that hinders effective use of new technologies to achieve these objectives. Many African youth lack access to new technologies, despite the growing popularity of mobile phones and other digital devices in urban and rural parts of the continent. The situation is serious but even more so among university students.

Some of the basic technologies that are taken for granted in western university campuses are noticeably absent in many African universities. It is this paucity of technologies in public places that was highlighted by Ani, Uchendu and Atseye (2007) in their study that noted the huge inequalities existing in the level of access to new technologies in public and private sectors of Nigeria. They found that 'In most public institutions, such as universities, polytechnics, primary and post-primary schools, and government ministries, access to ICT, if not completely lacking, is inadequate' (Ani et al., 2007, p. 355). Also in Nigeria, Omotayo (2006) notes that the National Universities Commission's (NUC) Internet project for universities has remained a pipe dream for many years. This is the key challenge that faces African youth and indeed the wider society.

Compared to the situation in western countries, the picture that emerges is one of digital divide and digital poverty between developed and developing countries. For example, Kandell (1998) reported in his study that college students in the United States are introduced very early in life to computer technology. According to him, in the United States, 'Computer use by college students is strongly encouraged, implicitly if not explicitly, and in some courses is required' (Kandell, 1998, p. 16). This is consistent with the findings by Jones et al. (2009), who reported in their study that 'College students continue to be early adopters of new Internet tools and applications in comparison to the general U.S. Internet-using population.' They noted the students' overall fondness for using the Internet as an instrument for social communication.

The inability of African youth to gain wider access to new technologies means they will be unable to harness the technologies effectively to empower themselves, to express their views, to contribute to deliberative democracy in the public sphere and to challenge established authorities in their countries. Lack of access to new technologies will seriously constrain African youth from using new media to advance democracy. This is very important because, in various countries, new media contribute to the development of the democratic process. Tambini (1999, p. 306) exemplifies how new media are enabling citizens to participate in the democratic process. So, if African youth must participate in public discussion of issues that are fundamental to the development of their countries, they must have access to information. A well informed citizen is an active participant in a democratic society. For African youth to make well informed decisions about their welfare, wellbeing, security and everyday life, it is crucial that they have access to information to assist them to make those judgments. This implies they must be free to gather information that is important to their lives. Information is an important element that contributes to the development of a healthy democracy.

The use by African youth of new media implies that new media, including social media, are perceived as alternative and credible sources of information. New channels of communication and social interaction are gaining wide popularity because of the greater degree of freedom they confer on citizens, particularly freedom from political, social and economic control by political leaders. New media are also attractive because of their interactive nature and their relatively low cost. However, despite their attractive qualities, new media have certain shortcomings, as Tambini (1999, p. 319) explains:

> The very characteristics that are seen as positive in encouraging participation (cheapness, anonymity) are seen as a problem when they foster less appealing forms of online political organization.... The legal status of inflammatory or libellous material posted in the semi-public worlds of discussion groups remains contested, and the links between the virtual identity of users and the real identity unclear.

Tambini (1999) argues that how new media will help to develop various types of participatory democracy could depend on the regulatory mechanisms that new media are subjected to, as well as how the complex problems of access are resolved. In discussing the strengths and weaknesses of new media as essential tools for the advancement of democracy, it is important to recognise the main characteristics of new media, as well as the structural problems in society, the political and economic factors, and the individual differences that make it possible for some people to access new media while others lack access.

Cybercafés as sites for cultural expression

A range of literature exists on how people use new technologies in their workplaces and at their homes, in particular how cybercafés serve as a public sphere (Brants, 2005; Dahlberg, 2007; Dahlgren, 2005; Papacharissi, 2002), as well as the underlying reasons why people use cybercafés and the particular needs they aim to satisfy through the use of the Internet (Kaye, 2007; Kaye and Johnson, 2004). Lloyd, Dean and Cooper (2007) found in their study of technology use and its effects on students that new technologies have affected the way students communicate, interrelate and participate in social activities. In Nigeria, one study examined the level of Internet use by undergraduate students of Obafemi Awolowo University (Awoleye et al., 2008, p. 84) and found that the Internet was used 'mostly for e-mail, information search and online chatting'. In a related study, Omotayo (2006) revealed that, among the reasons given by university students for accessing the Internet, email communication and search for academic and sport-related information, as well as the search for pornographic material, featured prominently.

Wasserman and Kabeya-Mwepu (2005) studied the use of information and communication technologies by Congolese refugees who were studying at tertiary education institutes in Cape Town, South Africa. In Tanzania, Chachage (2001) looked at the use of Internet cafés, while a related study of Internet use in Gaborone city, Botswana, was conducted by Sairosse and Mutula (2004). Similarly, Jain and Mutula (2001) examined the distribution of information technology in Botswana. Across Africa, Mutula (2003) studied the cybercafé industry. Other studies of the Internet and cybercafés in Africa include Ugah and Okafor (2008), Alao and Folorunsho (2008), Ani et al. (2007), Anunobi (2006), Olatokun and Bodunwa (2006), Oyelaran-Oyeyinka and Adeya (2004), Jagboro (2003) and Adomi et al. (2003).

Overall, research evidence suggests that students tend to be attracted to cybercafés because cybercafés offer useful services and are regarded as convenient sites for users. This is reflected in the results of a study conducted in Gaborone, Botswana by Sairosse and Mutula (2004, p. 61), who note that

> Cybercafés are becoming preferred Internet access points because most of them open for long hours, charge reasonably, provide assistance to users, have diverse services and are generally convenient and flexible places for searching the Internet. Students studying in various universities through distance education, for example, find using cybercafés to access course syllabuses and material convenient.

The interactive and social nature of cybercafés was also cited as one of the reasons why they are popular among users in Botswana. Sairosse and Mutula (2004, p. 65) point out that 'cybercafés provide Internet access points for users to socialise, provide meeting places for different people, are centres of communication through e-mail, and pursuit of education through e-learning'. Through these services, cybercafés serve not only as a public sphere for participatory communication among youth in Botswana but also as spaces for cultural expression. Research conducted in Africa provides an important framework to understand how African youth use new technologies to empower themselves, to express their views and to engage in participatory communication in the public sphere. The next section examines the theoretical frameworks of uses and gratifications, media richness theory and Jürgen Habermas's (1989) theory of the public sphere.

Theoretical frameworks

Many of the research studies that examined how people use new technologies were based on the theoretical framework of uses and gratifications. Examples include Kaye (2007), Kaye and Johnson (2004), Charney and Greenberg (2001), and Papacharissi and Rubin (2000). Morris and Ogan (1996) suggest that the uses and gratifications framework serves as a fundamental tool for investigating Internet use. The uses and gratifications theory is particularly valuable because it provides insights into reasons why people use or select certain media over other forms of communication channels (Flanagin and Metzger, 2001). The literature also shows that different media satisfy different kinds of audience needs (Dobos, 1992; Perse and Courtright, 1993).

Apart from uses and gratifications, other theories applied in this chapter include the media richness theory and Habermas's public sphere concept. The media richness theory explains the behaviour of Internet and email users because it proposes that media users tend to determine the richness of a medium by evaluating the difficulty or ease of the services the medium provides. These two theories explain why media (and other new technologies) are selected and used by audience members. They also offer insights into how media technologies are used. Therefore, there are theoretical implications for how and why people use new technologies such as the Internet. The next section starts with an analysis of the uses and gratifications theory.

Uses and gratifications theory

The uses and gratifications theory focuses on media users and how they use media. The theory perceives media audiences as effective users of media content. A key point is that media users make deliberate choices about media and media content they expose themselves to. Kaye (2007, p. 129) states that 'Uses and gratifications studies investigate how the audience uses the media rather than how the media use the audience.' McQuail (2005) states that uses and gratifications research explores why people use media and what people do with the media. Bucy, Gantz and Wang (2007, p. 149) highlight the main postulations of uses and gratifications theory as follows:

(a) that the audience for news and other genres of media content is active and goal directed, (b) that media are an important source of need gratification whose fulfillment lies with audience choices, and (c) that media compete with other sources of need satisfaction.

Kaye and Johnson (2004, p. 198) explain that uses and gratifications theory is particularly suited to the study of the Internet because 'online technologies such as e-mail, bulletin boards and chat rooms are interactive applications that require audience members to be active users'. Drawing on previous research, Kaye and Johnson (2004) argue that, in terms of gratifications that people seek through the use of the Internet, 'the Web tends to satisfy entertainment, escape and social interaction needs' (Kaye and Johnson, 2004, p. 199). However, they point out that 'because different components of the Internet are functionally different than the Web and from each other, they may gratify different needs' (2004, p. 199). With regard to specific uses of the Internet and

email, some researchers reported that Internet and email users identified information collection (and the ease of collecting information on
the Internet) as major gratifications they received through the Internet.

In its early years, uses and gratifications research marked a major shift
away from the trend in mass communication research because it projected the media audience as active individuals who make conscious
decisions about types of media and purposively selecting media contents
to satisfy their needs. Prior to the emergence of the uses and gratifications theory, mass communication scholars had presented media
audiences as a 'passive' and 'unthinking' group of people. However,
following the emergence of the Internet and the range of choices available to Internet users, the uses and gratifications approach has been
deemed particularly relevant to studies that analyse why and how people use the Internet because 'the role of electronic media audiences has
evolved from passive "viewers" or "listeners" of media content into
active "users" of information and communication technologies' (Bucy
et al., 2007, p. 149).

Littlejohn (1992, p. 365) points out that the satisfaction that people
seek to derive from media use is influenced by 'one's beliefs about what a
medium can provide and one's evaluation of the medium's content'. For
example, people who appreciate the entertainment value of situation
comedies as valuable activity will seek to gratify their entertainment
needs by viewing the situation comedies. However, people who perceive situation comedies as worthless will aim to stay away from such
comedies.

Media richness theory

The media richness theory argues that an individual's choice of media
technologies is influenced by the characteristics of each medium. The
theory arranges media on a scale ranging from 'lean' to 'rich' based on
attributes such as 'speed of feedback, variety of channels, personalness
of source, and richness of language used' (Flanagin and Metzger, 2001,
p. 157). This model of media use incorporates into its framework of analysis the proposition that media users tend to determine the richness of a
medium by evaluating the difficulty or ease of the services the medium
provides.

Critique of theories

Despite its theoretical and methodological relevance, uses and
gratifications theory has been criticised for its excessively descriptive

orientation, its theoretical inadequacies and for 'relying too heavily on audiences for reporting their true motivations for media use' (Bucy et al., 2007, p. 150). More significantly, uses and gratifications theory has been criticised for ignoring 'the dysfunctions of media in society and culture' because it 'sees media primarily as positive ways in which individuals meet their needs, without any attention to the overall negative cultural effects of media in society' (Littlejohn, 1992, p. 373). This is consistent with evidence in the literature that shows that, rather than serve as facilitators of social change and development, the media often serve as agents of destabilisation in society.

One limitation of media richness theory is that it fails to recognise the impact that collective experiences with, and perceptions of, media technologies will have on how audience members evaluate and select media (Flanagin and Metzger, 2001). As Flanagin and Metzger (2001, pp. 157–158) argue, 'it is not primarily the attributes of media that determine use, but rather such factors as assessments of needs fulfillment, appropriateness, social norms, and peer evaluations of media'. In fact, the social presence model of media accepts that the perceptions that people have of media are not only biased but are also influenced by their social milieu. 'Influences can come from others, through vicarious learning, and from situational factors such as individual differences or those factors that facilitate (e.g., training, support) or constrain media use (e.g., geographic barriers and time constraints)' (Flanagin and Metzger, 2001, p. 158). In essence, group dynamics, as well as individual and cultural differences, can influence the way people perceive and use media technologies. The third theoretical framework applied in this chapter is examined in the next section.

Jürgen Habermas's public sphere

Jürgen Habermas's (1989) theory of the public sphere has received wide attention from scholars investigating the impact of new technologies on the development of participatory communication and deliberative democracy in the digital age. This is significant because the public sphere in the 17th and 18th century Europe that Habermas described, including the rules and characteristic elements that underpinned the public sphere of that era, may not reflect the principles that guide the public sphere in the modern era. In his widely cited scholarly book, Habermas pointed to the growth of capitalism in Europe in the 17th and 18th centuries as the key factor that engineered the emergence of the public sphere.

The public sphere is an unofficial meeting of members of the public to discuss, deliberate, and communicate information and opinions. One key component of the public sphere is that it operates without persuasion or manipulation by government officials, the church, political organisations, educational establishments and other elements that operate in the market. Last Moyo (2009b, p. 140) identifies four elements of an ideal public sphere to be 'participation, nondiscrimination, autonomy and rational critical discourse'. However, Calhoun (1992, p. 3) states that 'The early bourgeois public spheres were composed of narrow segments of the European population, mainly educated, propertied men, and they conducted a discourse not only exclusive of others but prejudicial to the interests of those excluded.' He points out that, in modern times, a credible public sphere that should facilitate deliberative democracy must aspire to enhance two elements, namely the 'quality of discourse and the quantity of participation' (1992, p. 2).

Calhoun states that, although the development of the public sphere must be attributed to the free participation of more people, it must be noted that it was the exclusive participation of all kinds of 'men' in the public sphere of that era that eventually undermined the quality of discussion. Another element that worked against the quality of the dialogue in the public sphere was the pursuit of commercial interests by the media. Indeed, Habermas (1989) acknowledged that the same capitalist elements that contributed to the growth of the public sphere were also instrumental in its demise.

With specific reference to the effect of the public sphere on modern democracies, Dahlberg (2004, p. 2) argues that 'a public sphere of informal citizen deliberation is central to strong democracy'. Ho, Baber and Khondker (2002, p. 128) express a similar sentiment, stating that 'a public sphere that allows for free and unconstrained public deliberation of matters of common concern is essential for democratic legitimacy'. On this point, Chambers and Costain (2000, p. xi) agree, noting that 'Healthy democracies need a healthy public sphere where citizens (and elite) can exchange ideas, acquire knowledge and information, confront public problems, exercise public accountability, discuss policy options, challenge the powerful without fear of reprisals, and defend principles.' They assert that there are critical questions that must be answered by civil society in order to sustain a healthy public sphere. The questions include:

Who speaks, and what idiom predominates? Who has access to what venues, and do we have sufficient knowledge of and control over new technologies that will shape the public spaces of democracy? How do market forces and power differentials affect the free exchange of ideas? What cultural trends are sweeping the public sphere and subtly altering the public topic of conversation?

(Chambers and Costain, 2000, p. xi)

Similarly, Ferree, Gamson, Gerhards and Rucht (2002, p. 289) pose some important questions, namely:

What qualities should the public sphere have to nurture and sustain a vigorous democratic public life? More specifically, who should be participating and on what occasions? What should be the form and content of their contributions to public discourse? How should the actors communicate with each other? What are the desirable outcomes if the process is working as it should be?

Embedded in these questions is the contested nature of the debate in the public sphere. In his contribution to the debate, Dahlgren (1991, p. 2) suggests that the public sphere should promote 'the institutional sites where popular political will should take form and citizens should be able to constitute themselves as active agents in the political process....'

Critique of Habermas

Habermas's concept of public sphere is not without its critics. One criticism is that Habermas's public sphere privileged men and remained silent about the valuable contributions of women and less privileged people such as the old and the young (Banda, 2010). Another criticism is that Habermas attempted to privilege upper-class interests over the interests of working-class people (Last Moyo, 2009b). He emphasised the bourgeois public sphere and underplayed other forms of public spheres. As Allan (2004, p. 39) points out, 'The basic ruling out of half the population (women) demonstrates that Habermas' claims of widespread participation in the "classical" period of the public sphere are far from warranted.'

Another view notes that the public sphere of the 17th and 18th centuries was restricted to a few educated and privileged men, who could afford the time and willingness to express their views. Other areas in which the public sphere theory has been criticised include its oversight of alternative ways through which people participated in public discourse and information exchange in the 17th and 18th centuries, as well as the misleading notion that individuals who participated in the public sphere possessed equal abilities to express themselves, and also had equal access to information (Allan, 2004, p. 41). For more criticisms of Habermas, see Garnham (1992).

The public sphere in the electronic age

The resurgence of scholarly interest in the public sphere has been attributed to technological transformations in which technologies are seen to empower civil society, to enable people to express their views and to allow them to engage in participatory communication. It is perhaps for these reasons that optimism has grown about how new technologies might encourage and strengthen participatory communication and deliberative democracy in modern society. A key question is: does the presence of new technologies suggest that people will use the technologies and, if so, how they will use the technologies?

Optimism over the ability of new technologies to empower people and contribute to social and political change seems to be based on public perceptions of technologies. Ho et al. (2002, p. 128) argue, for instance, that 'the rapid expansion of information and communications technologies has influenced the development of the public sphere'. Hurwitz (1999, p. 656) notes that 'The Internet has become a new tool and venue for political groups of all stripes. Advocacy and interest groups use it to organize their supporters for online lobbying of local, national, and foreign officials – who themselves need e-mail addresses to be credible in this Information Age.' In fact, Tanner (2001) points to how Chileans utilised Internet discussion forums to engage in public debate on political issues, particularly the discussion that followed the capture in London of Chile's former dictator and president Augusto Pinochet in October 1998. Against the backdrop of the Chilean example, it is necessary to ask how African youth use new technologies to express their voices by setting up their own public sphere for political discussion. Ho et al. (2002, p. 145) identify one of the qualities of the Internet that endears it to public use:

> The fact that the Internet allows for many-to-many communication and comes bundled with a multiplicity of functions are critical elements that have enabled a wide range of public interest groups and civil society organizations to recruit members, propagate their views to a larger audience and even to challenge existing rules and regulations.

Hurwitz (1999, p. 655) explains that the Internet is particularly suited to promoting the public sphere because the 'libertarian and communitarian visions built on the Internet's technology, particularly its non-hierarchical structure, low transaction costs, global reach, scalability, rapid response time, and disruption-overcoming (hence censorship-foiling) alternative routing' make the technology suitable for communication by all classes of people. These elements promote greater democratisation of information on the Internet, allowing civil society groups and activists to meet online, to make their voices heard and to spread their ideology worldwide. It has been pointed out that, through the use of new technologies, individual members of society can

> gain more and more information on various social and democratic issues by having access to the ICT.... Large segments of the population are now, and more so in the future, able to form personal educated opinions on common issues.... In modern societies, many people want to shift from being 'the governed' into having 'self-government'... They want to have more power and control to conduct their own life as they want.
> (Keskinen, 1999, cited in Dahlberg, 2001, p. 159)

In its early years, doubts were cast on the ability of the Internet and other new technologies to accomplish public expectations. Hurwitz (1999) cautions that regardless of the freedom associated with the Internet, there are instances in which national governments have successfully resisted political activists and thus limited their liberal use of the Internet. Not only do governments in China and Singapore, for instance, post their own preferred political messages on the Internet in order to counter opposing views, they also require Internet 'users to register and make a pretense of logging their online activities' (Hurwitz, 1999, p. 656). Nevertheless, one significant consequence of the emergence of new technologies and social media is not only that they encourage people to engage in participatory communication, therefore strengthening the public sphere, they also make it possible for civil society to gain 'greater access to information, more opportunities to engage in public speech, and an enhanced ability to undertake collective action' (Shirky, 2011, p. 29).

Various ways through which ordinary citizens use social media to press for political changes in different countries have been documented, including in some cases the successful overthrow of governments (Shirky, 2011). In the Philippines, for example, citizens successfully used social media to oust the government of President Joseph Estrada in 2001. Other instances include Spain in 2004, when text messages were used to galvanise public demonstrations that eventually led to the overthrow of Prime Minister José María Aznar. And in Moldova in 2009, civil protests engineered through social media (text messages, Facebook and Twitter) were organised to protest the outcomes of the election (Shirky, 2011).

There were also instances in which demonstrators failed to use social media to achieve political change. One example was the contested 2009 Iranian presidential election in which the government cracked down on protesters. The same situation occurred in Thailand in 2010 when the government used extreme force to break up protesters that resulted in a number of deaths. On account of the mixed outcomes of the use of social media to achieve political reforms, Shirky (2011, p. 29) argued that 'The use of social media tools – text messaging, e-mail, photo sharing, social networking, and the like – does not have a single preordained outcome.' He further argued that 'social media have become coordinating tools for nearly all of the world's political movements, just as most of the world's authoritarian governments (and, alarmingly, an increasing number of democratic ones) are trying to limit access to it' (Shirky, 2011, p. 30).

One of the key objectives of liberal democracies is to maximise citizen participation in decisions that affect them (Ferree et al., 2002). 'Participation enhances the public sphere, allowing for the emergence of something approximating a general will, and improves the individual, by drawing on and developing the person's highest capacities for action' (Ferree et al., 2002, p. 295). Dervin and Schaefer (1999, p. 20) note that the level of participation by individuals should be qualified because 'Ordinary people participate cooperatively, usefully, and well in public spheres if those spheres are fair and useful and serve their interests.'

Ho et al. (2002, p. 129) argue that web forums serve as 'a space for discussion and re-education of citizens about participation in public affairs'. They underline an important point about online forums. Although the Internet accommodates various discussion groups that utilise the web to publicise their views, Ho et al. (2002) note that participation in online discussion forums is voluntary. This raises the question about the usefulness of online forums and, in particular, the value of the information generated in those forums. In essence, the emphasis should be as much on Internet access as on what people do with information they receive from online forums.

From theory to practice

Research in Africa shows that access to the Internet does not determine the purpose to which the Internet will be put, or how frequently people will use the Internet. A number of studies conducted among African university students show that email communication was the most common reason why the students use the Internet. A study conducted among university students in Ghana (Kwansah-Aidoo and Obijiofor, 2006) found that 'an overwhelming majority of respondents use the Internet mainly for sending emails' (2006, p. 363). In terms of gender difference, over 80 per cent of female students used the Internet mostly for sending mails while fewer than 60 per cent of male students reflected a similar practice. Only a few students used the Internet for research. For example, 21.4 per cent of male students used the Internet for research and about 10 per cent of female students did the same (Kwansah-Aidoo and Obijiofor, 2006). In a study of students at the University of Lagos (Nigeria), Obijiofor (2009c) found low use of the Internet for purposes other than email communication. In terms of access, although a majority of the students said they had Internet access, only about one-third of them used the Internet more frequently.

Among the reasons often mentioned for the prevailing low frequency of Internet use are lack of basic computing skills and lack of access to Internet services. Other studies that found a predominance of email communication in Internet use in Africa include Awoleye et al. (2008), Ugah and Okafor (2008), Sairosse and Mutula (2004), Jagboro (2003) and Robins (2002).

In comparative terms, outside Africa Lee (1999) found that email was the main purpose for which people used the Internet in southern England. In the United States, Haythornthwaite (2001) drew on a range of studies to highlight the predominant use of email by Internet users. She notes that 'Users rank e-mail as the number one reason for being online' (Haythornthwaite, 2001, p. 369). She cites studies in the United States which showed that the second most frequently mentioned reason for using the Internet was related to information seeking in the areas of pastimes, healthcare, travel or shopping. In their study of Internet café users in Indonesia, Wahid, Furuholt and Kristiansen (2006, p. 287) conclude that 'Seeking information, emailing and chatting are the most popular single activities for the Internet café users.' They also note that the use of the Internet for business related activities and computer games was less popular. Drawing on their own research and results from other studies, Kaye and Johnson (2004, p. 199) echo the results of previous research, saying that 'Sending and receiving e-mail continues to be the major activity people engage in online.'

The results that relate specifically to Africa show the under-utilisation of the Internet for other activities. However, two studies conducted in different universities in Nigeria found that academic activities constituted the major reason why students use the Internet. In a study that examined the level of digital divide at the University of Calabar, Ani et al. (2007) reported that the search for academic and research information was the main reason why the students used the Internet. Similarly, Anunobi's (2006) study of Internet use at the Federal University of Technology, Owerri, found that academic purposes topped the reasons why the students use the Internet. Results from these two studies differ clearly from much of the evidence in the literature on African university students' use of the Internet. It is not only students who use the Internet mostly for email communication. University academic staff also do so. See Chapter 2 for a discussion of the results of the study conducted by Oyelaran-Oyeyinka and Adeya (2004) on Kenyan and Nigerian university teachers.

It is important to clarify that using the Internet for email communication is not necessarily a bad form of activity. There are social advantages associated with using the Internet in this way. Howard, Rainie and Jones (2001, p. 399) report that not only does email enlarge the social worlds of Internet users but also a 'majority of those who e-mail relatives say it increases the level of communication between family members'. In general, the researchers found that 'the Internet allows people to stay in touch with family and friends and, in many cases, extend their social networks' (Howard et al., 2001, p. 399).

Omenugha (2009) notes that, while new technologies could be regarded as channels that provide space for students to express themselves, there remain concerns about inappropriate use of the technologies:

> The fact that more students own, use and access Information Communication Technologies is a welcome development, but there is bad news as well. Existing literature shows that the ICT can be used in both positive and negative ways. Youths who are said to be the major users of these technologies appropriate them in various ways – impacting negatively and positively on them.
>
> (Omenugha, 2009, p. 1)

She found in her study that the commonest technologies used by students of Nnamdi Azikiwe University, Awka (Nigeria), were the mobile phone and the Internet. The students said they used mobile phones to access Facebook. As Omenugha (2009, p. 12) reports, 'The students find the use of Facebook empowering too as they meet people who otherwise they may not have had the opportunities to meet in "real life".' So, the students use Facebook to meet friends, to relax and for entertainment. The students said using Facebook enabled them to meet people they would not have met in real life. While they admitted the negative consequences of addiction to Facebook, the students said the benefits of using mobile phones far outweighed the negative aspects. The students said it was no longer necessary for them to go to Internet cafés as they could access the Internet through their mobile phones.

To the students, the mobile phone represents a symbol of power and status which has compelled them to own expensive and sophisticated models with 3G features that can also perform multiple tasks. Students who do not own sophisticated mobile phones are perceived as belonging to a lower socioeconomic class. In this context, Omenugha reports that some students were driven to steal sophisticated phones just to be accepted by their peers. However, use of mobile phones has negative implications too. It has made the students to be more audacious in disregarding ethical behaviour. Some of the students have become undisciplined as they disregard widely accepted norms of society. Consequently, a youth culture that venerates consumerism, unconventional English language use, excessive pursuit of material wealth and fraudulent practices has developed (Omenugha, 2009).

While research shows that African youth are engaging more actively with new technologies, such as mobile phones, Internet, online forums and social media, questions remain about the extent to which they are using these popular forums to empower themselves, to engage in participatory communication, to express their views in the public sphere and to promote deliberative democracy. Although African youth are using new technologies in various ways, their involvement in the public sphere and in promoting civic deliberation can only be described as moderate or low. This is consistent with the literature, which suggests that access to new technologies does not necessarily determine what people do with the technologies and how frequently they use the technologies (Obijiofor, 2009b). Studies in Nigeria, Ghana and Senegal show African youth using new technologies mostly for email communication to maintain social relations, for communication with friends and family, and for entertainment (see Kwansah-Aidoo and Obijiofor, 2006; Obijiofor, 2011, 2009c; Robins, 2002).

The voices of African youth remain absent in the public sphere and in most online discussion forums, as only a few young people contribute to participatory communication in the public sphere owing to a range of problems identified in this chapter (Albert, 2010; Brinkman, Lamoureaux, Merolla and de Bruijn, 2011; Obijiofor, 2011). And yet research shows that cybercafés serve as sites for popular participation by citizens. Cybercafés as well as other new technologies enjoy popular appeal because they promote interactivity, freedom of expression, participatory communication and, above all, serve as popular spaces for public debate and for expression of popular culture. In a talk he delivered on 23 November 2004 at the second Nelson Mandela Foundation Lecture, renowned South African Archbishop Desmond Tutu told the audience: 'We want our society to be characterized by vigorous debate and dissent where to disagree is part and parcel of a vibrant community, that we should play the ball, not the person and not think that those who disagree, who express dissent, are ipso facto disloyal or unpatriotic' (cited in Albert, 2010).

The importance of new technologies in engineering a politically conscious citizen in Africa has been highlighted by Adesanmi (2011) who states that 'Africa is not only the fastest growing market for the technologies of the infotainment age, she also presents the rest of the world with a public sphere that has most radically been inflected by social media.' He points to the effective role that social media played in the 2011 uprisings in the Arab world and specifically in Nigeria, where social media were used by the citizens at different times to achieve successes against political leaders. On this basis, he states: 'the age of the citizen has now been replaced by the age of the netizen. The netizen carries his weapon in his hand. S/he is nowhere and everywhere at once. The netizen has powers that existed only in the restless imagination of the citizen.' This might be true of the situation in some parts of the world but debate persists about the extent to which African youth use social media to challenge established authorities, to contribute to civic deliberation and to participate in the public sphere.

Omenugha (2009) found in her study that the students of Nnamdi Azikiwe University in Nigeria used mobile phones for diverse activities, most notably to join Facebook in order to meet friends and other people they would not otherwise encounter physically in the social world, as well as for entertainment. There is no doubt that these students recognise the power of new media and are using the technologies to satisfy their personal needs. However, the point must be made that, while the students owned and used their mobile phones in various ways, they did not use the phones to contribute to public discourse in the public sphere. The main appeal of using their mobile phones was to fulfil the need for personal (private) communication with friends, family and other associates.

So, when Adesanmi (2011) writes that the Nigerian citizen 'has a weapon in the palm of his hands. He has a blackberry or an iphone. He can take pictures that could go viral online within seconds', one wonders whether ownership of mobile devices has encouraged Nigerian youth to participate actively in the public sphere, to use the mobile devices to contribute to political discourse and to advance civic deliberation. Obviously, research conducted among university students does not uphold the view that a majority of the youth use the new technologies for the higher goal of participating in the public sphere. This is not to deny instances in which Nigerian citizens have used digital technologies to report human rights abuses that occurred in public spaces. However, even these cases were episodic and irregular. Two examples that come to mind are the brutal treatment meted out to Ms Uzoma Okere in 2008 by naval ratings who were enraged that she did not move her car out of the way for a naval convoy to pass through heavy traffic. Another incident of human rights abuse was the controversy that erupted over the killing of the former leader of the Boko Haram insurgent group, Mohammed Yusuf, who was arrested by the army and handed over to the police before he was reported dead. On a national scale, these two events stand out as instances in which ordinary Nigerian citizens used their digital technologies to inform the world about events in their society. If these events were not recorded in digital cameras and distributed to online discussion forums where they were widely reported, the world and Nigerians in the diaspora may not have been informed of what happened.

More than five years after the emergence of the Boko Haram insurgent group, the Nigerian government has continued to fight the group. Boko Haram, in response, has been more audacious. In mid-April 2014, Boko Haram militants invaded the Government Girls' Secondary School in Chibok, Borno State, and kidnapped over 250 female students. At the time of writing, more than 200 days after the event, the girls have not yet been released and the Nigerian soldiers fighting Boko Haram have not been successful in freeing the girls. This is one of the sensitive political topics that dominate discussion in Nigerian online forums.

The predominant use of the Internet for email communication by African youth suggests that the youth make very limited use of Internet technologies, implying also lack of knowledge of various uses to which they can put the Internet. This lack of knowledge of various uses of the

Internet extends to university teachers as well. As Oyelaran-Oyeyinka and Adeya (2004) reported in their survey of Kenyan and Nigerian university teachers, only a few said they used the Internet mostly for electronic commerce, as against the majority who said they used it for email communication. However, we must not forget Omenugha's (2009) study, which showed that students used mobile phones for various private purposes. The use of mobile phones for private communication suggests that youths are more attracted to new technologies for private reasons rather than using the technologies for participatory communication in the public sphere as a way to advance deliberative democracy. The youth did not seem keen to use the technologies to empower themselves in the public sphere.

Another point to note is that, regardless of the role that Internet discussion forums play in encouraging and sustaining participatory communication and deliberative democracy in other parts of the world, scholars have identified some of the shortcomings of Internet discussion forums as a tool for deliberative democracy in Africa. One suggestion is that online forums are restricted to a few people owing to factors such as 'lack of capacity (intellectual ability, resources for accessing the Internet and so on)' and other problems, namely poverty, unemployment and a general feeling of political indifference (Albert, 2010). This is consistent with research evidence. In their study of websites managed by English speaking Cameroonians residing overseas, Brinkman et al. (2011) reported that the contents of the websites and the involvement of the citizens in generating the contents were controlled by elite male Cameroonians who interpreted their own 'position as marginal so as to garner support for a political cause' (Brinkman et al., 2011, p. 249). Studies of other African countries such as Sudan, the Democratic Republic of Congo and Angola reported similar findings. Brinkman et al. (2011) found that the issues discussed on the websites dwelt on matters of special appeal to the elite. More significantly, the contents were produced by privileged people who were technologically savvy and had more access to the Internet than other members of their community. On account of these findings, Brinkman et al. (2011) advised that the presumption that 'the Internet offers a voice to the marginalized, that it allows for democratization through popular participation, that it offers a natural space for the diaspora to create and perpetuate a virtual nation' must be taken with a great deal of cynicism (Brinkman et al., 2011, p. 248).

Albert (2010) argues that the main reason why few Africans contribute to political debate in the public sphere is not because the majority lack interest in public debate. It is, he says, partly because of political indifference but also because a majority of African youth lack the capacity and the financial means to access the Internet. He believes that lack of participation in public discourse by African youth could be attributed to factors such as ignorance, lack of knowledge of politics and lack of interest in politics. He says that a majority of African youth 'lack the resources of physical and intellectual capacity for contributing to online fora and have little appetite for the kind of abstractions and arguments that online deliberation of public issues requires' (Albert, 2010).

Citing Nigeria as an example, Albert said:

> The salary of a fresh university graduate in Nigeria, like in many other African countries, is about $200. More than 60% of young school leavers in the country are unemployed. Those employed on $200 definitely cannot afford the monthly Internet access rate of about $100 ... A casual survey of 10 different cybercafés in Ibadan (Nigeria) suggest that most of these young people use the internet for sending scam messages to unsuspecting people, for monitoring football fixtures and results, for desktop dating ..., for watching x-rated videos, ... for filling admission and examination forms, for checking examination results ... It was difficult throughout my search to come across one young person that was browsing the Internet for things having to do with public discourse.
>
> (Albert, 2010)

There are other factors that constrain African youth from using the Internet. In Nigeria, they include 'slow response time, network fluctuation at cyber café, and the lack of financial capacity' (Ani et al., 2007, p. 362); 'slowness of the server, inadequate knowledge of how to navigate on the Internet, financial problems and insufficient cyber cafés' (Omotayo, 2006, p. 219); irregular supply of electricity and high cost of access and use of the Internet (Ugah and Okafor, 2008); low connectivity (Jagboro, 2003); as well as 'financial constraint, erratic power supply, inefficient Internet links and servers, not having enough time, no personal access to the Internet, not being computer literate, cyber congestion, lack of reliable storage facilities, long distance and pop-up of pornographic sites (spyware)' (Awoleye et al., 2008, pp. 88–89). In Tanzania, Chachage (2001, p. 230) reported similar problems such as 'slow responses or server not working, junk mail and failure of previous users to sign out, which causes the new user to use their own time to sign out their predecessors'.

Lack of Internet skills deriving from poor training of Internet users has also been identified as a problem that hinders Internet use (Omotayo,

2006). In her study, Omotayo (2006, p. 222) argues that a 'majority of the respondents use the Internet only for e-mail, because they lack the skill to use it effectively for other purposes. University libraries in Nigeria also do not have any training programmes for the students on how to use the Internet.' Chachage (2001) makes a similar point in her study, which found that 56 per cent of Internet café users in Tanzania did not have any form of Internet training.

Conclusion

The media, including social media, play an important role in the democratic process, in strengthening the institutions of society and in creating a space that allows citizens to express themselves by engaging in participatory communication in the public sphere. Despite the advantages that cybercafés and Internet discussion forums offer to African youth, research shows that African youth are yet to use new technologies to express themselves, to contribute to the political process in their countries, to engage in civic deliberation and to participate in the public sphere. Indeed, some scholars have questioned the ability of African youth to participate in the public sphere and to contribute to political discourse in an environment in which they are constrained by economic problems, lack of infrastructure, poverty, high cost of accessing cybercafés, illiteracy, instability in supply of electricity, lack of basic computing skills and political indifference owing to lack of knowledge of politics.

It could be that African youth consider the Internet and other new technologies as forms of popular media to be used essentially to satisfy their personal communication needs. Research shows that African youth use the Internet essentially for email communication. This implies that the youth use new technologies to gratify personal communication needs in the private, restricted sphere. The higher goal of using the Internet and online discussion forums for civic deliberation or participatory communication in the public sphere is yet to be achieved. Factors that account for the absence of the voices of African youth from the public sphere were identified in this chapter. They comprise poverty, lack of basic computing skills, and general technical, infrastructural and structural problems that impede wider access to the Internet. Other factors are ignorance of the value of political participation, as well as ignorance of the personal fulfilment to be derived from participating in public spheres, in online discussion forums and in the use of other new media.

6
Changing Technologies and the Changing Role of Citizens

Introduction

New technologies are having profound impacts on the way journalism is practised across the world. Technological changes have also challenged traditional forms of journalism, redefining the relationship between professional journalists and citizens. In the digital era, Singer (2006) argues that the free, participatory and democratic appeal of online media has encouraged all types of news, resulting in different kinds of news reporters and different genres of news. One implication of this technological transformation is that 'Journalists' hegemony as gatekeepers is threatened by an audience able to actively participate in creating and disseminating news' (Singer, 2006, p. 268). Before the emergence of new technologies, news was assembled and distributed by professional journalists. Now, that is no longer the case. The outlets for news gathering, production and reporting have broadened to include citizens with computer access, digital cameras, mobile phones and other electronic devices. Access to new technologies has empowered citizens to produce and distribute news. Africa is also experiencing these changes in journalistic practices.

This chapter examines how new technologies have transformed journalism practice in Africa, including the various ways that technological changes have expanded the outlets for news production and dissemination in Africa and beyond. The analysis looks at how digital technologies have enabled African citizens to participate in news reporting, to promote civic deliberation, to express their views and to present accounts of events that often differ from reports provided by professional journalists and political leaders. The chapter analyses new forms of citizen journalism, not only from western scholarship but also from non-western contexts, as shown in research conducted in Africa (e.g., Atton and Mabweazara, 2011; Dumisani Moyo, 2009, 2007; Mabweazara, Mudhai and Whittaker, 2013; Mudhai, 2013, 2011; Paterson, 2013; Paterson and Doctors, 2013). The analysis therefore contributes to our knowledge and understanding of how new technologies are shaping African journalistic practices in the 21st century. One of the key questions examined here is the extent to which African citizens use new technologies such as the Internet, mobile phones, digital cameras and email, and social media such as Facebook, Twitter and YouTube to communicate news of national and international events to a global audience.

Civil society as an agent of change in Africa

The role of civil society as an agent of social and political change has been documented. In Africa, the limitations of institutions of democracy such as the legislature, the courts and political parties have compelled civil society organisations to assume the role of catalysts for political change (Mudhai, 2004). Essentially, new technologies have strengthened the position of civil society groups and enabled them to engineer social and political change on the continent. In various African countries, civil society has actively challenged political leaders. Examples include the popular uprisings that occurred in 2011 in three north African countries – Tunisia, Libya and Egypt. Not only did the protests lead to the overthrow of governments in those countries, the uprisings were also seen as a positive development because they signalled to other autocratic political leaders on the continent that their citizens expect them to be more responsible and accountable when they hold political office.

In a deeper analysis of the role of communication technology in promoting democracy, Grossman (1996) identifies various ways through which the power of individual members of society is enhanced. These are principally through enormously increased access to and ability of citizens to influence decision-makers and the political process. Access to new technologies implies that citizens can reach their political representatives much more easily and quickly. They are also able to access political decisions and outstanding legislative matters that could affect them. Similarly, citizens can convey their opinions more directly to parliamentarians and ultimately through civil society groups (Grossman, 1996, cited in Ott, 1998). This is one way that new technologies have empowered citizens in the political process. Essentially, new technologies enhance participatory democracy by strengthening public access to information and also by creating the environment for people to express their views. Ott (1998) states that the Internet has the potential to stimulate and strengthen the development and preservation of democratic processes and values in Africa in positive and negative ways.

Theoretical contestations: Technology and African journalism

Claims about the impact of communication technologies on African journalistic practices deserve systematic research attention (Atton and Mabweazara, 2011). Given the different levels of technology adoption and uses in different cultural contexts and platforms of journalism practice, the claims must be seen as valid. The changes in journalistic practices brought about by technological transformations in western newsrooms have received greater research attention than the situation in Africa. Scholars such as Singer (2003), Deuze (2007, 2003), Bruns (2005) and Ahlers (2006) have examined the impact of technology on newsroom practices. While Atton and Mabweazara (2011) contend that there is a lack of clarity on how African mainstream journalists grapple with the challenges of new technologies in their newsrooms, including how they have adjusted their professional practices and conventions in order to cope with the challenges, it is important to clarify that there is indeed emerging research on how African journalists are using new technologies in their professional practices.

There is, without doubt, growing knowledge of how African journalists are using new technologies in the 21st century. The diverse literature cited in this chapter attests to the existence of that scholarship. However, western theoretical perspectives have dominated research on this topic and therefore underplayed the unique circumstances of Africa. Some African scholars have pointed to how western perspectives failed to capture a range of technological, political, cultural, structural and socioeconomic problems that encumber the ability of African journalists to serve as watchdogs of their society in the new electronic age. Scholars such as Nyamnjoh (2005a, 2005b, 1999), Louw (2001), and Wasserman and de Beer (2009) have called for media research that recognises Africa's circumstances and contexts.

The dominance of western perspectives about journalism practice tends to produce a homogenous worldview that excludes other non-western experiences. Wasserman and de Beer (2009, p. 428) have argued that a conception of journalism as 'an Anglo-American invention' (reference to Chalaby, 1996, p. 303) prevents non-western journalistic practices from being seen as authentic journalism. The exclusion of some areas of the world, such as Africa, from discussions about the way journalism is practised has diminished intellectual efforts to map global media models. 'The end-result is too often that the Western democratic model of liberal democracy remains the implicit or explicit normative ideal against which journalism in non-Western societies is measured, with media-state relations as a primary determinant of journalistic standards' (Wasserman and de Beer, 2009, p. 431).

This chapter contributes to our knowledge of what is occurring in African journalism in the electronic age. The call for an inclusive understanding of journalistic practices that accommodate perspectives from the non-west is timely. Wasserman and de Beer point out that 'Theories about how journalism should be defined, what its relationship with society is, how it should be taught and how it should be practiced ought to be constructed within a globally inclusive, dialogic setting' (Wasserman and de Beer, 2009, p. 429). While debate continues about public knowledge of journalism, including ethical issues that straddle the profession, the choices available to the audience and technological advancements that have spawned citizen journalism practices, 'scant attention is paid to the situation in other parts of the world where these technologies are less pervasive, but where journalism producers and consumers are finding more and more creative ways of dealing with lack of access in order to compete in a globalized media world' (Wasserman and de Beer, 2009, p. 431). Quite appropriately, the situation in Africa is examined in the following sections.

New technologies, new threats to journalists

Kupe (2004) acknowledges how the environment for journalism practice in Africa has changed significantly in the past two decades. Changes in African journalistic practices are consistent with media reforms that are driven by globalisation and technological transformations. Atton and Mabweazara (2011) argue that research on the impact of new technologies on African journalistic practices tends to celebrate new forms of journalism practice without reflecting on the various political, economic, cultural, structural and social conditions in which the technologies are appropriated by journalists. Supporting the view of Nyamnjoh (2005a), they call for emphasis on what journalists do *with* the technologies, rather than what the new technologies do *to* journalists (Atton and Mabweazara, 2011, p. 668). New technologies in African newsrooms have to be examined in the context of the role they play in professional practice, in the society and in the existing sociocultural and political environments in which journalists operate. The values that journalists and ordinary citizens attach to new technologies inform their greater use, not only in news reporting but also in the development of social networks and in facilitating interaction with peers, community members and social groups.

Mudhai (2011) notes that the use of new technologies in journalism practice in Africa reflects national contexts and circumstances, pointing out how governments have responded to greater journalistic freedom offered by new technologies. Examples include the Zambian government proscription of the *Post* online and the demonisation of bloggers in parts of Africa, such as the Egyptian government's crackdown on bloggers. Where governments have suppressed free expression of opinions, journalists, particularly those operating in environments in which dictators hold political power, tend to engage in self-censorship. They also adopt evasive and underground journalistic practices that were more common in some African countries in the 1990s. One example is 'guerrilla journalism' or subversive journalism in Nigeria during military dictatorship in the 1980s and 1990s, which may have paled in comparison to the violence visited on journalists in Kenya in the 1990s when gunmen invaded and seized computers in the oldest media organisation in the country. Other examples include the beating of staff of the Standard Group or shutting down of signals from Kenya's Television Network or the incineration of copies of the *East African Standard* newspaper (Mudhai, 2011). Clearly, professional practice comes with risks to journalists. All this goes to show that even as journalists and ordinary citizens celebrate new technologies, they still face dangers to their lives in environments in which security agencies have little or no regard for the human rights of citizens.

Use of mobile phones by journalists

A number of studies have examined how African journalists use mobile phones in professional practice. Mabweazara (2011) analysed the use of mobile phones by Zimbabwean print journalists in their professional practice and found that new technology is changing established news reporting and production conventions. The sociocultural uses of the mobile phone by Zimbabwean journalists indicate that the phone has taken on new values in the society. The frequency of mobile phone use by journalists has obscured understanding of the borderline between the journalists' work and their private life. Mabweazara argues that little research exists to show the relationship between new technology and journalists' professional practice, in particular how mobile phones contribute to the increasing collaboration between professional journalists and ordinary citizens in news reporting practices. In his view,

> While traditional gate-keeping processes persist and determine what news is covered in the newsrooms, a closer examination of the uses of the mobile phone suggests a widening exposure of journalists to news and a widening participation of citizens in mainstream newsmaking – mainstream journalists no longer speak *ex cathedra* as they used to before the advent of new media.
>
> (Mabweazara, 2011, p. 694)

Chapter 9 explored the various ways in which the mobile phone has transformed public communication in Africa.

Other scholars have highlighted the role of mobile phones in the socioeconomic development of Africa (Aker and Mbiti, 2010; Hahn, 2012; Hahn and Kibora, 2008; Nyamnjoh, 2005a; Obijiofor, 1998). In his study, Mabweazara (2011) identified the pervasive use of short message service (SMS) text messaging because of its relatively low cost, 'beeping' or 'flashing' features and other elements. SMS text messaging is popular in Africa and is regarded as an effective tool for communication essentially because of its affordability to the majority of people, as well as its convenience and dependability, particularly in those remote and rural locations where weak network services constitute impediments to making a phone call (Mabweazara, 2011, p. 696). As other scholars have acknowledged, SMS technology facilitates unhindered distribution of information and messages, especially during general elections and outbreaks of political unrest in parts of Africa (Dumisani Moyo, 2009).

In Zimbabwean newsrooms, Mabweazara (2011) found that mobile phones have given mainstream journalists the freedom to report without necessarily being close to news locations. Thus, the mobile phone has become, to Zimbabwean journalists, an essential tool for performing their daily tasks. 'The oral and textual contact with people that the mobile phone facilitated was seen as enabling a flexible work regime in which journalists were available to their sources and colleagues while on the move – on work-related assignments or engaging in personal business' (Mabweazara, 2011, p. 698). Additionally, the mobile phone has redefined the relationship between Zimbabwean journalists and their sources, as journalists and sources can work around their busy routines and bureaucratic obstacles to communicate by mobile phones. There are other ways in which the mobile phone has empowered journalists. For example, it serves as a source of news stories which journalists receive through SMS alerts from civil society groups, and calls from members of the public.

Mabweazara (2011) notes that the access that the public has to journalists' mobile phone numbers, as well as the secrecy that mobile phones offer to users have facilitated easy interaction and communication between news sources and people who report illegal activities in public and private offices. This has expanded the scope of news coverage and decreased the time it takes for journalists to cover news.

For a related discussion, see Hendrickson (2006). All this is not to suggest that the use of mobile phones by Zimbabwean journalists has gone on without impediments. There are challenges involved in journalists' use of mobile phones in their daily news reporting routines. The problems include but are not limited to weak or poor network services, censorship worries, high cost of mobile phones and little or no support provided to journalists by news organisations (Mabweazara, 2011). Nevertheless, mobile phones have contributed to the emergence of network-convergent journalism in Africa and other parts of the world.

Network-convergent journalism

Networked journalism has been defined as a combination of conventional news journalism and newer forms of collaborative media facilitated by Web 2.0 technologies that include mobile phones, email, websites, blogs, and social networks. This form of journalism promotes active citizen involvement in news production through various forms of collaboration. Networked journalism has changed the news process from its original narrow form that is controlled by senior journalists and turned it into a more cooperative process involving citizens (Beckett, 2010).

Beckett adds that networked journalism is designed to challenge journalists, citizens and policymakers to deliberate on the purpose of journalism, its function in society, its relevance to the economy and individual members of society. It asks the question: what is the significance of journalism to society? (Beckett, 2010). One advantage of networking with the public is an increase in breaking news gathering. Networking also contributes to local news.

The values of networked journalism are: it encourages public involvement or collaboration in the news production chain; it is founded on the principles of interactivity and connectivity; it transforms the working relationship between the professional journalist and their media organisation; it links the mainstream media with a broader network of independent, individual and social media; and it has the potential to change the public value that journalism can offer in a networked society (Beckett, 2010). Networked journalism holds editorial value for the consumer in three ways: it promotes diversity in editorial content; it provides a variety of news that allows consumers to access news content that meets their interests and requirements; and it enhances connectivity and interactivity by delivering news in various ways that attract and hold the attention of the public by getting them involved at all stages of the news process. Interaction with the public creates a feeling of community among news consumers; networked journalism engages audiences and subjects in various ways to produce innovative ethical and editorial relationships to news; and it is a transparent process that encourages the building of trust (Beckett, 2010).

Networked journalism should not be confused with convergent journalism, which Quinn and Filak (2005, p. 7) describe as 'doing journalism and telling stories using the most appropriate media'. Although convergent journalism may be radical in its orientation, it differs in different countries and cultural contexts (Quinn and Filak, 2005). Mudhai (2011) points out growing concerns expressed by Kenyan trade unions about the impact of convergence on news quality, although he notes that concerns have eased owing to increasing participation of citizen journalists in news reporting and production for little or no remuneration. What is really important with regard to networked and convergent journalism is the prospect of reformulating the bond between news producers and content consumers in a culture that promotes sharing (Mudhai, 2011).

Although immediacy and openness have been noted as strengths of networked and convergent journalism that are driven by new technologies, in some cultures immediacy may offend political leaders. As Mudhai (2011) notes, immediacy allowed Kenyans to observe events at vital periods, such as the coverage of the 2007 national elections that worried the government to the point that it had to stop real-time coverage of the elections on television. Of course, immediacy has consequences, such as unfairness and inaccuracies. These could be contested or rectified.

Of course, openness that is facilitated by new technologies is harder to stifle, as some governments in Africa and elsewhere have discovered. Even as journalists and citizens celebrate the advent of new technologies that have enabled them to challenge political leaders and to provide alternative accounts of events in their societies, the same technologies have often been used in ways that constrained the freedom of citizens.

One form of networked journalism that has gained popularity in parts of the world is mobile journalism, otherwise known as 'mojo' or mobile news (cited in Mudhai, 2011, pp. 682–683). Governments in Africa (e.g., Nigeria and Kenya) have reacted to the development of mobile news or the increasing use of mobile phones to take photographs and to report breaking news. SMS is perceived differently by citizens and government officials. To citizens, SMS is a tool of liberation. To government officials, it is an instrument for social destabilisation (see Chapter 9 for more on this). The widespread demonstrations that erupted in the Arab world in 2011 have been attributed to the power of mobile phones, SMS text messaging and camera phones that were used to mobilise citizens and to spread messages about planned demonstrations.

Camera phones in particular were used by civil society in Nigeria to dispute official accounts of the circumstances that led to the death of the leader of the Boko Haram sectarian group, Mohammed Yusuf, in 2009. Camera phones were also used to capture the brutalisation of a young Nigerian woman in November 2008. That event outraged the Nigerian public and the global community. Details of these events are discussed later in this chapter; see the section titled 'Citizen journalism in Kenya and Nigeria'.

The convergent use of mobile phones to record and report events in Africa and elsewhere is growing. Webb (2004), for instance, notes the social uses of the mobile phone:

> Mobile phones are no longer used purely for phone calls. They have now taken on a convergent form, where the user can access the Internet, listen to the radio, download polyphonic ringtones, text message other mobile phones using SMS, take photos and send emails all from their mobile handset. One group in particular that has heavily adopted this technology is youth. This new media technology has spread rapidly and has created a whole new youth culture, particularly in urban centres.
>
> (Webb, 2004)

This is clearly evident in the way Nigerian and Kenyan citizens used mobile phones and other digital technologies to record and post news events on online discussion forums, YouTube and social networking sites such as Facebook and Twitter. One important way in which new technologies have transformed news reporting is the phenomenon of 'citizen journalism'. Livingston (2007, p. 52) notes that the explosion in camera phones and digital cameras (and other portable devices) has spawned a generation of 'pocket paparazzi'. He cites an example of this phenomenon during the funeral of Pope John Paul II in 2005. In an effort to restore some respectability to the funeral, officials at the Vatican ordered a ban on the use of 'cameras' by many people who looked at the body of the Pope as it was rested at the Vatican. However, the officials didn't understand that the meaning of camera has changed from what it used to be. Many of the mourners captured the body of the Pope in their camera phones (Livingston, 2007).

McNair (2011, p. 42) describes the phenomenon thus: 'Since the late 1990s, and accelerating after 9/11, we have seen the rise of the content-generating user – the blogger, the citizen journalist, the accidental eyewitness in possession of a digital camera and access to the Internet.' The growth of online journalism has not been without tensions between government officials and citizens, between citizens and professional journalists, as well as between editors and bloggers, citizen journalists and other genres of online news producers. Paulussen and Ugille (2008) contend that professional journalists will have to relax their power over the processes of news production, as online news consumers are getting more keenly engaged in the construction of news. This will result not only in journalists using content produced by news consumers but it will also generate more partnership between trained journalists and untrained journalists.

Not only are new technologies helping citizens to question political leaders and to provide alternative accounts of events in their society, the technologies have dramatically altered public understanding of journalists and editors as gatekeepers. With the aid of new technologies, citizens are able to report news, supply photos that serve as eyewitness accounts of events and also provide feedback on news stories reported by mainstream media (see, for example, Hendrickson, 2006; Williams and Delli Carpini, 2004). New technologies are also helping African citizens who serve as correspondents to foreign media to challenge and reconstruct skewed reporting by western journalists who create images of the continent as a region that is rife with violence, hunger, diseases and political instability (see also Mudhai, 2011; Obijiofor, 2012).

The wind of political reforms that blew across the world in the late 1980s helped to generate sustained demands for democratisation in various African countries in the 1990s. Campbell (2003) notes that these agitations were influenced specifically by the political changes that occurred in Eastern Europe and the former Soviet Union resulting in the collapse of the Berlin Wall and the disintegration of the Soviet Union. In Zambia, harsh restrictions on the press were reduced in 1990. The new climate of press freedom contributed to the defeat of the government of President Kenneth Kaunda in the 1991 election. Nigeria, where military governments owned and controlled the broadcast media and some newspapers, witnessed changes to media ownership laws, leading to new legislation that facilitated private ownership of the broadcast media in the 1990s (Campbell, 2003). The global movement for democracy impacted on citizen involvement in journalism in various ways. First, it raised questions about the representativeness of traditional forms of journalism practice. Second, it called for reforms of traditional journalistic practices in order to encourage greater citizen participation and expression of diverse viewpoints. Third, the culture of journalism practice was examined in the context of its importance to and connection with other democratic institutions (Banda, 2010).

Citizen journalism defined

Citizen journalism represents one way in which new technologies have transformed journalism practice, extending the world of journalism beyond the roles attributed to, or monopolised by, professional journalists. In different parts of the global community, technological changes have opened new opportunities for popular participation in news generation, as well as multiple channels for information dissemination. Different scholars have defined citizen journalism in different ways (e.g., Atton, 2002; Banda, 2010). Citizen journalism is the form of practice in which ordinary citizens engage in news reporting, or news commentary related to events in their community. 'Citizen journalists gather, process, research, report, analyse and publish news and information, most often utilizing a variety of technologies made possible by the Internet' (cited in Banda, 2010, p. 26). The underlying element that features in most of the definitions is that citizen journalists generate, collect, investigate, handle, provide accounts of events and disseminate news with the aid of new technologies. Citizen journalism is a natural reaction by citizens to the inadequacies and limitations of mainstream media.

Citizen journalism takes different forms, such as online discussion forums. Some online discussion forums are set up by individuals, independent groups or organisations. Others are set up by established media such as the BBC, CNN and *OhmyNews.com* – a South Korean

Internet-based newspaper – not only to report news but also to promote greater interaction between journalists and audiences. Such interaction and discussion are designed to engender healthy democracies through vigorous debate.

Akinfemisoye (2013) reports on how the announcement of an unprecedented increase in the price of petrol per litre by the Nigerian government on New Year's Day in 2012 sparked mass protests by the citizens not only on the streets but also on social media. The protests were tagged 'Occupy Nigeria' on Twitter and Facebook. She wondered whether Nigerian journalists who reported on the protests through social media and other alternative forms of media aided discussions in the public sphere that were different from the way the mainstream media reported or constructed such public events. Drawing on a critical analysis of notions of citizen, citizenship, citizen media and citizen journalism, Berger (2011, p. 713) observes that 'citizen journalism' should be seen as a term that is designed to inform the journalism that is produced from unpaid work that originates from outside of the mass media. He contends that this definition still stands even if this kind of journalism is conveyed via mass media channels. Similarly, the definition will stand even if the outputs of journalists who are employed by media organisations relate to citizen activities, which imply that they could also engage in citizen journalism.

In arguments that echo the views of Mare (2013), Berger states that it is misleading to attribute to citizen journalists the position of alternative journalists because various journalists who work in traditional mainstream media are similarly dedicated to citizenship. Therefore, the issue, in his view, is not really competition among people outside the media industry and people within the industry but a conscious collaboration between citizen journalists who work outside traditional media and journalists who work in the media industry (Berger, 2011).

Critique of citizen journalism

Despite the positive role that citizen journalists play in reporting news across the world, critics of citizen journalists express uneasiness about their impact on professional journalism practice. For example, citizen journalists are seen as encouraging unethical journalism practices and diminishing the role of professional journalists as gatekeepers of news and information. Citizen journalists are also criticised for disrupting established business models of journalism through encouragement of free access to online news (Mare, 2013). Criticisms of citizen journalists echo the views of Samuel Freedman, who expressed disapproval of the concept (see, for example, Profita, 2006).

Samuel Freedman, a journalism academic and newspaper columnist, expressed serious doubts about the ability of citizen journalists to render professional journalists irrelevant in the contemporary world. He defined a citizen journalist as 'anybody with a video camera or cell-phone or blog who posts photographs, live-action film, or written reports on news events' (Profita, 2006). He argues vigorously that 'Citizen journalism does not merely challenge the notion of professionalism in journalism but completely circumvents it.' In his view, 'citizen journalism forms part of a larger attempt to degrade, even to disenfranchise journalism as practiced by trained professionals', even as he acknowledges the strengths of citizen journalism, such as the provision of eye-witness accounts of major events across the world and democratisation of news media (Profita, 2006). Nevertheless, Freedman believes that citizen journalists are less equipped with necessary skills to evaluate, reflect on, examine and explain the events they report on (Profita, 2006). Fenton (2010) and Mabweazara (2011) have identified some ethical issues that arise in news reporting in the new electronic environment.

Role of social media in engineering change

The growth of the Internet and the rapid adoption and use of mobile phones in African countries have facilitated the growth of social media and other platforms of news production and distribution (Jordaan, 2013; Mabweazara, 2011; Moyo, D., 2009; Mudhai, 2011). Paterson (2013) argues that social media will play a role in social and political change in Africa but what is uncertain is the nature of that transformation – whether it will be steady and planned or disorderly, abrupt and far-reaching. He makes an important point about the impact of social media on journalism in Africa and whether they will assist Africans to achieve control over the way Africa is represented in western media. African representation is crucial, as social media will help to correct the stereotypes that have been constructed about Africa, African people and the history of Africa. Stereotypical stories about Africa have been a huge part of the misrepresentations of the continent in western media. If used appropriately and effectively, social media could serve as tools for the economic, social and political emancipation of Africa. The use of social media to demystify the image of Africa constructed by western media is important because, according to Paterson (2013, p. 5),

Africa has long been subject to a prejudiced form of reporting which has focused almost exclusively on specific types of negative events, with little attention to long-term processes. Do social media amplify the negative or give new voice to the positive? Do they provide a new avenue to reach journalists outside of Africa directly, to facilitate more nuanced reporting, and to critique that which falls into the old Afro-pessimist paradigm?

Social media provides unlimited opportunities to citizens and professional journalists to circumvent established channels of information flow. However, uncertainty remains about the extent to which social media have substituted traditional information outlets, the degree to which they are being integrated into African journalistic practices and the extent to which they are engineering the development or emergence of varieties of citizenship in Africa (Mare, 2013). It has been argued that during the popular revolt that occurred in Egypt in 2011, the interaction between social media and mainstream media empowered news consumers to become effective contributors to the creation, distribution and consumption of news, thus 'giving a voice to people who had previously been limited to more passive and non-interactive forms of news consumption' (Mare, 2013, p. 84).

The rise of social media, the increasing uptake of mobile phones and the use of the Internet have encouraged the development of a public sphere that provides alternative discourses about governance that affect people in various parts of Africa. Nevertheless, debate continues about whether new media have provided adequate opportunities for citizens to express their views about events in their societies and the performance of their political leaders.

Atton and Hamilton (2008) have described various ways in which citizens engage in alternative forms of journalism practice in developing and developed countries. Similarly, the growing phenomenon of networked journalism (discussed in this chapter; see Bardoel, 2002; Beckett, 2010) offers many opportunities through which citizens and communities can collaborate with established mainstream media in the service of society. However, Paterson (2013) wonders whether increasing interaction between citizens and professional journalists in news reporting and production has raised concerns about the temptation for journalists in resource-poor news organisations to rely on information published online without cross-checking or confirmation.

Theoretically, there are three areas in which scholars have discussed the relationship between social media and traditional journalistic practices. They are: scholars who support the open and unrestricted character of social media; scholars who dispute the role of social media because they see it as a source of problems for traditional journalists; and the third group who encourage views that are not extreme as a way to combine and promote efforts at cooperation between traditional journalists and social media (Mare, 2013). Regardless of whether these positions are sound or unsound, scholars agree that social media have strengths and drawbacks (e.g., Berger, 2011; Mabweazara, 2011; Newman, 2009). For example, social media are associated with opening up of public spaces for news dissemination and unrestricted discussion. In this way, social media are linked to the promotion of free expression of views by citizens. More significantly, social media have been recognised for the important role they played in reporting various events across the world, such as: the 2011 floods in Queensland (Australia); the riots that followed the outcome of the 2009 Iranian presidential election; the unrest that erupted in north African countries in 2011; the earthquake in Haiti (Mare, 2013); the 2011 earthquake in Christchurch, New Zealand; the London bombings in 2005; and the 26 December 2004 tsunami that claimed many lives in different parts of Southeast Asia and the Pacific.

In a study of the relationship between social and mainstream media in their reporting of the civil unrest that erupted in Zimbabwe, Malawi and Mozambique at different times in history, Mare (2013) identifies various reasons why social media were included in the processes of news gathering and dissemination in traditional media. He found that in these three countries, social media were used to discover story ideas, to collect news stories, to follow and develop news sources, to interact with news sources, to discover and monitor powerful campaigners, to talk about forthcoming events, to assess public views about current events, to convey and shed light on stories, and to collect and distribute news (Mare, 2013). In this way, social media promote active audience participation in news reporting and production processes. On this basis, Mare (2013, p. 95) concluded that the evidence that social media provided news alerts to southern African journalists shows the rising relevance of citizens as sources of news and information. Mare also notes that during political uprisings in southern Africa, social media served as alternative spaces for political debate and communication by citizens and professional journalists. The outcome is cooperative journalism practices by professional and untrained journalists who operate as watchdogs of society.

As Akinfemisoye (2013) found in her Nigerian study, alternative media platforms do influence how media agendas are constructed.

Journalists also monitor social networking sites for breaking news and news ideas that warrant further investigation. Nevertheless, there is still public recognition and acceptance of the way things are done when it comes to news reporting practices. Akinfemisoye's (2013) view that journalists in Nigeria use social media to some extent in their news reporting practices resonates with Paterson's (2013) observation that African journalists incorporate social media in their news work, disregarding the fact that many people lack access to social media. Paterson (2013, p. 2) identifies challenges of social media in Africa owing to poorly developed telecommunications infrastructure, 'limited (though rapidly increasing) extra-urban mobile access, and bandwidth limitations in many areas'.

Jordaan (2013) investigated the extent to which professional use of social media such as Twitter and Facebook affected news selection and reporting cultures and conventions in the South African media. She found that, although journalists who worked with *Rapport* and the *Mail & Guardian* newspapers used social media for various reasons (mostly to keep informed of events in the news and in the general society), many of the journalists said that social media did not have a significant impact on their news selection and presentation routines and practices. However, the journalists believed social media served as complements to their work rather than pose a threat to their job. Jordaan defines social media as 'communication technologies that enable connections between individuals and groups where these connections lead to information-sharing and mutual influence' (Jordaan, 2013, p. 24).

Research by Newman (2009) shows a steady rise in the number of journalists across the world who access and use social media. He observes that journalists are embracing social media such as Twitter, blogs and Facebook but states clearly that they have not displaced journalism, although they are producing additional levels of information and various opinions. On the basis of his study, Newman (2009) submits that social media and contents produced by users are transforming the mode of breaking news. They add to the compact nature of the 'news cycle' that increases the burden on editors to decide what to report and at what time. Newman believes that media organisations are discarding their goal to be first with the news and are now concentrating on being the leader in authenticating news.

With specific reference to South Africa and the role of social media in contributing to social change, Wasserman and de Beer (2005) argue that multiple channels of news and information should facilitate the development of an open and deliberative public sphere that should enhance democracy in post-apartheid South Africa.

Last Moyo (2011) analysed the use of blogs to intervene during a violent election in Zimbabwe, especially how citizens communicated and distributed information about their sufferings and difficult situations in the face of the state crackdown on the citizens. He examined various forms of alternative media in Zimbabwe during the crisis. He argued that a driving force of alternative media, whether they are online or offline, is that they are used to serve the community. Atton (2002), as well as Atton and Hamilton (2008), have written extensively on alternative media, their characteristics and the various uses to which they are put. Participation is one key element of alternative media. Atton (2002, p. 25) states that alternative media is designed to facilitate 'wider social participation in the creation, production, and dissemination [of content] than is possible in the mass media'. Last Moyo (2011) identifies the close relationship between citizen participation and citizen journalism, noting that the two are inseparable. Yet the point has been made that alternative journalism is not the same as citizen journalism.

One element of alternative media is that they are 'counter-hegemonic' (Last Moyo, 2011), which could imply that they tend to promote political and social extremism (Atton, 2002). In his study of the Kubatana bloggers in Zimbabwe, Last Moyo (2011) found that the bloggers used no sources or bylines, and never sought to reflect objectivity or balance in their reports. Although the bloggers informed and educated the citizens about the political violence in Zimbabwe, they never perceived themselves as objective and impartial reporters of news and events in the country. Indeed, according to Last Moyo (2011), the language used by Kubatana bloggers echoes the resentment the writers have against the state of affairs in the country that appear to be submissive to the bigger reason for opposition to dictatorship rather than to safeguarding some journalistic values. Kubatana bloggers seem to possess numerous personalities. They are dynamic citizens, worried campaigners, and at the same time 'journalists' because they generate and disseminate news of events in their neighbourhoods.

This shows that Zimbabwean citizens cannot be regarded as passive recipients who are deluged with news and information from the mass media. Assisted by the Internet, the citizens actively engage in the production of news, and in the distribution of news between the people and the outside global community. For example, the bloggers disseminated photos of victims of human rights abuses which would not normally have found space in mainstream media in Zimbabwe. This is seen as evidence of 'the health and effectiveness of the Fifth Estate as an alternative space for uncensored news' (Last Moyo, 2011, p. 755). Nevertheless, problems of access and participation challenge the ability of Zimbabwe's alternative media (described as the Fifth Estate) to function as a credible and effective channel.

As many citizens in Zimbabwe lack access to the Internet, bloggers in Zimbabwe, and the Fifth Estate generally, lack the ability to reach a majority of the population and therefore the impact of alternative media remains low because they are unable to influence public opinion in the country. Beyond this, questions have been raised about the appropriateness of Kubatana bloggers to campaign for political rights against the more important economic rights in a country in which many people suffer economic deprivation (Last Moyo, 2011). Hence, 'Kubatana bloggers are not revolutionaries seeking to uproot Zimbabwe's political and economic status quo. They are only moral reformists who are concerned with the particular leadership style or the grammar of politics, and not the entire edifice of the ruling elite' (Last Moyo, 2011, p. 758).

Years after the uprising that overthrew Egyptian President Hosni Mubarak in 2011, questions remain about the role that social media played in moulding public opinion against the government and in galvanising public support for the revolt. Some people argue that social media should not be regarded as the facilitator of the Egyptian uprising because the people were already motivated to protest because of 'decades of oppression, poor socioeconomic conditions, and demonstrators' bravery...' (Loudon and Mazumdar, 2013, p. 52). This is perhaps a sound argument because, even after the government had denied people access to the Internet and closed mobile phone services across the country, the protests grew louder, more defiant and more persistent.

Other people hold the view that social media contributed to the collapse of unpopular regimes across the world such as those of President Joseph Estrada of the Philippines in 2001 and Spanish Prime Minister José María Aznar in 2004 (Shirky, 2011). In both instances and indeed in others, social media devices such as text messages, electronic mail, photo sharing and social networking tools were identified as the weapons that empowered citizens to organise popular protests against their governments. As Shirky (2011, p. 36) notes, 'Social media increase shared awareness by propagating messages through social networks.' In the two instances cited here, Shirky (2011) observed that the opposition against Estrada in the Philippines benefited from the simplicity of using sms text messages to coordinate a large group without the requirement to put in place some control mechanisms. Similarly, opposition to Aznar in Spain gained impetus quite rapidly because the people who spread the information did not belong to any organisation that is hierarchical in structure.

Two arguments have been advanced to support the notion that social media do not shape the nature of national politics across the world. The first argument is that social media devices are unproductive and useless. The second view is that the devices are detrimental to the growth of democracy, as authoritarian regimes have in-depth knowledge of, and experience with, using the tools to repress the opposition (Shirky, 2011). In essence, the same social media devices that activists and civil rights groups use to resist suppression are also used by despotic leaders to stifle free expression.

A counter argument to the first view is that, while not every social group that uses social media in its campaign will achieve success, a growing number of political movements are using social media to create awareness about social issues, even if awareness does not lead to social or political change. Although the Chinese authorities are widely cited for their skill in using digital technologies to monitor, censor and constrain dissident groups and their views, the strategy has also backfired. When governments ban the use of certain technologies or public space, they invariably spread awareness of such issues to groups that were previously unaware of the technologies or contested public space. Shirky cites an example in Bahrain about which he notes that 'When the government of Bahrain banned Google Earth after an annotated map of the royal family's annexation of public land began circulating, the effect was to alert far more Bahrainis to the offending map than knew about it originally' (Shirky, 2011, p. 39).

These discourses position social media and other new technologies as both a facilitator of political protests and a device used by authoritarian governments to repress citizens. In research that investigates whether social media are changing traditional channels of information flow in and about Swaziland, and whether social media can be seen as a vehicle for empowering the people, Rooney (2013) argues that social media have widened the public sphere and created opportunities for various people inside and outside Swaziland to produce, disseminate and discuss information about the country, particularly information relating to the need for political change. However, he also identifies impediments to public participation such as disparities in access to new technologies, and imbalanced capabilities among citizens to contribute to the digital public sphere (Rooney, 2013).

In a study of the use of social media as outlets for alternative journalism by civil society activists during the 2010 G20 summit in Toronto, Canada, Poell and Borra (2011) note that organisers of the protests encouraged the protesters to publicise news through Twitter, YouTube and Flickr. However, the researchers found that with the exception of Twitter, social media did not aid the protesters' use of alternative reporting channels. They report that in covering protests, mainstream media have been criticised for undue focus on the demonstrations and the violence that go with protest movements, and for paying little attention to the causes of the protest (Poell and Borra, 2011, p. 705). This seems to go against the spirit of alternative journalism which is to correct reporting by mainstream media by focusing on the social, economic and political factors that underpin protest movements.

One of the difficulties of relying on reports provided by activists is that their accounts tend to be based on the comments and knowledge of a small but influential group of people with privileged information. This obviously contradicts the ideal of alternative journalism, which is to include as many diverse viewpoints as possible in news reports (Poell and Borra, 2011). Incidentally, they found in their study of protests at the 2010 G20 summit in Toronto that the use of Flickr and to some extent YouTube in reporting the event was built on the opinions of a few users of the social networks. Against this background, they suggest that 'the result of activist social media reporting is just as tragic: the attention is drawn away from the original issues at stake in the protests' (Poell and Borra, 2011, p. 709). Issues that underpin protest movements and the reporting that takes place on social media should be open to greater public scrutiny.

Strengths and drawbacks of social media

Despite criticisms of aspects of citizen journalism practices, Dumisani Moyo (2009, p. 555) makes the forceful point that 'The ability of ordinary citizens to be where events are taking place, which is not always possible for professional journalists, means that citizen journalism can make a tremendous contribution in bringing to light issues and events that may otherwise go unreported.' Nevertheless, he notes the dangers that ordinary citizens expose themselves to when they engage in journalism practice in societies in which certain privileges and protections that are accorded to professional journalists in the constitution are not extended to ordinary citizens.

With reference to the use of online forums as an intervening force in the political crisis in Zimbabwe, Dumisani Moyo (2007) states that the news websites do not only serve as alternative media that 'give voice to the voiceless and articulate viewpoints that would otherwise not see the light of day under Zimbabwe's tightly controlled media environment' (2007, p. 101), but have also reduced the significant role that mainstream state-owned and controlled media have over the society. This is achieved through publication of stories about corruption, human rights abuses and abuse of office that would never have been publicised in the government-controlled media (Dumisani Moyo, 2007).

Impediments to public use of social media

The ability of African citizens to use new technologies is dependent on the extent to which they have access to the technologies. As stated in Chapter 2, access to and use of digital technologies such as smartphones is highly restricted in Africa, despite the rapid diffusion of mobile phones on the continent. Similarly, wireless Internet services are not cheap. Berger points out that these factors restrict the ability of ordinary citizens to use new technologies to engage in citizen journalism. Owing to these constraints and other sociocultural factors, Obijiofor (1998) argues that the technology that will transform the mode of communication in Africa is the telephone. Limited access to technologies also affects skills development. In countries in which access to new technologies is limited, many people lack the technical and communication expertise required to operate and use the technologies to produce and distribute news.

Berger (2011) points out that skills development serves as an ancillary to access. Similarly, Banda (2010) reinforces the point that an assessment of the production and consumption of citizen journalism in Africa is particularly problematic owing to problems associated with access to new technologies. The Internet in Africa could be described as a medium that is largely accessible to the elite. Thus, 'the practice of Internet-based forms of citizen journalism, while clearly a novelty for many, is still a long way from becoming a "mass" reality that can transform African societies' (Banda, 2010, p. 16), particularly rural and remote communities. This is the point that Albert (2010) underlined when he argued that popular participation in Africa's online forums is limited to a few people owing to factors such as 'the lack of capacity (intellectual ability, resources for accessing the Internet and so on)', as well as underlying problems of poverty, unemployment and a general feeling of political indifference (Albert, 2010). Brinkman, Lamoureaux, Merolla and de Bruijn (2011) echo this view.

Whether new technologies facilitate greater freedom for citizen participation in the news process will be determined by the degree of access that citizens enjoy. Citizens must have unimpeded access to technologies if they are to contribute to news reporting and production. In Africa, an enormous gulf exists between citizens who have access to new technologies and those who do not. This is what is generally referred to as the digital divide, that is, the inequalities that exist between those who have access to technology and therefore have greater access to information and those who lack access to technology. The digital divide exists at several levels. In addition to this divide there are others such as the gender divide, the poverty divide, the urban–rural divide, the age divide and so on. In Africa, several factors account for lack of access to new technologies. They include but are not limited to high cost of technologies, poverty, illiteracy, unsteady supply of electricity, cost of accessing Internet services and limited public Internet sites. For these reasons, Berger (2009, p. 361) cautions against optimism about widespread use of the Internet.

If citizen journalism is being practised on a massive scale in western countries, it does not follow that a similar experience is occurring in Africa or other developing regions. As Tuinstra (2004, p. 102) notes, 'There are still many countries, of course, where most people are not connected to the Internet, and so this makes its use as a mass communication tool still problematic there.' With specific reference to Internet presence and use in Africa, Wall (2009, p. 399) agrees that 'most African countries are far from wired, and use of the Internet, much less a video site such as YouTube, is limited'. In Nigeria, Ani, Uchendu and Atseye (2007) have observed inequalities in access to new technologies in the private and public sectors of the economy.

Online discussion forums

Despite these shortcomings, some privileged groups and individuals in Africa continue to use new technologies to report news, to reach out to the rest of the world and to expand public spaces for deliberative democracy. As Obijiofor (2009b, p. 197) concluded in his study of the press framing of the Niger Delta conflict in Nigeria, new technologies such as email and the Internet

> serve as a forum through which marginalized groups and minorities such as the Niger Delta activists tell their stories and communicate their problems to the rest of the world ... The Niger Delta activists use

these technologies as tools for their economic, social, and political emancipation in their struggle for self-determination.

A common feature among civil society groups is the establishment of online discussion forums that serve as a watchdog over political leaders across Africa. In Nigeria, there are sites such as the Nigeria Village Square (www.nigerianvillagesquare.com) that presents itself as 'The marketplace of ideas FOR THE THINKING NIGERIAN and friends', the Saharareporters (www.saharareporters.com) which states on its website that 'Sahara Reporters is an online community of international reporters and social advocates dedicated to bringing you commentaries, features, news reports from a Nigerian-African perspective' (http://saharareporters.com/page/about-sahara-reporters) and Elendureports operated by Jonathan Elendu (http://www.elendureports.com/). These are by no means all the active online discussion sites operated by civil society groups and individuals in Nigeria or indeed Africa. In Kenya, a popular online platform is Ushahidi.com. A brief history of the website states that

> 'Ushahidi', which means 'testimony' in Swahili, was a website that was initially developed to map reports of violence in Kenya after the post-election fallout at the beginning of 2008. Since then, the name 'Ushahidi' has come to represent the people behind the 'Ushahidi Platform'. Our roots are in the collaboration of Kenyan citizen journalists during a time of crisis. The original website was used to map incidents of violence and peace efforts throughout the country based on reports submitted via the web and mobile phones. This website had 45,000 users in Kenya, and was the catalyst for us realizing there was a need for a platform based on it, which could be used by others around the world.
>
> (http://ushahidi.com/about-us/)

Citizen journalism in Kenya and Nigeria

Following the disputed outcomes of the national elections in Kenya in December 2007, there was widespread violence that took on an ethnic dimension in early 2008. Many Kenyan citizens were murdered. The mainstream media took sides in the conflict. Some sections of the media condemned the killings and the ethnic undertones of the political violence, while other media simply stayed away from reporting on the conflict. The controversial role of the mainstream media in Kenya in reporting the violence or in underplaying the magnitude of the killings showed how the media could easily be used as a medium for incitement of political violence. The confusion that prevailed during the ethnic riots highlighted the challenges that many Kenyans and the international community faced in accessing correct accounts of the scale of the violence. It was this state of affairs that compelled some Kenyan citizens to set up the 'Ushahidi' online site. According to the administrators of the web site, Ushahidi, which literally implies 'testimony' in Swahili, is an online site that was formerly developed to register accounts of violent behaviour in Kenya after the post-election results at the start of 2008. Ushahidi emerged as a result of collaboration by Kenyan citizens during a political crisis. (http://www.ushahidi.com/about)

Certainly, the emergence of the 'Ushahidi' website could be attributed to the failure of Kenya's mainstream media to provide accurate reports of the post-election violence. The lesson learnt from the Kenyan experience is that when traditional media fail to serve as the channels of credible information, non-professional journalists and ordinary citizens will open up alternative channels for news and information circulation and public discussion. Through the 'Ushahidi' website, Kenyan citizens opened up an opportunity for other Kenyans at home and overseas to report and deliberate on political events within their country. Apart from sharing information through the online site, some Kenyans also took photographs of the post-election violence with their mobile phones which they distributed through video sharing networks such as YouTube. Banda (2010, pp. 43–44) argues that not only did ordinary citizens contribute to public knowledge of the events in Kenya but also 'the online communities expanded the democratic space and allowed people to share their opinions'. Mudhai (2004) states that one of the more appealing features of online journalism is interactivity, which allows users to post comments, and provide reactions to and participate in conversations about contentious issues.

One major aspect of the Kenyan incident was the difference between the journalistic practices followed by ordinary citizens and the reporting styles adopted by professional journalists. In general, Kenyans distributed information and mentioned issues they felt were disregarded or underplayed by the mainstream media. A major significance of the 'Ushahidi' online discussion forum is that it generated lively citizen participation in the democratic process in Kenya. Although Kenya's mainstream media have a responsibility to furnish citizens with true and accurate accounts of news events, the inability of the media to fulfil public expectations implied that the citizens could no longer expect the media to perform their task. The Kenyan experience underlined some important messages for Kenyans at home and those who reside overseas. In reporting on the crisis, Kenyan citizen journalists offered national and international audiences more than a mere report of the political situation. The citizens outlined the key causes of the violence as a way to map solutions to the conflict. In that experience, citizen journalists encouraged national integration in Africa. Zuckerman (2009) explained that Kenyan citizen journalists used their online discussion forums to advance peace. This meant that personal views, essays and other material that prompted inter-ethnic tension and dislike were disapproved. Unfortunately, in the Kenyan experience the technologies that were used effectively to inform the citizens about the post-election hostility and also to encourage peace were also employed to cause violence. In this regard, Zuckerman (2009) notes that,

> communication tools can be used to spread strife as well as to promote harmony. Mobile phones allowed reporting from rural locations, but also permitted messages spreading ethnic hatred. Website operators found themselves moderating hateful messages and struggling to maintain online civility.
>
> (Zuckerman, 2009: 195–196)

Therefore, the technologies that were used to unite different people and to aid cross-cultural awareness of the conflict were also used to foster ethnic divide.

In Nigeria, civil society groups used the social networking sites Facebook and Twitter and online discussion forums to actively draw public attention and response to events that centred on violation of the human rights of the citizens. When the Nigerian government announced the sudden increase in the prices of petroleum products on New Year's Day (1 January 2012), civil society responded vigorously by organising street demonstrations and by reaching out to Nigerians in the diaspora through Twitter, Facebook and other online discussion forums maintained by Nigerians in the diaspora. Civil society set up a movement that was tagged '#OccupyNigeria' on Twitter. The movement served as citizens' rallying cry against the increases in the pump prices of petroleum products. The organisers campaigned and recruited ordinary citizens through social networking sites Twitter and Facebook. After days of industrial gridlock marked by strikes and demonstrations during which protesters confronted fully armed police on the streets, the government retracted the decision. At the time of the protests, the online discussion forums such as the Nigeria Village Square and Saharareporters became the sites for the struggle. Citizens used the sites to express their rejection of what was seen as a unilateral government decision that was taken without consultation with the people and civil society groups such as labour unions, student groups and market women's organisations.

Again, Nigerians woke up in mid-April 2014 to learn that the sectarian Islamic group, Boko Haram, had kidnapped over 250 female students at the Government Girls' Secondary School in the town of Chibok, in Borno State. For two weeks, the government took no action when news of the event broke out. In fact, some government officials even denied that any students were abducted. Some government officials described the news as unfounded media propaganda. As the reality dawned on the Nigerian Federal Government that Boko Haram insurgents had indeed abducted female students in Chibok, public anger rose as civil society groups began to coalesce. Civil society received support from high profile international personalities such as Michelle Obama, British Prime Minister David Cameron, media stars such as Beyoncé and others. Within weeks of confirmation of the kidnap of the girls, civil society responded forcefully by organising demonstrations and sit-ins in government offices and other public spaces. The movement was tagged '#Bringbackourgirls' on Twitter, Facebook and other social media. It was the outcome of the civil society reaction to the Nigerian government's apathy over the abduction of the students on15 April 2014. The movement served as a reminder of the unresolved fate of the female students. Public events were organised to highlight the fate of the students, to maintain pressure on the government and to sensitise Nigerians to the event.

The 2014 Nobel Peace laureate, Malala Yousafzai of Pakistan, visited Nigeria to meet President Goodluck Jonathan and to plead with the government to rescue the female students. Several countries, including the United States, the UK, Israel, China and others pledged to provide military and intelligence assistance to Nigeria to help the government to track the movement of the schoolgirls to facilitate a rescue mission by soldiers.

In 2008 and 2009, Nigerian citizens used technologies such as mobile phones, digital cameras, social media and online discussion forums to report on two events that occurred in the country. On 3 November 2008, a young Nigerian woman – Uzoma Okere – was beaten by a group of six naval men. She was brutalised, dragged out of her car, her clothes were torn, as the naval men assaulted her in full public view. Some citizens recorded the event on their mobile phones and digital cameras. Hours later, news and photos of the event were posted on the video sharing network YouTube (http://www.youtube.com/watch?v=VHdkyvn41us) and on popular Nigerian online discussion forums such as the Nigeria Village Square (http://www.nigeriavillagesquare.com/index.php?option=com_content&view=article&id=10648&Itemid=46) and the Saharareporters (www.saharareporters.com). Okere's offence was that she refused to pull her car out of the heavy traffic on that day, as the Naval Commander's car blared its sirens to beat the traffic. The video of Okere's beating that was distributed worldwide and watched by thousands of people across the world drew immediate national and international response.

Another major incident of human rights abuse occurred in Nigeria in July 2009. The outbreak of religious unrest in one northern Nigerian state later spread to five other states. The revolt was led by Mohammed Yusuf, the head of the 'Boko Haram' sectarian group, whose members openly express opposition to western education and cultural values. Yusuf and his 'Boko Haram' members wanted recognition of the Sharia Islamic law that existed in some northern Nigerian states. They also asked for the law to be imposed on the rest of the nation, regardless of the fact that other religious faiths existed in the country. The problem that led to public anger and requests for investigation was the way that Mohammed Yusuf, the 'Boko Haram' leader, died. There were contradictory accounts by the police, soldiers and civil society organisations. Earlier accounts by the police mentioned that Yusuf died when he wanted to escape from police custody. However, soldiers who initially captured Yusuf said he was still alive when they handed him over to police. Video images posted on YouTube (http://www.youtube.com/watch?v=ePpUvfTXY7w) and the Nigeria online discussion forums (e.g., www.nigerianvillagesquare.com and www.saharareporters.com), and broadcast on the BBC online site (http://news.bbc.co.uk/2/hi/africa/8180475.stm) contradicted police reports on how Yusuf died.

These reports show that the Internet, online discussion forums and other digital technologies have become highly important tools of communication with which citizens report events in their society and contest official accounts provided by government officials and agents. In the hands of citizens and civil society groups, digital technologies and social media are used to challenge government officials. These events show that new technologies have allowed citizens to participate in news reporting and civic deliberation, to resist oppression, to challenge established authorities and to provide alternative accounts of events that occur in public spaces. New technologies have therefore given voice to the voiceless in Africa.

Conclusion

New media, social media and other forms of digital media have empowered African citizens in various ways such as enabling them to express their views, to report events in society, to resist tyranny and to fight against injustice and human rights abuses that occur in society. New technologies have also facilitated increasing involvement of citizens in news reporting. Active participation of citizens in news reporting and production processes has transformed journalistic practices in Africa and at the same time widened the platforms for news and information dissemination on the continent. This has resulted in the emergence of multiple channels of news dissemination that are independent of the mainstream news media. New media have also facilitated increasing civic deliberation in the public sphere in Africa, especially in specific African countries where the people's freedom of expression has been violated and severely restrained by authoritarian regimes.

The ability of Nigerian and Kenyan citizens to report news of events in their countries, such as human rights abuses, crimes like election manipulation and acts of negligence, encouragement of inter-ethnic hatred and offences that violate the rights of citizens, show how technological transformations have expanded the landscape of news reporting to allow citizens to participate in news reporting. What these show is that citizens have as much capacity as professional journalists to report news.

A number of reasons have been adduced to explain why citizen journalism is thriving in Africa. Not only have new technologies encouraged citizen journalism and use of social media for civic deliberation and the construction of a vibrant public sphere, citizen journalism is growing because of public unhappiness with the performance of mainstream media that have abdicated their obligations to society. Citizen media have grown because the audience for news and entertainment in Africa is consistently searching for credible and alternative sources of news that will satisfy their news and entertainment needs.

The role of civil society as credible agents of social and political change in Africa has been strengthened owing to the shortcomings of the institutions of democracy such as the legislature, the judiciary, political parties and religious organisations. Civil society groups have occupied the space left by other institutions of society and therefore serve as vehicles for advancement of democracy. New media, including social media, have reinforced the important role that civil society plays as facilitators of social, political and cultural change on the continent. In various African countries, civil society is perceived as an important agency that defends the human rights of citizens.

7
Tradition Versus Modernity in HIV/AIDS Prevention

Introduction

Since the discovery of the Human Immunodeficiency Virus (HIV) and Acquired Immunodeficiency Syndrome (AIDS) in 1981, the global race to halt the spread of the virus has accelerated. There are many reasons to be concerned about the spread of HIV/AIDS. If the global community does not respond to the pandemic, there will be catastrophic consequences for the human race. Healthcare systems will be overwhelmed, economies will be under severe pressure, the labour force will be depleted and the health of future generations will be endangered. When too many people are hospitalised or are compelled to take sick leave to look after their health, human and economic development will be slowed.

Research shows that the virus that causes HIV/AIDS is transmitted through various channels in different societies. For example, in the United States, the virus was reported to have been transmitted originally through sexual relationships among men. In Africa, Asia and Latin America, transmission was mainly through heterosexual contact (Rogers, 2000, p. 1). Researchers in the health sector, medical doctors, governments, NGOs, aid agencies, communication scholars and civil society are committed to investigating and understanding the main causes of the virus, how it is spread, the factors that slow or hasten the spread of the virus, the existing course of treatment for the virus and the future outlook for developing a vaccine.

General overview

More than three decades after the discovery of HIV, researchers are making good progress toward developing a vaccine to fight it. One example is the availability of antiretroviral medicaments that are used to halt the spread of the virus and therefore prolong the lives of people living with HIV/AIDS. Despite this progress, the prevalence rate of the disease remains high in sub-Saharan Africa, the region that has attracted much of the international attention. In Nigeria as in other African countries, governments and aid agencies are fighting the virus on two fronts, namely cultural practices and traditional belief systems that inform general apathy to public health information campaigns designed to stop the spread of the virus. These cultural practices and beliefs constitute some of the obstacles that impede official efforts to rein in the virus. Research shows that culture is a major factor that influences human behaviour and response to HIV/AIDS (Rogers, 2000). In many developing countries, HIV/AIDS is a particularly sensitive topic because, to deal with the problem, one must talk about sexual habits and preferences, sexual relationships and personal feelings (Lie, 2008). However, sex is a taboo subject in some African countries. In Nigeria, for example, sex education is often perceived as an indirect pathway to promiscuous behaviour.

In the early years following the discovery of the virus, a large number of people paid little attention to public service messages disseminated through the mass media with regard to HIV/AIDS and how to prevent infection. Radio and television announcements about safe sex practices and other preventive measures were either dismissed outright or were treated with scorn. To a large extent, public ignorance served as fodder for the spread of the virus. In many parts of the world, particularly in remote and rural areas of developing countries, opinions differed about the causes of HIV/AIDS, how the virus is spread or contracted and the best way to treat people with the disease. In those early years of the virus, official responses by governments and the medical and scientific community were sluggish because the epidemiology of the disease was largely unknown.

All these have not stopped the global community from commemorating in December of every year the World AIDS Day which is designed to sensitise the public to the need to take action to stop the virus. Nearly 33 years since the HIV/AIDS virus was first discovered, the battle against the spread of the disease has gained momentum because the virus is still spreading across the world. HIV/AIDS is truly a global health problem. The Joint United Nations Programme on HIV/AIDS reports that as of December 2008, approximately 33.4 million people were living with HIV. A little over 31 million people were adults, about half (15.7 million) were women and 2.1 million were children under 15 years of age (UNAIDS, 2009). The European Commission reported that the number of people living with HIV/AIDS in 27 European Union member countries rose from 1.5 million in 2001 to 2.2 million in 2007. About 50,000 new cases of the virus were discovered in the European Union in 2007 (Australian Associated Press, 2009). The rapid spread of the virus is a cause for worry. For this reason, Treichler (1999, p. 11) has described the virus as an 'epidemic of significance'.

HIV/AIDS in Africa

The Organisation for African Unity (OAU – now known as African Union or AU) acknowledged more than a decade ago that 'HIV/AIDS, tuberculosis and other related infectious diseases constitute not only a major health crisis, but also an exceptional threat to Africa's development, social cohesion, political stability, food security as well as the greatest global threat to the survival and life expectancy of African peoples' (OAU, 2001, p. 3). The AU believes HIV/AIDS and other diseases that ravage the continent are aggravated by poverty and endless conflicts that have encumbered the economy, resulting in depletion of vital human resources and decreased agricultural production.

In sub-Saharan Africa, an estimated 23.5 million people were identified to be living with HIV in 2011. This represents an increase of about 1 million people since 2009, when about 22.5 million Africans were discovered to be living with HIV. Of this number, 2.3 million were identified as children. These figures were reported by AVERT, a UK-based international HIV and AIDS charity that aims to prevent or 'avert HIV and AIDS worldwide, through education, treatment and care' (AVERT, n.d.). In Africa, South Africa has the highest number of people living with HIV at 5,600,000, followed by Nigeria with 3,400,000 people. Kenya and Tanzania have the same estimated number of people living with HIV (i.e., 1,600,000 people in each country). These numbers are for the year 2011 (AVERT, n.d.). On a global scale, the Joint United Nations Programme on HIV/AIDS (UNAIDS, 2013) reports that as of 2012, an estimated 35.3 (32.2–38.8) million people were living with HIV. The agency also reports there were 2.3 (1.9–2.7) million new HIV infections across the world. The figure, according to UNAIDS, represents a 33 per cent decline in the number of new infections from 3.4 (3.1–3.7) million in 2001 (UNAIDS, 2013).

Seven years ago, over 40 million people were estimated to be living with HIV/AIDS. Of that number, 25 million (more than half) were reported to be in sub-Saharan Africa (Tufte, 2008). Over a decade ago,

HIV/AIDS killed an estimated 2.2 million people in 1999 alone. The World Health Organisation (WHO) and the United Nations (UN) have been at the forefront of global efforts to halt the spread of the virus. The consequences for the global community of further spread of HIV/AIDS can be catastrophic. For example, Lie (2008, p. 279) identifies the effects of HIV/AIDS on the young and old, men and women, including its impact on present and future generations. The consequences include a growing number of orphans, deficiency in generational knowledge sharing, lack of ability to work and raise income, withdrawal of children from schools so they could help to produce income, and youths migrating to city centres.

Outside Africa, the Caribbean is also confronted by the challenges of HIV/AIDS. It is regarded as the region with the second highest infection rate in the global community. Among adults aged between 15 and 44, HIV/AIDS is the leading cause of death two decades after the virus was discovered (de Bruin, 2006), regardless of the fact that many countries in the region have launched their national AIDS programmes to halt the spread of the virus. This is a worrying figure. Adults aged between 15 and 44 constitute an important productive age group in any country's working population. The HIV/AIDS prevention campaign in the Caribbean has been undermined by a range of problems such as inadequate resources, movement of staff, need for qualified healthcare staff, reliance on political leaders who have shown little or no commitment to the prevention campaign, and external aid programmes that have conditions attached to them even when the conditions do not reflect national or regional needs and reality (de Bruin, 2006).

Apart from health-related illnesses that are associated with HIV/AIDS such as chronic diarrhoea, dementia, blindness, loss of weight and Kaposi's sarcoma (cited in Frey, Adelman, Flint and Query, 2000, p. 54), the cost of healthcare and provision of resources to people with HIV/AIDS has also magnified the need to prevent further spread of the virus. Since the outbreak of HIV/AIDS, attention has focused more on strategies of prevention while researchers look at the possibility of developing a vaccine to deal with the virus. Prevention intervention programmes have also focused on behaviour and attitude change. Communication researchers have been in the vanguard of the campaign to design behaviour change strategies, backed up with relevant theories, to overcome entrenched attitudes and practices that are resistant to public information campaigns against the spread of HIV/AIDS.

Theoretical background to understanding HIV/AIDS

HIV/AIDS has been examined from theoretical frameworks such as diffusion of innovations, health behaviour and hierarchy of effects. The diffusion of innovations theory is associated with Rogers (2003). The theory outlines the processes of introduction, adoption and use of new ideas or new technology. Diffusion of innovations explains how new ideas or objects or behaviour are diffused in society. In the diffusion of innovations theory, there are five stages that determine the success or failure of the introduction of an innovation.

For HIV/AIDS prevention education, change in attitude and behaviour toward sexual practices is key. In this case, the necessary stages of diffusion of innovations aimed to achieve attitude and behaviour change involve: the extent to which the general population or target group perceives the proposed behavioural changes as superior and valuable to the existing attitude and behaviour – that is, the more useful the proposed attitude and behaviour to the target group, the more likely it is that it will be adopted much more quickly; as well as the extent to which the new attitude and behaviour is perceived to be in harmony with existing values within a group or in a society. Where the new behaviour is seen to be at variance with existing values, it is less likely that it will be adopted. Also, the easier it is to understand or make sense of the new behaviour, the more quickly it will be adopted. In essence, the more difficult it is to understand the new behaviour, the more unlikely it is that it will be adopted.

Furthermore, the easier it is to experiment with or trial the new behaviour without difficulties, the less it will be doubted by the group or target population. Finally, if the outcomes of the new behaviour are clear to the target group or population, the easier it will be for the group to make a decision about whether to adopt the innovation. According to Rogers (2003), these stages determine to a large extent how groups decide to adopt or not to adopt innovations or new behaviour. Despite its widespread application, the diffusion of innovations theory has been criticised for 'being too linear, for having a pro-innovation bias, and for widening the gaps between the "information haves" and "have-nots" in a social system. This gap has certainly been observed in AIDS awareness and knowledge ... ' (Freimuth, 1992, p. 103).

One theoretical framework that has been applied to studies of HIV/AIDS prevention programmes is Bandura's social learning theory. Social learning highlights the significance of role models and practical examples as facilitators of new behaviours (Pratt, Ha and Pratt, 2002).

According to the theory, individuals learn through personal experiences and also through observing role models. Social learning theory states that human beings learn through an open relationship with the environment in which they live. Bandura (2002) used social learning in his studies of the effects of television. He identified a number of circumstances that influence children to mimic what they see on television. The conditions are concentration, ability to retain knowledge of what they see on television, the ability to reproduce what has been observed on television and the motivation to display the observed behaviour (Bandura, 2002). These processes influence what is noted and chosen for reproduction or recreation. Retaining what is observed involves storing the information in the memory. Bandura argues that individuals will behave in a certain way if they expect a reward for enacting that behaviour.

Another theoretical model that has been applied in studies of HIV/AIDS prevention is the hierarchy of effects model. The hierarchy of effects model states that, for anyone to advance to a higher spot, they must walk through the lower stages. The seven stages of the hierarchy of effects theory are 'exposure to the entertainment-education soap opera; knowledge of what is being broadcast or transmitted, understanding the message, convincing someone to change their attitude through the soap opera, demonstration of willingness to change behaviour or conduct, real modification or adjustment in behaviour, persistent acceptance of behaviour' (cited in Sherry, 1997, p. 78).

In discussing the role of theory in the design of HIV/AIDS prevention programmes, culture is considered a critical factor. Airhihenbuwa and Obregon (2000) identify some important theories and models of behaviour change that have been applied in HIV/AIDS prevention programmes. They include the health belief model (HBM), the theory of reasoned action (TRA), Albert Bandura's social learning theory and diffusion of innovations. Developed in the 1950s, the HBM was founded on an individual's apparent perception of the seriousness of a disease, gravity of the disease, supposed advantages of the services provided and the obstacles to gaining access to the services provided (Airhihenbuwa and Obregon, 2000). The TRA, proposed by Fishbein and Ajzen (1975), states that human behaviour is determined by an individual's intention. The theory presupposes that individuals are reasonable in their decision-making (Airhihenbuwa and Obregon, 2000). The theory states that human behaviour is determined by intention to perform and the intention to act serves as a signal of willingness to carry out a particular action.

In the theory of social learning, two key aspects applied in HIV/AIDS prevention programmes are modelling (copying the behaviour of a role model) and self-efficacy (an individual's ability to adopt a prescribed behaviour). Airhihenbuwa and Obregon (2000) point out quite rightly that although social learning theory has been effective in the HIV/AIDS prevention campaign in the United States because of its application at an individual level, doubts remain whether the theory would be effectively applied in cultures in which group norms are more highly regarded than individual values. For example, theories and models of human behaviour that are based on individual cultural practices in western societies may not be relevant in Africa, Asia, Latin America and other developing parts of the world in which the family and the community have major influence on the construction of an individual's identity. In these non-western cultures, the family and the community tend to regulate how individuals express themselves and their wellbeing.

In a critique of research designed to collect data from individuals in developing countries, Airhihenbuwa and Obregon (2000) identify a major flaw – the tendency to structure the research instruments in such a way to capture the feelings of individuals about their health status. They point out that

individuals are not always accustomed to expressing their attitudes and beliefs by using extreme descriptors often found on social science survey instruments such as 'strongly agree' or 'strongly disagree'. In fact, to do so within such a cultural context is considered disrespectful. Yet instruments designed to measure health behaviour, for example, self-efficacy, often are presented on such a continuum of two extremes (strongly agree to strongly disagree) in cultures where such measures are not only irrelevant but could also be considered offensive.

(Airhihenbuwa and Obregon, 2000, p. 9)

Noting that most theories on which HIV/AIDS prevention and health behaviour change are formulated do not recognise the value of culture as the central pillar of society, Airhihenbuwa and Obregon (2000, p. 13) suggest that culture should play a central role in HIV/AIDS prevention education programmes. This should allow for variations in designing regional and national communication strategies for HIV/AIDS prevention. In terms of communication messages designed to promote HIV/AIDS prevention, they also suggest segmenting messages in order for the messages to reach diverse populations that have different ways of generating and obtaining information (Airhihenbuwa and Obregon, 2000).

Related to specific cultural practices are the concepts of individualism and collectivism. The usefulness of this theoretical framework, propounded by Dutch social psychologist Geert Hofstede (2001) in his studies of the dimensions of national cultures, is that it helps to explain whether an individual is practically responsible for the decision to undertake or observe HIV prevention measures. Hofstede (2001, 1997) proposed dimensions of national values, namely power distance (the extent to which people handle inequality), uncertainty avoidance (how individuals deal with uncertainty in life, i.e., whether people are at ease or ill at ease in unfamiliar situations), individualism versus collectivism (already explained above) and masculinity versus femininity (the extent to which masculine or feminine characteristics are dominant in a culture). An example cited more frequently comes from African and Asian cultures in which a wife cannot make a unilateral decision to accept or decline her husband's use of condom during sexual intercourse without consulting him. One of the reasons why family planning programmes fail in rural and remote parts of Africa is that messages are often targeted at the people with limited power, who do not have the sole authority to make decisions about the adoption of family planning strategies. Questions about gender equality and empowerment of women dominate discussions about family planning and HIV prevention in traditional societies in Africa, Asia and Latin America.

Pratt et al. (2002, p. 890) identify three theories they consider to be relevant in the study of healthcare issues and the prevention of diseases in Africa and other developing countries. These are agenda-setting (including media framing), community power and social learning. Bandura's (2002) social learning theory has already been discussed here. Agenda-setting theory describes how media construct news events through the amount of coverage and prominence the media give to the events. Pratt et al. (2002, p. 891) argue that one consequence of agenda-setting theory for media coverage of health issues in Africa is that intense media coverage is essential to position the issues high on the public agenda. Community power theory states that communities pass on social values and conventions that either endorse or disapprove of the behaviour of individuals in their communities (cited in Pratt et al., 2002). The theory states that communities may be organised as 'information, education, and change agents to achieve expected behavioural outcomes' (Pratt et al., 2002, p. 891). The theory has two implications for disseminating health-related messages in Africa. First, it encourages social support networks of individuals and groups that are necessary to accomplish intended ways of living or behaviour change. Second, it accentuates widespread appeal and participation of audience members in health education campaigns (Pratt et al., 2002, p. 891). Pratt et al. argue that the theory encourages people who share common ideas to express their opinions and therefore enhance the role of the community as a force for social mobilisation.

While scholars have offered a number of theories or models to effect attitude and behaviour change in the fight against HIV/AIDS, Bandura (1994, p. 25) has argued that in any campaign aiming 'to achieve self-directed change, people need to be given not only reasons to alter risky habits but also the behavioural means, resources, and social support to do so. It will require certain skills in self-motivation and self-guidance.' In other words, attitude and behaviour change will not be achieved automatically without convincing people about the benefits to be derived from changing their sexual behaviour, for example. Attitude and behaviour change will be much easier if people are provided with a range of social, financial and logistical support.

Some of these theoretical models have been criticised because they do not take into consideration structural and sociocultural factors, as well as individual contexts in some countries. These variables include the social environment in which people exist, their economic situation, religious practices, cultural conventions and structural impediments, as well as race and ethnicity. For example, it has been argued that 'People who are poor are not only economically deprived but also find themselves with severely restricted access to information. This has led to an unequal distribution of knowledge in the population resulting in "knowledge gaps" between people of low and high socioeconomic statuses (SES)' (Melkote, Muppidi and Goswami, 2000, p. 20).

The knowledge gap hypothesis, first advocated by Tichenor, Donohue and Olien (1970), argued that an information crusade in society has a tendency to amplify the gap in knowledge between people of low and high socioeconomic status, as people of higher socioeconomic status tend to obtain information at a faster pace than people of low socioeconomic status. Melkote et al. (2000) argue that, although attitude and behaviour change is important in the campaign against the spread of HIV/AIDS virus, there are other socioeconomic, cultural, political and structural factors that affect the spread of the virus. These include 'poverty, access to formal education, income inequality, gender inequality, knowledge inequality, vested interests, lack of democratic norms, and so on' (Melkote et al., 2000, p. 25). Similarly, Myhre and Flora (2000, p. 42) state that communication programmes aimed at HIV prevention should endeavour to magnify the significance of HIV prevention programmes, and the programmes should project HIV prevention as a community challenge. Additionally, HIV prevention programmes should expand the amount and value of public and private conversation about HIV prevention, and also enhance the relevance and degree of public involvement in HIV prevention programmes.

Tufte (2008) outlined a range of theoretical and practical flaws that have undermined global attempts to halt the spread of HIV/AIDS. The problems include but are not limited to: a simplistic and one-dimensional link between awareness and action which does not recognise the differences in the socioeconomic, cultural and political circumstances that people face; outside administrative procedures that respond to closely concentrated temporary concerns which tend to neglect the advantages of long-standing internal remedies; the notion that raising awareness through mass media crusade will automatically result in behavioural modification; the belief that a simplistic approach aimed at generating a one-off behaviour such as vaccination would be sufficient to achieve and sustain lasting behaviours such as regular use of condoms; a concentration on the endorsement of condom use which disregards the value of sociocultural circumstances, socioeconomic status, cultural factors, gender and religion; and using strategies that are founded on conventional family planning methods that have a tendency to direct HIV/AIDS prevention programmes at women, thereby making women instead of men the chief decision makers about condom use (Tufte, 2008).

The following section examines practical strategies involving the use of media technologies in campaigns aimed at preventing the spread of HIV/AIDS.

From theory to practice: Entertainment-education

A number of practical strategies are used to promote HIV/AIDS prevention. One of them is entertainment-education, which is a deliberate communication programme that seeks to entertain and educate in order to produce favourable attitudes that will lead to behaviour change. Entertainment-education has been defined as 'the process of designing and implementing an entertainment program to increase audience members' knowledge about a social issue, create more favorable attitudes, and change their overt behaviours regarding the social issue' (Singhal and Rogers, 1999, cited in Vaughan, Rogers, Singhal and

Swalehe, 2000, p. 82). Through entertainment such as theatre and soap operas, the programme demonstrates to audience members how they can overcome public health problems through attitude and behaviour change (Singhal and Rogers, 1999). Entertainment-education is also known as 'info-tainment', 'enter-educate' and 'edutainment' (Brown and Singhal, 1993, p. 92; Papa, Singhal, Law, Pant, Sood, Rogers and Shefner-Rogers, 2000, p. 32).

Tufte (2008, p. 329) defines entertainment-education as 'the use of entertainment as a communicative practice crafted to strategically communicate about development issues in a manner and with a purpose that can range from the more narrowly defined social marketing of individual behaviours to the liberating and citizen-driven articulation of social change agendas'. According to Papa et al. (2000, p. 32), entertainment-education, as a strategy, 'involves media programs that intentionally incorporate one or more educational issues in an entertainment format in order to influence audience members' knowledge, attitudes, and overt behavior regarding an educational issue'. The strategy involves the use of radio, television, soap operas, popular music and books, among other communication channels, for the dissemination and endorsement of educational campaigns mostly in developing countries. Some of the programmes in which educational and entertainment media are used to disseminate messages include family planning, sexual practices and literacy, as well as HIV/AIDS prevention.

The outcomes of a field experiment conducted in Tanzania to evaluate the impact of an entertainment-education radio soap opera – *Twende na Wakati* (Let's Go with the Times) – on adoption of HIV/AIDS prevention behaviours showed that radio led to a decrease in the number of sexual partners that men and women had, and a rise in the number of people using condoms (Vaughan et al., 2000). These changes in behaviour were influenced by radio soap opera through individual assessment of the risks associated with getting infected with the HIV/AIDS virus, self-assessment with regard to HIV/AIDS prevention, group discussions about HIV/AIDS and association with the characters that are shown on the radio soap opera (Vaughan et al., 2000).

Other than the HIV/AIDS prevention programme in Tanzania, HIV/AIDS prevention and control programmes have also been deliberately promoted through television and radio soap operas such as *Soul City* (the South African entertainment-education programme that is widely cited for its success in communicating attitude and behaviour change relating to HIV/AIDS prevention), *Tinka Tinka Sukh* ('Happiness Lies in Small Things') in India and *Nshilakamona* ('I Have Not

Seen It') in Zambia. There are also radio talk shows in different countries such as Costa Rica (*Dialogo*) and Uganda (*Good Times with DJ Berry*) (Vaughan et al., 2000). Similarly, popular music and concerts, feature films and animations, as well as competitive events have been used or staged in different countries to promote HIV/AIDS prevention in countries such as Zaire, Cameroon and Thailand (Vaughan et al., 2000). These researchers argue that evaluations of the programmes show that entertainment-education approaches were successful in promoting HIV/AIDS prevention.

Tufte (2008) argues that one difficulty in the campaign against the spread of HIV/AIDS is the limited clarity in explanation and understanding of the problem which has produced restricted response to the disease. He states that 'HIV/AIDS is obviously a significantly different and more difficult communicative challenge than for example communicating about tobacco and arguing for the audiences to stop smoking' (Tufte, 2008, p. 331).

In studies that seek to explain HIV/AIDS prevention behaviours at the individual level, the prevailing variables identified by researchers include '(1) perceived susceptibility to HIV infection, (2) perceived severity of AIDS, (3) perceived benefits of prevention behaviours, (4) perceived barriers of adopting prevention behaviours, and (5) the individual's perceived ability to adopt the prevention behaviour (self-efficacy)' (Vaughan et al., 2000, p. 83). However, theories such as diffusion of innovations (Rogers, 2003) and social movement (Friedman, Des Jarlais and Ward, 1994) highlight the significance of group communication, opinion management by credible local people, reliable agents of change, tying behaviour change to local cultural norms, and community management designed to endorse HIV prevention (Vaughan et al., 2000). Drawing on theory and research, Galavotti, Pappas-DeLuca and Lansky (2001, p. 1062) state that intervention programmes designed to halt the spread of HIV/AIDS are most effective when 'they are personalized and affectively compelling, when they provide models of desired behaviours, and when they are linked to social and cultural narratives'.

In some of the programmes disseminated through entertainment-education media, positive attitude and behaviour change was reported among the target population (e.g., Valente and Saba, 1998). In fact, Vaughan et al. (2000) found in their study of use of radio soap opera for HIV/AIDS prevention in Tanzania that the programme encouraged adoption of HIV/AIDS prevention behaviours. They concluded that 'The entertainment-education strategy represents a potentially viable approach to address the global public health crisis posed by AIDS'

(Vaughan et al., 2000, p. 98). Similarly, between 1975 and 1981, Mexican television programmes known as *telenovelas* (i.e., 'television novels') 'promoted adult literacy, good health practices, family harmony, sex education, nationalism, women's status, better treatment of children, good citizenship, and family planning' (cited in Brown and Singhal, 1993, p. 94).

In the HIV/AIDS prevention campaign, attitude and behaviour change has been the focus of attention because of the lack of a medical cure for the ailment. This is based on research evidence that suggests that transmission of HIV/AIDS is dependent on sex and drug-related behaviour by individuals (Melkote et al., 2000, p. 17). Communication is promoted as the main channel of spreading awareness about how to reduce the risk of contracting HIV/AIDS. In the early years following the discovery of HIV, a public campaign against the spread of the virus was aimed at getting people to change their sexual behaviour and to avoid using intravenous needles. Although some progress has been made in the campaign to prevent the spread of HIV/AIDS through the discovery of antiretroviral drugs, a large number of people living with HIV/AIDS reside in developing countries in which access to antiretroviral medication is severely limited or non-existent (Airhihenbuwa, Makinwa and Obregon, 2000). This makes prevention of the spread of HIV/AIDS virus through attitude and behaviour change crucial.

As a part of the entertainment-education campaign for HIV/AIDS prevention, the Global AIDS Program advanced an ideal strategy for behaviour change. It is called the MARCH approach, which is short for Modeling and Reinforcement to Combat HIV. MARCH encompasses two main strategies designed to induce behaviour change. The approaches are entertainment-education communicated via radio and television, and strengthening of interpersonal networks at the community level (Galavotti et al., 2001). The literature on effective behaviour change campaigns suggests that programmes designed to achieve behaviour change must be positive in outlook and result-oriented; the programmes must enhance people's sense of self-worth; and they must remove structural and cultural obstacles to behaviour change. 'Positive-outcome expectations can include physical or material rewards (e.g., good health or prosperity), social rewards (e.g., recognition or support), or personal rewards (e.g., fulfilment of role of good mother or responsible son). Such strategies are most effective with people who already believe they are capable of changing their behavior' (Galavotti et al., 2001, p. 1603).

In developing regions such as Africa, there exist social, cultural and structural problems that impede people's ability or willingness to engage in attitude and behaviour change. These can manifest through absence or poor quality of healthcare assistance, general poverty, the shame attached to HIV illness, and cultural impediments that define and constrain what women can do and what they cannot do. According to Galavotti et al. (2001), there are two important parts of the MARCH programme. The first involves use of role models who can be friends, relatives and opinion leaders. The second involves interpersonal strengthening through community support. In the first part, role models serve a number of purposes. They can educate through provision of important information on how people can change their behaviour and the stages they can follow. They can influence and encourage people by changing how people perceive the costs and benefits of the proposed behaviour change. Role models are particularly effective in influencing attitude and behaviour change. 'When a man or woman sees a role model similar to him or herself overcome an obstacle and achieve a desired reward, this provides information for social comparison, that is, "If he or she can do that, perhaps I can too"' (Galavotti et al., 2001, p. 1603). The researchers argue that

> One reason serial drama can educate is because it is closely aligned with the customs and norms of its audience and uses narrative forms with which they are familiar. Entertainment focuses on emotional as well as cognitive factors that influence behaviour, and thus it keeps the attention of the intended audience.
>
> (Galavotti et al., 2001, p. 1603)

In Ghana, Panford, Nyaney, Amoah and Aidoo (2001) examined the use of folk media in two districts of the country – Wassa West and Adansi West – as a part of a health initiative in the HIV/AIDS prevention programme. Residents of the two districts were mostly illiterate and this made the prevention programme a lot more difficult to implement. The researchers focused on folk media because of its characteristic elements that reflected the people's cultural practices, norms and ways of living. In the literature on HIV/AIDS prevention, various terminologies are used to refer to folk media. They include 'oramedia' (Ugboajah, 1985), 'traditional media' and 'informal media' (Panford et al., 2001, p. 1560). 'Oramedia', for example, are regarded as credible and effective communication channels because rural people in Africa consider them to be accessible, interactive, immediate and user-friendly (Ugboajah, 1985). These traditional channels are also more actively used, more commonly recognised, more credible and purposeful than the mass media

(Obijiofor, 1995). Owing to their interactive nature, folk media provide opportunities for instant feedback. Traditional media also facilitate face-to-face interaction and sharing of information.

Despite the effectiveness of traditional media as credible channels of communication in rural and remote parts of developing countries, Panford et al. (2001) point out that they have not been fully utilised in health education campaigns such as HIV/AIDS prevention. They believe the functions of folk media could be associated with Albert Bandura's social learning theory, which proposes that human behaviours are learned through role modelling. Social learning theory indicates that human beings learn by watching role models perform on television or in movies. This relates also to the diffusion of innovations theory proposed by Rogers (2003) in which new ideas, behaviours or objects are adopted by groups after they have been exposed to group leaders who are seen to be favourably disposed toward the new behaviours or ideas. Panford et al. (2001) suggest that folk media can be used to persuade people to change their behaviour because they facilitate open discussions about the problems that confront rural dwellers and the need for them to take action to change their behaviour. 'The power of folk media to change behaviour makes it an appropriate complement to the HIV/AIDS behaviour change communication project being implemented in Ghana' (Panford et al., 2001, p. 1561).

South Africa is regarded as the country with the highest number of people living with the HIV virus in sub-Saharan Africa. The financial, logistical and political impediments that have undermined efforts to make antiretroviral treatment widespread across South Africa have refocused attention on prevention programmes that are aimed at achieving attitude and behaviour change. In HIV/AIDS prevention, communication is a vital tool that helps to decrease the shame and isolation of HIV-positive people, and enhance public awareness of the rights of individuals and the alternatives available in terms of prevention mechanisms, treatment regimes and opportunities (Goldstein, Usdin, Scheepers and Japhet, 2005).

Soul City entertainment-education against HIV/AIDS

In South Africa, a national health promotion that has been deployed since 1994 in the fight against health-related illnesses and the spread of HIV/AIDS is known as Soul City.

Soul City uses 'edutainment' to convey carefully researched and structured messages to previously disadvantaged South Africans... The Soul City Series is a 13-part prime-time television drama, a 45-part radio drama transmitted in nine languages through the SABC stations (the public broadcaster), and three basic full colour booklets, a million of each distributed through 10 newspapers nationally. The health messages are integrated into the drama through an 18-month process of research, development, testing, and partnership development in order to ensure the optimal messaging and advocacy... The dramas depict the lives of ordinary South Africans dealing with very real issues that affect their lives.

(cited in Goldstein et al., 2005, p. 466)

Goldstein et al. (2005) found in their study of Soul City Series 4 that the messages were conveyed to 82 per cent of the respondents via television, radio and print media. This means an estimated 17 million South Africans received Soul City messages. The researchers reported that exposure to Soul City influenced people's perceptions about AIDS. 'Respondents with high access to Soul City television were significantly more likely to understand that people are at risk of getting HIV/AIDS because their partner may have exposed them to the virus, despite their being monogamous' (Goldstein et al., 2005, p. 472). The success of Soul City was attributed to several factors. They include: the development of mass media in an all-encompassing way that enabled the audience to identify with stories that mirrored their lives and the options they were confronted with; the addition of subjects apart from HIV/AIDS that helped to prevent monotony and predictability; the inclusion of positive messages that gave people the feeling of being in a position to make informed decisions; and use of multi-platform strategy with various media strengthening one another (Goldstein et al., 2005).

Critique of entertainment-education

Despite the successes achieved through entertainment-education as an effective tool for promoting HIV/AIDS prevention and other health-related campaigns, certain drawbacks are associated with the strategy, such as ethical dilemmas that arise from use of the approach (Brown and Singhal, 1993), and the likelihood that the purpose of entertainment-education programmes may be misunderstood (e.g., Sherry, 1997). Five critical ethical questions that should be considered by government officials, popular media programme producers and media scholars with regard to the use of entertainment media for educational campaigns have been raised. The questions are:

(1) Is it ethical to use communication and marketing strategies to systematically influence societal beliefs and behaviours? (2) Who is best qualified to make the decision about prosocial and antisocial messages in the popular media? (3) Is it ethical to target messages to a particular audience group in exclusion of others? (4) Is it ethical for nations that control the media to export their own cultural values and beliefs? and (5) Should we risk the unintended consequences of media designed to promote social change?

(Brown and Singhal, 1993, pp. 94–95)

Brown and Singhal contest the notion that entertainment culture is value-free. They say this is not the case because television and films are known to have effects on people. Another ethical concern is the use of popular or entertainment media to create demands or appetites for material acquisitions that can never be achieved. Furthermore, directing media messages to a defined population may result in the exclusion of a group for whom the media messages might be more valuable. Additionally, the entertainment-education framework lacks sufficient theoretical depth in its attempt to explain how and why human populations change when they are exposed to entertainment-education programmes (Papa et al., 2000, p. 33). Studies of this nature 'report aggregate changes among audience members' knowledge, attitudes, and behavior, but do not illuminate the social process through which such changes occur' (Papa et al., 2000, p. 33).

Studies that are based on entertainment-education are perceived as linear because they overlook the difficulties that intervene in processes of social change that involve interrelationships, reflection and engagement by members of a group (Papa et al., 2000). The authors see value in collective efficacy because it aids the advancement of important social change. Collective efficacy is the extent to which members of a social group have faith in their ability to arrange and implement actions that are essential to accomplish their group objectives (Bandura, 1997, cited in Papa et al., 2000). Collective efficacy is important in social change processes because it is entrenched in a system in which members influence one another to achieve common goals. As they state, 'Individual and community change require that people in a system work together to change their lives for the better. For this process to begin, people need to believe that they can solve their mutually experienced problems through unified effort' (Papa et al., 2000, p. 36).

A typical example of collective efficacy is the way rural women in Bangladesh deliberated on how they should deal with moneylenders who charged them high interest on their loans. Through exchange of ideas, the women realised they could break the power of the moneylenders through collective action, if they were united in pursuit of their common goal (cited in Papa et al., 2000). In their study of an entertainment-education radio soap opera – *Tinka Tinka Sukh* – in an Indian village, Papa et al. found a relationship between members of the audience and mass media characters. They found that discussions among audience members of the content of a media programme provided a meaningful learning environment that enabled people to assess ideas they held prior to exposure to the media content. The relationships between audience members and mass media characters also helped audience members to think about their choices, and to map strategies that will enable them to achieve social change. On this basis, they argued that 'Interpersonal conversations can lead to collective efficacy and to community action when individuals in a system believe that unified efforts can solve social problems' (Papa et al., 2000, p. 50). However, the authors acknowledge that not all entertainment-education programmes lead to expected outcomes. Some outcomes may contradict the original intentions of the programme producers. They also identify ethical issues associated with entertainment-education.

In entertainment-education programmes directed at a mass audience, how can programme producers aim to achieve social change at individual and system levels without taking upon themselves the responsibility for the changes that might accrue from the programmes? Papa et al. (2000) conclude with an important piece of advice that has been repeated in many entertainment-education studies – the importance of not seeing audience members as passive receivers of media content. Meaningful social change is achieved when everyone – researchers, programme producers, media audiences and policymakers – maintains a learning environment that facilitates mutual learning among all stakeholders.

In his critique of South Africa's Soul City education-entertainment programme for the prevention of HIV/AIDS, Tufte (2008, p. 338) points out:

there is a discrepancy between Soul City's written representation of their work on one side, and their practice on the other. The fact is that

Soul City has been developed as a health communication project, but mainly by health scholars and with no substantial participation of communication scholars. As such the scientific connotations in the communication discourse they apply seemingly plays less of a role in their practice.

Despite this shortcoming, Tufte identifies some of the lessons learned from Soul City's education-entertainment approach, such as: recognising the potency and limitations of integrating communication approaches in the audience's popular culture; recognising that successful education-entertainment approaches need strong support elements; and recognising that education-entertainment activities require follow up action (Tufte, 2008). He calls for a clear understanding of the diverse factors that influence appropriate communication strategies that are applied in the campaign to prevent the spread of HIV/AIDS. Those factors include but are not limited to:

- The meanings (stigma, fear and denial) attached to HIV/AIDS in the respective settings.
- The sexual practices and the inherent gender roles and relations of target audiences.
- The local institutional capacity to tackle the HIV/AIDS problem (with particular focus on the health and educational systems).
- The national policies and communication practices informing and guiding HIV/AIDS prevention in the chosen countries.

(Tufte, 2008)

Support for people living with HIV/AIDS

Reeves (2000) identifies one of the difficulties of HIV-positive people coping with their illness. It is not just a matter of the person dealing with the physical implications of the illness. It is more about the ability of the HIV-positive person to deal with public fear and social exclusion, including the emotional and psychological trauma they experience. She states that with the exception of leprosy, no other illness compares in terms of public fear to the stigma associated with HIV illness (Reeves, 2000). It was against this background that education campaigns were mounted by medical and scientific communities, including government officials to dismiss public anxiety about HIV/AIDS and to encourage greater public understanding of the disease.

In helping people living with HIV/AIDS to cope with their illness, social support is crucial. Drawing on the literature, Kalichman, Sikkema and Somlai (1996) identify three types of support that are provided to people with HIV/AIDS. These are: emotional support that comprises loving and caring, reassuring and helping the HIV-positive people to have that feeling that they belong to a society and that they are valued; informational support which enhances knowledge and awareness; and instrumental support that provides practical help with everyday life (Kalichman et al., 1996). They argue that these support systems can help to reduce psychological suffering linked to recurring ill health and can cushion the impact of traumatic life experiences. Social support is usually provided through the network of friends, family, workplace colleagues, members of professional organisations, health-related NGOs and community organisations. Nevertheless, the Internet is seen as a viable alternative source of support for HIV-positive individuals who are unwilling or unable to access mainstream support services. The Internet is a valuable health resource because it helps people to develop the sense of self-assurance and personal ability that enable them to cope with health problems.

Reeves (2000, p. 49) argues that the research literature is silent on how individuals who are dealing with the HIV virus use the Internet to access valuable health resources, including social support services. Her study found that HIV-positive people 'considered the Internet beneficial in coping with HIV and identified three ways it is particularly helpful: Internet use promotes empowerment, augments social support, and facilitates helping others' (Reeves, 2000, p. 54). Empowerment in this context refers to the HIV-positive person taking steps to modify their circumstances in an active way. However, one drawback of the use of the Internet by HIV-positive people is the phenomenon of information overload, which leads to the inability to differentiate between what is important and what is not.

Cultural factors in HIV/AIDS prevention

In many parts of Africa and other developing regions such as Asia, the Pacific islands and Latin America, misunderstandings exist about HIV/AIDS. Vaughan et al. (2000) found in their study that 'Widespread misunderstandings about HIV transmission exist in Tanzania. For example, many young people do not associate illness with sexual activity, or believe that they cannot contract HIV' (2000, p. 85). The researchers identify some other traditional beliefs about HIV/AIDS such as the notion that young people cannot contract the virus, and that it is easy to identify an HIV-positive person by looking at the person. In Nigeria, the Catholic Church discourages the use of condoms on the basis that it encourages promiscuity and impedes the normal process of procreation (Olokor, 2013). In Nigeria also, being HIV-positive is seen as a dishonour to one's family, friends and local community. HIV-positive people are discriminated against on the basis of certain fallacies about the virus. In some instances, some people believe they might contract the virus if they interact with an HIV-positive person.

Owing to the stigma attached to HIV-positive people, those who are diagnosed with the virus are reluctant to identify themselves in the public domain. In fact, sexually transmitted diseases are not talked about in Nigeria's public spaces. For example, in 2001 the national advertising regulator – the Advertising Practitioners' Council of Nigeria (APCON) – halted an advertisement that cautioned the youth about the dangers of unprotected sex because of the graphic language used in the advertisement. Previously, sex education was a taboo subject in secondary school curricula because of the misunderstanding that it could promote immoral practices among youth. Another aspect of the Nigerian cultural practices that relate to public misunderstanding about HIV/AIDS is the view that sex-related illnesses represent evidence of bad behaviour. This explains why HIV-positive people are not likely to admit in the public sphere that they are carriers of the virus. To admit to carrying the virus would suggest that the HIV-positive person is morally lax.

The nature of the society also affects public perceptions of people living with HIV/AIDS and indeed general response to the virus. In the Nigerian cultural context, people identify first with their families, villages or communities. What happens to an individual has social implications for their family, village or community. Once someone is known to be HIV-positive, there is a sense that the virus has effectively affected members of that person's family or community. This is one of the reasons why HIV/AIDS is not discussed openly, particularly in the rural areas. To identify an HIV-positive person publicly is akin to condemning an entire family to social exclusion or discrimination in the community. In a traditional society in which everyone knows everyone, social exclusion serves as a severe punishment. This is consistent with the argument advanced by Galavotti et al. (2001, p. 1607): 'For many in sub-Saharan Africa, the story of HIV and other threats to reproductive health is essentially a story of isolation, stigmatization, and social paralysis.'

Obijiofor (2001) noted that HIV/AIDS was seen in Nigeria more than a decade ago as a western imported disease that did not exist. In 1997, a famous Nigerian musician – Fela Ransome-Kuti – argued publicly that HIV/AIDS did not exist. However, in August of the same year, he died of the virus. His brother, who was at the time Nigeria's Minister of Health, admitted that Fela died of AIDS. The news shook the nation and awakened everyone to the reality that was HIV/AIDS. Fela's experience showed that people have to acknowledge that HIV/AIDS exists before they can attend to prevention messages aimed at checking further spread of the virus. If people perceive HIV/AIDS as a western-oriented disease that does not affect people in developing countries, they are likely to switch off attention to public information campaigns designed to prevent the spread of the virus.

Airhihenbuwa and Webster (2004) examine the role of culture in influencing individual behaviours in HIV/AIDS prevention. They argue that culture is the platform on which health behaviour and HIV/AIDS are communicated and through which health should be clarified and comprehended. As they argued, 'behaviour, particularly health behaviour, occurs in the context of cultures and, furthermore, is either reinforced or resisted through family, government and spiritual institutions' (Airhihenbuwa and Webster, 2004, p. 6). According to them, research shows that in Africa, a public health intervention approach that focuses on the individual person has not been successful, essentially because of the group dynamics that influence human behaviour. In Africa, decisions are made in groups, not by individual members of society. This relates to Hofstede's (2001, 1997) concepts of collectivism and individualism which suggest that while collective decisions are valued in some developing countries, individual-based decisions are appreciated in developed western countries. As discrimination against and social exclusion of people living with HIV/AIDS occur in families, communities, peer groups, social organisations, educational institutions, workplaces and even in churches, Airhihenbuwa and Webster (2004, p. 10) call for culture-based solutions to the spread of HIV/AIDS in Africa. This implies that HIV/AIDS prevention programmes that focus on individual behaviours rather than cultural practices will not be successful.

In Zambia, the Zambian government is collaborating with community youth organisations in the fight against the spread of HIV/AIDS (James, 2013). The organisations support open conversations about HIV education and prevention methods. One common feature of the Zambian culture, as is the case in most parts of Africa, is the helplessness that women suffer through conforming or acquiescing to their husbands' sexual needs. In some parts of Africa, women lack the authority to say no to their partners whenever they demand sex. They are raised to understand that it is their responsibility to satisfy their male partners at all times. This cultural practice exposes women to the risk of contracting HIV/AIDS, as the men are seen to be free to have many sex partners while women are required to remain loyal to their husbands and partners. Another difficulty is the perception by men that sex with condoms does not offer the 'real' experience. For Africa to make an impact on the campaign against the spread of HIV/AIDS, there is a need to reconsider some cultural practices. Women must be empowered to protect themselves against the virus, not to be perceived by men as objects of sexual satisfaction. People living with HIV/AIDS must be allowed to tell their stories, not to be excluded from society, so they can spread the message about the need to avoid or halt inappropriately risky behaviours that encourage the spread of the virus.

In a study of the obstacles that prevent male-partner participation in programmes to prevent mother-to-child HIV transmission in Tshwane, South Africa, researchers Koo, Making and Forsyth (2013) found structural and psychological impediments such as the widespread view that clinics were not 'male-friendly', emphasis on undertaking HIV tests rather than overall wellbeing and limited avenues for fathers to take part in activities designed to maintain good health (Koo et al., 2013). They point out that while research relating to prevention of mother-to-child HIV transmission had tended to concentrate on women, little attention had been paid to male partners.

While mass media and folk media have been deployed in the HIV/AIDS prevention campaigns, attention has now shifted to use of social media to spread the HIV/AIDS prevention message and to reach an important segment of our population – the youth.

Use of social media in HIV/AIDS prevention

A United Nations Joint Programme on AIDS (UNAIDS, 2011a) panel discussion at Stellenbosch University, South Africa, in 2011 examined how social media could be used to prevent the spread of HIV/AIDS. A number of innovative ideas and strategies were identified. There were also questions about how new media could assist in the fight against HIV/AIDS. Executive Director of UNAIDS, Michel Sidibé, said in his opening address: 'The potential of new technologies to re-energize the AIDS-movement is clear. We need nothing less than an HIV prevention revolution, with social media and mobile technology at its core' (UNAIDS, 2011a). Participants noted the significance of social media as an effective and appropriate media to engage young people in the campaign against the spread of HIV/AIDS.

Research has shown that young adults are attracted and attuned to social media in various ways, including use of social media in social communication. Social media could be used to communicate health messages, in particular HIV/AIDS prevention messages. Helen Alexander, who works with the Sonke Gender Justice Network, told the participants at the panel discussion:

> In South Africa at least, the cell phone is an important tool of the trade for sex workers, as it helps them connect to their clients, and helps to keep them safe. So mobile phones are actually a great way to reach sex workers. It's anonymous, you don't have to track people down, and often these are people who are not comfortable coming to a community event.
>
> (UNAIDS, 2011a)

At the end of the workshop in South Africa, Olga Rudneva, the executive director of the Elena Pinchuk ANTIAIDS Foundation, declared the start of a competition for developing mobile applications for HIV prevention designed to encourage the world to initiate a social network project for prevention of HIV/AIDS. She said the organisation's project should:

- Raise awareness about HIV/AIDS, ways of using transmission social media platforms or mobile applications.
- Establish communication platforms using social media to discuss safe sex, HIV/AIDS, stigma and discrimination issues.
- Create innovative ways of communication using social media.
- Create easy-to-use mobile applications to spread information and news about HIV/AIDS, safe sex and HIV/AIDS resources.
- Establish blogging and photo blogging platform to exchange ideas about fight against HIV/AIDS.

(UNAIDS, 2011b)

The shift to social media is understandable. Young people are known to use social media and the Internet across cultures. Given the rapid growth, adoption and use of the mobile phone in Africa, social media can serve as an appropriate and effective channel for communicating health-related messages to young and old, and men and women in

Africa. In the fight against HIV/AIDS, mobile phones can be used in various ways to educate young people, to create awareness, to reach out to them through various social networks, to train them and to empower them. With mobile phones, young people can share ideas about prevention strategies, appropriate sexual behaviours, and benefits to be derived from prevention of HIV/AIDS infection. Equipped with mobile phones, the Internet and social media, the much-needed HIV prevention revolution can be initiated by young people. Patel (2014) notes the promising role that social media can offer in the campaign to reduce the spread of HIV/AIDS, particularly among young people.

Social media such as Facebook and Twitter, including other social networking sites accessible through mobile phone technology, provide unique opportunities to access and actively engage with youths in remote and rural parts of the world, in particular the developing world in the fight against the spread of HIV/AIDS. This innovative idea resonates with research evidence. For example, research by the Pew Research Center Internet Project (2013a) shows that as of September 2013, 73 per cent of online adults in the United States use social networking sites. More significant, though, is the number of young people aged between 18 and 29 who use social networking sites in the United States. The research shows that 90 per cent of young people aged 18–29 use social networking sites. This makes the use of social networking sites as channels for disseminating HIV/AIDS prevention messages highly effective and appropriate, although this refers to the situation in a developed western country. However, given the high rate of mobile phone adoption and use in Africa, it is likely these social networking sites will also be used by young people in Africa.

A study of Internet and mobile technology use in 24 developing nations conducted by the Pew Research Center (2013b) from March to May 2013 found that the use of the Internet was notably more common among young people. Specifically in South Africa, 62 per cent of Internet users said they used social networking sites. In Nigeria, 83 per cent of Internet users said they used social networking sites. In Ghana, the figure is 77 per cent, Kenya (76 per cent) and Senegal (75 per cent). However, these figures relate to the general population. In terms of young people aged 18–29, the survey found that in Nigeria, 39 per cent of people in the 18–29 age bracket use online social networking sites, while in South Africa 35 per cent of young people in the same age bracket use online social networking sites. In Senegal, 37 per cent of young people in the same age group use online social networking sites, while in Ghana the figure is 32 per cent.

A study conducted by United Nations Children's Fund in South Africa supports research evidence presented here. In a study that examined the role of social networks in the lives of youth living in developing nations, UNICEF found that access to mobile phones is high in South Africa while access to computer and broadband Internet use is low (UNICEF, 2011a). In fact, UNICEF (2011b) sees Africa reaping huge benefits from increasing uptake of new technologies such as the mobile phone. This is facilitated by availability of inexpensive subscriber identity module (SIM) cards, access to low cost phone handsets and accessibility of pre-paid subscriptions that have allowed many mobile phone users to log on to the Internet through their mobile phones (UNICEF, 2011b). As Tanja Bosch, an academic at the Centre for Film and Media Studies at the University of Cape Town, South Africa, noted,

> The rise of the mobile internet in South Africa means that more peo-ple, especially youth, are using social networks as key tools in their identity formation. This timely report provides an important piece of the puzzle to understanding the formation of mobile youth cultures; and exploring the role that cellphone applications play in the lives of young South Africans.
>
> (UNICEF, 2011a)

The widespread use of mobile phones and social networking sites by young people in South Africa and other parts of the continent clears the way for NGOs, government officials, civil society, medical researchers and other agencies committed to the fight against HIV/AIDS to use these communication channels to reach the youth, to educate them, to encourage them to share their experiences and to clarify the bene-fits to be derived through safe sex practices in disseminating HIV/AIDS prevention messages. Citing research evidence on social media use in Nigeria, Ogunlesi (2013, p. 22) states that 70 per cent of social media users in Nigeria are aged 18–33, an indication of the extent to which social media has strengthened the public sphere and facilitated greater access to information, including free expression of opinion and a shift in the balance of power between political leaders and ordinary people.

UNICEF (2011a) notes that while the western world has seen the development of social networking sites such as Facebook, Twitter and MySpace in the early part of the 21st century, South Africa has followed suit by creating its own mobile-based application social network known as MXit. Thus,

> Created in South Africa in 2004, MXit is a free instant messaging and social networking application for people aged 13 and up that runs on multiple mobile and computing platforms. MXit allows its users to send and receive text and multimedia messages in one-on-one conversations as well as in public chatrooms. MXit users can also play games, download music, access movie clips and news, and buy and sell goods. With over 44 million registered user accounts in South Africa – 55 per cent male and 45 per cent female, with 47 per cent of users aged 18–25, 21 per cent aged 15–17, 5 per cent aged 13–14, and 20 per cent 26 years and older – MXit has become an important part of networking and communication in the lives of South Africans with diverse backgrounds.
>
> (UNICEF, 2011a, pp. 5–6)

The growing use of mobile phones and social networking sites by South African youth is not surprising. Research cited in Chapter 9 (in this book) shows Africa as the world's fastest growing market for mobile phones. It is therefore not surprising that new technologies such as mobile phones are regarded as the engines that drive socioeconomic, cultural, educational and political development in Africa and other parts of the developing world. It is in this context that mobile phones, the Internet and social media are regarded as vital platforms for promotion of an active and effective public sphere for deliberative democracy in the continent. In the fight against HIV/AIDS, it is important to use the technologies that are popular among young people but also the technologies that serve as credible pipelines for dissemination of HIV/AIDS prevention messages. Community organisations and agencies that are tasked with spreading HIV/AIDS prevention messages can mount online information campaigns through social networking sites and social media that are accessible to young people.

An online document, *HIV prevention goes social: Using social media to create, connect, and come together*, developed by the US National Minority AIDS Council in response to rapid growth of incidence of AIDS in communities of colour in the United States, identified social media as an important channel for communicating HIV/AIDS prevention messages. The document asked:

> Why should you consider social media? For one thing, over half of all Americans over the age of 12 use online social networks, most of which is driven by mobile access. Many of them are going online to research health questions or find support from a community. As

social media becomes more and more prominent, it is important to become better versed in these tools as a means of observing everyday conversations, understanding what's being talked about, who's doing the talking, and expanding ways to engage with specific communities.

(US National Minority AIDS Council, 2011, p. 5)

Another way that social media could be used to prevent the spread of HIV/AIDS is through monitoring the sexual behaviour of people at risk. Young, Rivers and Lewis (2014) suggest the possibility of using social networking data as a method of assessing and discovering HIV risk behaviours and outcomes. Based on a study of 553,186,061 tweets, the researchers reported that it is possible 'to use real-time social networking technologies to identify HIV risk-related communications, geographically map the location of those conversations, and link them to national HIV outcome data for additional analyses, and that these data were associated with county-level HIV prevalence'. This suggests 'that it may be possible to predict HIV and drug-use behaviors through peoples' tweets, map where those messages come from and link them to data on the disease to be used for prevention and detection' (Gladstone, 2014).

As in Africa, people living with HIV/AIDS in the Caribbean are widely stigmatised, isolated and discriminated against. In her critique of the media campaign against HIV/AIDS in the Caribbean, de Bruin (2006) notes the drawbacks of mass media as a sole channel for disseminating messages about HIV/AIDS. She draws attention to the changing role of media in the Caribbean and how it has affected the media use in HIV/AIDS prevention programme. This suggests the need to use social media in the campaigns. Social media are relevant channels of communication and networking among youth in various parts of the world. Social media are credible and can be used to reach the youth and spread messages about the need to take action to prevent the spread of HIV/AIDS virus, as well as to facilitate attitude and behaviour change and to avoid risky sexual behaviour.

In the campaign against the spread of HIV/AIDS, Wolf, Bond and Tawfik (2000, p. 64) note the important role that social factors play in influencing risky behaviours. In their view, the decision of a young person to use condoms may be affected by the opinions and practices of family members and friends, as well as mass media messages and conversations in schools. 'Social influence is substantial, shifting and shaping deeply rooted beliefs and perceptions. Individuals filter varying opinions and compare and shift their own opinions within group norms to

gain acceptance by other group members.' In their study of peer promotion programmes and social networks in Ghana, Wolf et al.
(2000) found that peer educators are more successful in reaching people who
have many similarities with them. In essence, youth tend to depend
more on family members and their peers. This is why peer educators
who are in school are able to reach their peers who are also in school.
In recruitment terms, they suggest that if the objective is to reach out-
of-school children, it would be more valuable to choose out-of-school
youth as peer educators (Wolf et al., 2000).

Even as the world confronts HIV/AIDS in Africa, another health crisis
has erupted in West Africa. This is the Ebola virus.

Ebola health crisis

The outbreak of the Ebola virus and the rapid rate of fatalities have taken
the world by surprise. Since the outbreak of Ebola in March 2014, it is
believed to have infected no fewer than 21,797 people and killed about
8,675 people in West Africa (as at the time of writing) (Dixon, 2015).
The deaths were reported in six countries, namely Guinea, Sierra Leone,
Liberia, Nigeria, the United States and Mali (as at the time of writing).
Among the countries worst affected in West Africa are Guinea, Liberia
and Sierra Leone. These three countries account for more than 97 per
cent of the fatalities. Mali has registered six cases, all of them resulting
in deaths (UNAIDS, 2014). In October 2014, the WHO declared Senegal
and Nigeria Ebola-free. In Nigeria, the virus claimed eight lives before it
was contained by the health authorities.

Ebola is not just a health crisis, it is also having serious impacts on
the economies of the three worst affected countries and indeed the
West African economy. Trade between countries in the region has also
been severely affected owing to the closure of borders and suspension of
flights among countries in the region. The latest strain of the Ebola virus
was first reported in West Africa in March 2014. It has grown to become
the most fatal outbreak of the disease since Ebola was first detected in
the Democratic Republic of Congo in 1976. What makes the disease
deadly is that there is no known cure or vaccine. The WHO and leading health laboratories in industrialised countries are racing to develop
a vaccine to be used to cure patients and to contain further spread of the
virus. In mid-January 2015, the first 300 doses of a trial Ebola vaccine
were transported to Liberia (Dixon, 2015). If the experimental vaccine
proves successful, there is hope that the Ebola outbreak and fatalities
resulting from the virus will be contained by the end of 2015.

Conclusion

HIV/AIDS as a global health problem and the worldwide efforts to stop further spread of the virus are examined in this chapter. HIV/AIDS prevention has been a story of sadness and hope; sadness in the sense that millions of men, women and children have lost their lives to the disease. It is also a story of hope in that the discovery of antiretroviral drugs has helped to slow down the infection rate and to prolong the lives of people living with HIV/AIDS. In the campaign to stop the spread of the virus, governments, civil society, the medical community, researchers and international aid agencies have found that cultural practices and traditional belief systems pose major obstacles. Cultural practices and beliefs influence people's willingness to adopt safe sex practices and other measures to avoid being infected. In various countries, people resist public education and information that clarifies the causes of the virus, as well as advice about how to relate with people living with HIV/AIDS. Essentially, discrimination against people living with HIV/AIDS does not offer a solution but cultivates a culture of fear in the community. In the years following the discovery of the virus, official government response to the disease was almost non-existent. There was little support for people living with the virus. Governments were also slow to provide funds for research aimed at finding a vaccine for the virus.

More than 33 years since the virus was discovered, significant progress has been recorded. The number of people dying from HIV/AIDS has slowed. The number of people being infected has reduced. However, the prevalence rate in some poor communities and developing regions of the world remains high. In the promotion of HIV/AIDS prevention messages, social media have been identified as useful and appropriate channels to communicate messages designed to reach young people. Research shows that young adults are fascinated by, and attuned to, social media in various ways such as the use of social media in social communication. Social media are being used to communicate health messages, in particular HIV/AIDS prevention messages. Social media are not only strategic and effective, prevention approaches that use social media to communicate HIV/AIDS messages differ significantly from previous health promotion campaigns that relied solely on mass media and folk media.

Among young adults, social media are seen as credible and effective. What makes social media different and effective is the familiarity of young adults with the technology. For example, the speedy diffusion and adoption of the mobile phone in Africa and other developing regions of the world has popularised the use of social media as an effective medium for circulating health-related messages. In HIV/AIDS prevention messages, mobile phones are used to inform young people, to create awareness and to reach out to them through their social networks. With mobile phones, youth can share ideas about HIV/AIDS prevention strategies and adopt correct and safe sex practices, as well as understand the benefits to be derived through prevention of HIV/AIDS infection.

While the world is grappling to stop the spread of HIV/AIDS, the deadly Ebola virus that has killed nearly 9,000 people in West Africa also poses a major health problem to the international community. However, the discovery of a trial Ebola vaccine might help to put an end to the spread of the virus and the toll on human population in West Africa, in particular, and the world, in general.

8
Ethnographic Research in 'Offline' and Online Worlds

Introduction

Despite decades of research investigations conducted via ethnographic tools such as participant observations, interviews, focus groups and document analysis, debate has persisted over the usefulness of ethnography as a valid research method. Researchers who hold the position that knowledge can only be obtained through direct examination and testing of phenomena argue that ethnography is methodologically unsound and unreliable because of lack of clarity in the way data are collected and measured. However, other researchers, particularly those who subscribe to qualitative methods of social inquiry, disagree. They suggest that ethnography, as a systematic qualitative method, is as valid as other empirical methods of investigation.

Ethnographic research methods are examined in this chapter as a tool to explore and understand the impact of new technologies on developing societies. The chapter shows how ethnography, as a credible research instrument, is used to collect data in research relating to new technologies and socioeconomic development.

Differences between qualitative and quantitative researchers have been attributed to differences in theoretical postulations, including distinctions in their epistemological and ontological foundations (Brewer, 2001; Gunter, 2000; Hammersley, 1992). In explaining the differences between qualitative and quantitative research, Servaes (1999, p. 108) states that 'Whereas the primary concerns of quantitative research are reliability and construct validity, qualitative research seeks external validity, not through objectivity, but rather through subjectivity.' Plows (2008) states that quantitative research methods tend to have broad scope and usually involve the use of methods such as surveys and questionnaires. In this research tradition, software packages such as the statistical package for the social sciences (SPSS) can be used to classify data and present results. There is also emphasis on statistical information and examination of large datasets. Plows states that one of the objectives of qualitative research is to gain access to the views and conduct of research participants. Qualitative researchers adopt various methods of data collection and there are various software packages that are used to analyse qualitative research data. Examples include NVivo and Leximancer.

Notwithstanding these basic epistemological distinctions, some scholars adopt the position that qualitative and quantitative methods should be seen as valuable methods of undertaking research (Baxter and Babbie, 2004; Merrigan and Huston, 2004). For example, Baxter and Babbie (2004, p. 103) argue that 'the strongest communication research is multi-method, in which both quantitative and qualitative methods are used to study a given communication phenomenon'. Although debate over the usefulness of ethnography as a reliable and valid research method has subsided, ethnographic research approaches continue to be used widely by social science researchers.

Ethnography is a part of the qualitative research paradigm that is widely applied in studies in which the researcher may not know much about the social groups or communities that are being investigated. Therefore, ethnography looks at how individuals or groups make sense of the world which they inhabit. For this reason, ethnography does not make predictions about the human world. This was the point that Servaes (1999, p. 108) highlighted when he said: 'Unlike quantitative inquiry, qualitative research does not, as a rule, seek broad generalizeability.' Understandably, ethnographic methods are best suited to undertaking research into the social world of groups of people or communities. There are examples of some classic studies that used ethnography to investigate various social problems. One African anthropologist and ethnographer of note is Victor Uchendu (1965), who undertook a case study of the Igbo of southeast Nigeria in the mid-1960s. Among contemporary African anthropologists/ethnographers is Francis Nyamnjoh (2005a, 2005b, 1999) who has written extensively on the anthropology of African societies, including media, democracy and politics in Africa.

Ethnographic methods have been used to study the influence that television has on Indigenous populations in Canada, New Zealand and Australia. Eric Michaels (1986) provides one classic example of ethnographic research that examined the impact of television on the

Warlpiri community at Yuendumu, South Australia, between 1982 and 1986. The methods he used provided deep insights into how television was introduced into the Warlpiri community. Michaels's work remains an inspirational reference material for anyone wishing to understudy the origins and effects of media in Indigenous communities.

One of the bases on which ethnographers criticise positivist research methods is their inability to recognise that human societies are underpinned by meaning systems and cultural practices that help them to create their own multiple meanings which are always dynamic and evolving. This is perhaps why ethnographers, in their attempt to understand the multiple realities that exist in various societies, do not start their research with fixed or prearranged propositions to be tested and confirmed or refuted. Ethnographic researchers rather start on the premise that human lives are socially and culturally constructed and social meanings cannot be predicted and measured with statistical instruments that are commonly used in positivist research. Rather than undertake research on the premise that there is one reality out there to be discovered and described, ethnographers proceed cautiously on the basis that there are multiple realities in human societies and those realities cannot be quantified and measured through strict scientific procedures.

To the ethnographer, understanding the social world and the realities that exist and describing them are more important than attempting to predict or hypothesise human behaviour. Ethnographers understand they cannot control human behaviour or cultural practices. They aim to understand human societies, their cultural practices, social world, belief systems, meaning making and other phenomena that are critical to understanding the social group or community under investigation. As Whitehead (2005, p. 7) argued, 'the ethnographer must be ontologically, epistemologically, and methodologically *flexible* and *creative* in the use of a range of methodologies that will help in understanding the people and study topic with the greatest emic validity possible'. One way to achieve emic validity is to continuously record daily field notes not only to ensure that observations are not forgotten or overlooked but also to underline the interpretive nature of the research, as interpretations are likely to change during the fieldwork. The ethnographer undertakes research in participants' natural world to observe them and their behaviour. Patton (1990, p. 55) clarifies the point this way:

> The neutral investigator enters the research arena with no axe to grind, no theory to prove and no predetermined results to support.

Rather, the investigator's commitment is to understand the world as it is, to be true to complexities and multiple perspectives as they emerge, and to be balanced in reporting both confirming and disconfirming evidence.

This chapter examines ethnographic research and the specific methods of data collection in conventional ethnography, including their drawbacks. Also discussed is online ethnography or what Kozinets (2010, 2009, 2002, 1998) described as 'netnography'. The chapter highlights the importance of online ethnography, as people interact in online spaces facilitated by computer-mediated communication. Online ethnography is recognition of digital spaces in which people operate and belong to make sense of their social world. Online ethnography is an important and growing field of research because people communicate and interact in diverse ways through the Internet, email, chat rooms, instant messaging, social media (Facebook, Twitter and YouTube, for example), new media and other digital technologies. Other issues discussed in this chapter include sampling procedures, sample size and the techniques for analysing ethnographic data, such as triangulation.

Definitions of ethnography

Reeves, Kuper and Hodges (2008, p. 512) define ethnography as 'the study of social interactions, behaviours, and perceptions that occur within groups, teams, organisations, and communities'. They trace the origins of the method to anthropological investigations of small communities that took place in the early years of the 20th century at a time when anthropologists such as Bronislaw Malinowski and Alfred Radcliffe-Brown engaged in long periods of participant observations of small communities and recorded their observations of the social practices and traditions of the people. Crang and Cook (2007, p. 35) perceive ethnography as 'participant observation *plus* any other appropriate methods' such as focus groups, video, interviews, photographs and archival material such as documents. Forsey (2010, p. 567) suggests that one main objective of ethnography is 'to listen deeply to and/or to observe as closely as possible the beliefs, the values, the material conditions and structural forces that underwrite the socially patterned behaviours of all human beings and the meanings people attach to these conditions and forces'. One key strategy for recording what people do in a group or in their community is to see them, to talk with them and to request them to narrate what they have done, why they did it that way and how that activity or action has had an impact on them (Forsey, 2010). Describing ethnography by its intention rather than its method would inspire the ethnographer to participate in, and connect with, the lives of people in various social settings. 'Being with people as they conduct their everyday duties and pastimes remains the preferred mode of ethnographic practice, but it does not have to be synonymous with it' (Forsey, 2010, p. 569).

Similarly, Reeves et al. (2008) believe one major objective of ethnography is to offer deep insights into the belief systems of communities or groups, and activities that people engage in, including things such as the setting where people reside. This is achieved through conducting in-depth interviews and undertaking personal observations. Hammersley (1992) believes the task of an ethnographer is to record the cultural practices and views of people in a given society in order to understand their worldviews. Indeed, ethnography is concerned with understanding and describing the social life of people. Katz (2002, p. 64) states that what marks out ethnography from positivist research is that ethnography focuses on 'what people are doing and how they are doing it'. On this basis, he argues that ethnography has made significant contributions to our understanding of social phenomena 'by noting the situated character of social life' (Katz, 2002, p. 69). Ethnographers draw readers into the social world of research participants by describing their social world and their behaviours. Katz (2002) asserts that ethnographers commence fieldwork by emphasising descriptive aspects that will provide them with the space to respond to questions relating to how social life progresses. From that point, they try to explain why connections emerge in their data.

Plows (2008, p. 1528) defines ethnography as 'embedded participant observation or field work – immersion in the research site and immersion in its practises'. She states that ethnography, as a research approach, assists researchers to comprehend activities and behaviour at a common, everyday level in concealed social situations; it also helps researchers to connect the knowledge gained to the research questions and also to theories. In this context, ethnography produces rich descriptions of social life in a community or group of people (Plows, 2008). Although there are different types of ethnography, the particular method used by ethnographers will depend on the objectives of each study and the specific conditions on the research site. Ethnography looks at human behaviour that occurs in particular social settings. This includes conduct that is moulded and limited by the environment and how people understand and construe their experiences (Wilson and Chaddha, 2009).

Some of the key features of ethnography outlined by Reeves et al. (2008, p. 512) include: a focus on the qualities of a given social event or phenomenon that does not entail testing hypotheses; working with raw data, that is, data that have not been coded at the point of collection; detailed exploration of a small number of situations, locations or communities; and clear, meaningful and detailed interpretation and description of actions, activities or practices of a group of people. Other forms of ethnographic research include auto-ethnography (the researcher's own views, based on their interactions with the subject of their research, become the key component of the research); meta-ethnography (qualitative research materials are examined and analysed to produce innovative ideas and data); and online ethnography which goes beyond traditional ethnographic practices to incorporate new forms of technology-driven exchange of ideas and interactions through online network and groups (Reeves et al., 2008).

Advantages and problems of ethnography

Of the various research approaches available to a qualitative researcher, ethnography is often selected because of the advantages it offers over other methods. One advantage of ethnography is that it enables the researcher to engage in participant observation. The researcher is able to submerge himself or herself into a group or community, thus producing detailed and meaningful research data. As Reeves et al. (2008, p. 514) point out, 'Participant observation also gives ethnographers opportunities to gather empirical insights into social practices that are normally "hidden" from the public gaze.' Ethnography, according to Plows (2008), is an important tool of research because it offers vivid and powerful stories that assist the researcher to add to theory through insightful examination of social systems and practices.

Regardless of the merits of ethnography as a research paradigm, there are problems associated with it. The long period of fieldwork in which the researcher stays in the field interviewing and observing people means that it is often difficult to obtain permission for repeat visits to the research sites, especially when the people being studied feel the research could portray their community or group in a negative way. The long period of fieldwork could affect the ethnographer in that the researcher becomes sympathetic to, or biased in favour of, the group or community being studied. In ethnography it is often difficult and time-consuming to secure approval from research ethics committees. As Reeves et al. (2008) mention with specific reference to the situation in the health sector, the interaction that develops

> between ethnographers and patients or clinicians during fieldwork can be regarded with suspicion, as traditional notions of health services research rest on researchers' detachment rather than involvement. Comprehensively recording the multifaceted nature of social action that occurs within a clinic or ward is a difficult task, as a range of temporal, spatial and behavioural elements need to be documented.
>
> (2008, p. 514)

Issues in ethnographic research

In ethnographic research, trust between the researcher and research participants is highly important. When research participants become suspicious of the intentions of the researcher, they are likely to withhold information. This could frustrate and jeopardise the research efforts. To gain more credible information from research participants, it has been suggested that 'insider' ethnographers should undertake the study. However, as Plows (2008) points out, there are both advantages and drawbacks to such a practice. While an insider is likely to gain more trust from the people being researched and therefore access valuable data, insider research has serious problems. The disadvantages of insider ethnographic research include 'concerns about seeing the wood for the trees; overly sympathetic accounts that are not rigorous enough, and ethical concerns about misuse of the trust placed in the researcher' (Plows, 2008, p. 1531). Of course, good ethnography does not have to be undertaken through an insider approach. There are also advantages in conducting ethnography as an 'outsider'. As Plows notes, the outsider can also gain rich viewpoints and can also gain the trust of the people over a period of time.

One of the questions that confront ethnographers when they are preparing to enter a research site is how they should introduce themselves to community members, and also how to respond to curious questions that community members might pose (Whitehead, 2005). Fine (1993, p. 276) states that scholars who criticise research that is concealed feel that participant observation which is hidden makes the researcher look like an undercover agent, which suggests a lack of respect for the 'right' of research participants not to be misled. This view is, however, contested in the ethnographic literature.

Fine (1993) identified three forms of information control in the research site. These are deep cover, shallow cover and explicit cover. In deep cover, the researcher withholds information about his or her research role. The researcher immerses himself or herself into the group under investigation as a complete member. In explicit cover, the researcher makes known, as early as possible, the objectives and propositions of the research, regardless of whether this revelation will have any impact on the behaviour of research participants. In shallow cover, the researcher reveals information about the intention of the research but remains unclear about the goals of the research (Fine, 1993). Fine challenged the accuracy of field notes which ethnographers record during fieldwork, arguing that it is misleading for researchers to produce spoken words that they attribute to research participants. In his view, it is impossible to reproduce the exact words used in a discussion or conversation, particularly if the researcher was not trained in shorthand or as a court reporter. On this basis, he argues: 'We claim that the scene really happened, but the scene did not happen in precisely the form we announce' (Fine, 1993, pp. 277–278). He insists that details of direct quotations and descriptions recorded by ethnographers are mere pointers or indications about what was said. There are many reasons for the inaccuracies.

Participant observation can be demanding as it requires numerous hours of observations and recording of observations. Accuracy may be affected when ethnographers rely more on their memory rather than on their field notes. Memories fade if they are not converted into field notes. As Fine (1993, p. 279) argued, 'the ability to be totally aware is imperfect. We mishear, we do not recognize what we see, and we might be poorly positioned to recognize the happenings around us.' What this highlights is the difficulty of participant observers being fully or completely objective in their field notes. As human beings, our abilities are limited, just as we have human flaws.

The role of theory in ethnographic research has been raised by some scholars. Wilson and Chaddha (2009) identify important questions about the role of theory in ethnography, such as whether theory should be largely inductive or deductive or be both inductive and deductive. While they acknowledge that there is an inductive role for theory in ethnographic research, they also point out that the important question is not whether theory can be used but how it is used. They identify some shortcomings of using theory to steer the ethnographic research process. One of them is that a precisely deductive method could steer the researcher to ignore critical behaviour that is incompatible with previous theoretical positions. Another weakness is that an inductive method could lead to an improper adoption of theoretical understanding to give meanings to research outcomes (Wilson and Chaddha, 2009).

One of the problems that confront ethnographers is whether they should copy the fundamental values in quantitative social science research in order to provide some kind of evidence for their qualitative data. As Small (2009, p. 10) explained it, 'The core predicament that many ethnographers face is deceptively straightforward: how to produce ethnographic work that keeps at bay the critiques expected from quantitative researchers while also addressing the thirst for in-depth studies that somehow or other "speak" to *empirical* conditions in *other* cases (not observed).' One of the major worries that researchers who adopt quantitative methods have about ethnography is 'generalizability' (Small, 2009, p. 11). This concern brings to mind the acrimonious debate that dominated academic research in the 1980s and 1990s over the comparative values of qualitative and quantitative research approaches. The debate has eased and both qualitative and quantitative methods are used interchangeably in some research situations, as both traditions are now seen as complementary.

Methods of data collection in traditional ethnography

There are different methods of data collection that are applied in ethnographic research. The most frequently cited method is participant observation. Others include in-depth interviews, focus groups and document analysis. However, technological transformations have introduced changes to the conventional ways of observation and accessing and analysing documents. In the electronic age, document analysis incorporates both print and electronic documents that are accessible on the Internet. Each of these methods has its own strengths and weaknesses. The methods can be used separately or in mixed forms. There is value in using mixed-method approaches in ethnographic research. Patton (1990) states that while a mix of interviews, participant observations and document analysis is valuable in ethnographic studies, those studies that use only one method are more susceptible to errors that are common within the specific method. Similarly, Glaser and Strauss (1967) argue there is merit in using multiple methods of data collection as it is difficult for anyone to 'trust all statements made by the other person in an interview or conversation, not merely because of his personal reasons for misleading the researcher but because of social rules about what can and cannot be told' (1967, p. 181). The following sections examine briefly participant observation, interviews and document analysis as some of the methods of data collection in ethnography.

Participant observation

Some scholars (e.g., Plows, 2008) have described ethnography as participant observation in one form or another. This is because, for many decades, participant observations were used by early anthropologists such as Margaret Mead and Bronislaw Malinowski to record information about people's behaviour and practices in the communities they studied. There is a wide range of literature that shows how ethnographers use participant observation in their research. Participant observation, which is a major tool of data collection, implies that the researcher has to be directly involved in the study by immersing himself or herself into the routines and practices of the group being studied. Participant observation requires the researcher to take field notes in which they record their observations. Forsey (2010) argues that listening to research participants is as important to an ethnographer as observation is to the researcher. He believes the ethnographer is more of a participant listener than a participant observer because what ethnographers do most of the time is to listen because 'it is mainly through listening to people that we access human consciousness' (Forsey, 2010, p. 563).

Participant observation and fieldwork in ethnography are often seen as similar, as fieldwork cannot be carried out without the participation of the ethnographer. Specific aspects of what should be observed during participant observation have been identified. These include the space used in the social environment; the objects that are in the social environment; the individuals in the research setting; the actor groups; the behaviours or actions; activities and events that occur in the social setting; the language used by the actors in the social setting; other forms of cultural expressions (examples include music, song, dance, art and architecture); types of interaction undertaken by actors in the social setting; emotional level of the conversation; the beliefs, attitudes and values that are present in the setting; and physical features in the setting (Whitehead, 2005).

Jeffrey and Troman (2004) point out that, although ethnographers are required to remain in the field collecting data for a long period, opinions are divided on the ideal length of time that an ethnographer should remain in the field. While some ethnographers consider the ideal length of fieldwork to be 24 months, others feel that 12 months should be sufficient. However, Jeffrey and Troman (2004, p. 538) argue that ethnographic research is never concluded because the reports are regarded as preliminary or tentative.

In ethnography, primary data collection is usually achieved through fieldwork. Fieldwork is important because it enables the researcher

> to observe and examine all aspects of a cultural system, especially those that could not be addressed through laboratory or survey research alone. Spending long periods of time in the field is considered the crucial aspect of the classical ethnographer's ability to comprehensively describe components of a cultural system as accurately and with as little bias as possible.
>
> (Whitehead, 2005, p. 5)

Of course, fieldwork is important in ethnographic research because it recognises that human beings live in different cultural and social situations and share different worldviews, belief systems and values. It is therefore through observation, interaction with and participation in human social world that the ethnographer can capture the social and cultural circumstances in which the people under study reside and make sense of their world. As Whitehead (2005, p. 6) notes, 'It is through repeated observations, conversations, and more structured interviewing that the ethnographer gets an emically valid understanding of the sociocultural contexts, processes, and meaning systems that are of significance to the study participants.' The word 'emic' refers to understanding the study participants from their own sociocultural contexts, belief systems and worldviews.

With regard to what researchers can learn from participant observation, Mack, Woodsong, MacQueen, Guest and Namey (2005) state that participant observation data can be used to cross validate a researcher's subjective beliefs and what they do. Participant observation is also a vital research tool to enhance understanding of the research participants' social world such as their physical, social, cultural and economic contexts, including their behaviours and actions, such as 'what they do, how frequently, and with whom' (Mack et al., 2005, p. 14). One of the greatest strengths of participant observation is that it provides researchers with the opportunity to witness events, activities and people, and to interact with research participants. As Mack et al. (2005, p. 14) state, 'Observing and participating are integral to understanding the breadth and complexities of the human experience....' Through participant observation, researchers are able to comprehend information gathered through other research approaches such as focus groups and interviews. This knowledge should assist in framing questions that should facilitate further understanding of the research problems. A further strength of participant observation is that it helps to reveal issues that are critical to comprehending the research problem that was previously unidentified at the research planning stage. This knowledge should help the researcher to ask the right questions (Mack et al., 2005).

Lewis and Russell (2011) proposed an embedded approach to ethnography, a concept that has been variously tagged 'collaborative ethnography' and 'engaged ethnography'. Regardless of how people describe embedded ethnography, Lewis and Russell note that one key characteristic of the concept is the use of fieldwork as a common method of investigation. As they argue, embedded ethnography

> allows the researcher to experience the 'worldview' of the organization, its members and their partners (and is akin, therefore, to immersion fieldwork), but also requires the researcher to assess that experience in the light of academic knowledge and give the resulting insights back to the organization critically and formatively (as with forms of action research or process evaluations), so that they can make operational use of those insights.
>
> (Lewis and Russell, 2011, p. 411)

They state that, essentially, embedded research allows the researcher to respond to their collaborators or research partners, as well as the needs and expectations of ethnography, while at the same time permitting the researcher to step back, consider and continue from a certain distance (2011).

Like other ethnographic research methods, participant observations have their merits and drawbacks. One of the challenges that confront participant observers is that it takes a lot of time to undertake participant observation, given that the participant observer is expected to stay in the field for a minimum of 12 months to observe and collect data (Mack et al., 2005). This contrasts with other research methods in which data collection lasts for a short period. Another disadvantage of participant observation, according to Mack et al. (2005), is the difficulty of recording information. This highlights the problem the researcher faces in recording everything they consider essential while at the same time participating and observing. This means the participant observer tends to rely more on his or her memory. As human memory can disappear so quickly, any decision to postpone the recording of the observations in the researcher's field notes can pose a risk that the observations could be lost or could lead to imprecise or erroneous documentation of data. One major disadvantage of participant observation is that it is seen to be highly subjective. Of course, researchers are required to be objective in the scientific tradition. Mack et al. advise that it is important for the researcher to acknowledge the disparity between recording and stating what they witness as against explaining what they observe.

Participant observation data are used in various ways, such as incorporating the information into data collected through other methods such as interviews. For example, when interviewing participants, the researcher can draw on knowledge of the participants' culture that he or she gained through observations. Furthermore, participant observation is valuable in enhancing and refining the planning of other research approaches, as well as in deciding how to study research participants and who should be enlisted in the study (Mack et al., 2005).

One problem in participant observation is that observations and interpretations made of the same phenomena at an earlier phase of ethnographic research can change from observations and interpretations made at a later stage of the research. Whitehead (2005) suggests that continuous recording of field notes should not only focus on the community under study but the researcher should also record their own responses and sentiments with regard to their fieldwork experiences. This reflexive action is designed to surmount the problem of researcher bias.

Another shortcoming of participant observation is the likelihood of observer bias. This is a situation in which the researcher could observe some events and ignore others. There is also the likelihood that the research participants might stage events and cultural practices to impress and influence the ethnographer. There are ways of overcoming these problems. For example, methods triangulation could be used to cross-validate data gathered through other approaches. One important way to establish the reliability and validity of participant observations is for the ethnographer to draw up their observation matrix or criteria that underpin their observations. Observations that are not based on defined criteria will be seen as haphazard and therefore open to criticisms relating to lack of reliability and validity. If, for example, an ethnographer is investigating how decisions are made with regard to adoption of new technologies in remote Indigenous communities, the ethnographer could draw up the following observation matrix or criteria to guide their observations:

- **cultural conventions, traditional ceremonies and practices** (list and describe community norms, practices and ceremonies that are highly valued in the community; note the practices that are restricted to certain gender and age and those that are generally open to everyone);
- **community governance** (record how the community is governed, who are the decision makers, who holds more power between men and women, how decisions are made, how decision makers are selected, and how they are perceived in the community);
- **role of elders in the community** (record the roles that elders perform in the community as repositories of knowledge and/or community leaders);
- **community communication technologies/channels** (record most active communication technologies/channels and least active technologies/channels; categorise them into technologies/channels most actively and least actively used by age and gender; also categorise them into traditional and modern technologies/channels of communication); and
- **sources of entertainment and leisure activities** (list and describe sources of entertainment by age and gender; list and describe leisure activities by age and gender).

These observation criteria will form categories that will be coded and used for analysis of data.

Interviews

Interviews, especially face-to-face interviews, are regarded as one of the primary methods of data collection in ethnographic research. Interviews offer a lot of advantages. They can help the researcher to uncover what the research participants are thinking about. They also provide opportunities for the ethnographer to seek clarifications from the interviewee and to confirm what the interviewee had said earlier. Interviews are regarded as a valuable data collecting tool in ethnographic research because they help to shed light on, and serve as a reflection of, the lives of people in various parts of the world. As Forsey (2010, p. 568) states,

Interviews, regardless of setting, can enable us to locate the biography of the individual, and groups of persons, in the broader cultural domains in which they live. Consequently, we should be able to link their personal story to the broader context and issues we are seeking to describe and analyse in the formal reports of our research data.

(Forsey, 2010, pp. 568–569)

When conducting face-to-face interviews, the researcher is able to observe non-verbal (facial) expressions and other signs and motions that the interviewee might make, including changes in tone of voice. The key element that the ethnographer must bring to an interview session is the ability to listen. Listening will give the researcher an opportunity to explore issues further by asking the interviewee follow-up questions. As some researchers have mentioned, what an interviewee may not say is as informative and revealing as what they may have said. Generally, what is covered during interviews depends on the objectives of the research, and the ethnographer's skills in extracting information through deep questioning. Reeves et al. (2008) state that ethnographic researchers adopt unofficial interviewing strategies that enable them to examine issues that arise and also to interrogate unusual practices or events. However, they clarify that ethnographers also use formal in-depth interviews and documentation such as official records of meetings, people's diaries and photographs.

Like every other ethnographic research method, interviews have disadvantages. One of these is the high cost of conducting interviews, including the cost of travelling to and from interview sites. Sometimes the outward appearance of the interviewer could pose obstacles to the research because the interviewee might feel a sense of unease about the physical appearance of the interviewer that could lead to unwillingness to answer questions. With regard to the nature of interview questions, it is often preferable to have standardised and open-ended questions that will enable the researcher to explore a wide range of issues. Using standardised questions which involve asking all interviewees the same set of questions will significantly reduce interviewer bias. Recording the interviews on audiotape and/or videotape is also highly recommended as this will make it possible for researchers to have easier access to the full interview transcripts. Recording the interviews will also provide evidence of reliability of data as future researchers can access the audio or video tape to cross-check the data reported by the ethnographer.

Sampling strategies

In ethnographic studies, there are diverse approaches to selecting interviewees. One process of selecting interviewees is what is commonly known as snowball sampling. In snowball sampling, the researcher asks key informants to suggest other respondents or interviewees (Weiss, 1994, cited in Small, 2009, p. 14). For example, the researcher can ask a few members of a community to identify people who have good knowledge of the research topic. If the researcher is looking at how decisions are made in remote Indigenous communities, he or she could ask some elderly members of the community to identify people who are well-informed about the processes of decision making in the community. When the ethnographer asks a number of elderly people such a question, the names that are mentioned continue to increase. The snowball sampling process entails the ethnographer compiling a list of the names of interviewees from the suggestions he or she received from elderly members of the community. What this means is that the ethnographer is able to access those people who are highly regarded and who have very good knowledge of cultural practices in the community. The people selected through snowball sampling constitute strategic contributors to the research.

There is another form of sampling that is used in ethnographic research. This is referred to as 'critical case sampling'. It relates to the selection of people who are seen as repositories of knowledge and information about community cultural and traditional practices. Patton (1990, p. 174) states that hints about the existence of a critical case could be located in an account by community members that suggests that 'if that group is having problems, then we can be sure all the groups are having problems'. As shown in the two examples discussed here, selection of a sample in ethnographic research can be wholly purposive. However, deliberate selection of a sample does not mean that the research participants are not representatives of their community. As long as the people selected are seen as knowledgeable about community practices, they should be regarded as genuine representatives of their community for this reason.

Despite its usefulness in ethnographic research, snowball sampling is not without problems. Small (2009, p. 14) states that one downside of snowballing is that 'the final interviewees are more likely to know one another than would be the case had they been selected at random'. The implication is that the respondents or interviewees selected are more likely to belong to the same network or group.

However, Small (2009) challenges the argument, pointing out that there is bias both in interviewing respondents selected through snowball sampling and in interviewing the sample selected through random process. While the sample selected through snowballing has a problem of bias in that the interviewees could belong to the same network or group, similarly the sample selected through a random process could be too small owing to unwillingness by community members to agree to participate or respond to the interview questions. As he puts it, 'What proponents of the random selection approach to small-n in-depth interviewing rarely mention is that many people who are cold-called will not agree to long, in-depth interviews on personal topics with a stranger. This often buried detail – how many people refused, hung up, or were not home? – is critical' (Small, 2009, p. 14). He states that sampling is more valuable when questions are asked about a population. Similarly, case study is more valuable or powerful when questions are asked about practices undiscovered before the commencement of the study.

Sample size

The literature on ethnographic research regards sample size as a contentious issue. Nevertheless, the literature states that it is worthwhile for the researcher to select the sample size that will provide insights into the key issues being investigated in a study. Patton (1990, p. 185) believes that the reliability and value of ethnographic research has 'more to do with the information-richness of the cases selected and the observational and analytical capabilities of the researcher than with sample size'. Additionally, the purpose of the study should determine the size of the sample to be selected. What is vital is for the ethnographer to select 'information-rich' cases that are important to the research. Once a resolution has been reached about a sample size, the researcher must indicate the number of interviewees selected, the procedure that informed the selection and the reasons for choosing that sample size.

Document analysis

Documents constitute an important part of ethnographic research. In the digital age, documents are no longer restricted to hard copies or printed papers. There are also electronic documents that are available online, in recognition of the changing nature of ethnographic research that has been spawned by transformations in technologies and computer-mediated communication. Whether in electronic or printed form, documents are considered legitimate ethnographic data. Documents are useful because they help us to understand events that occurred in a particular community in the past. They also provide insights into what is likely to happen in the coming years or decades. Regardless of their value in research, Glaser and Strauss (1967, p. 180) note one key weakness in using documents to analyse social groups: 'some groups or institutions evolve and disappear without leaving much, if any, documentary trace'. This is true especially in societies in which verbal communication is the main form of interaction and exchange of ideas.

In his classic and widely cited work relating to oral societies, Ong (1982) argues that there is less stress placed on writing but more emphasis on oral communication of messages. These oral varieties of communication can be in the form of metaphors, proverbs, parables and idioms that enable the people to make sense of their social world. As he puts it, 'In an oral culture, knowledge, once acquired, had to be constantly repeated or it would be lost: fixed, formulaic thought patterns were essential for wisdom and effective administration' (Ong, 1982, p. 24). Historical documents are also likely to contain the personal biases of authors of the documents. Nevertheless, historical documents remain relevant in ethnographic studies because they help researchers to unpack and understand past and present practices in various societies.

Data reliability and validity

Ethnography is often viewed with suspicion, particularly by positivist researchers who feel that ethnographic research procedures lack reliability and validity. That is not the case. There are different ways that ethnographers demonstrate reliability and validity in their research. One of their strategies is the use of various methods to collect data. For example, ethnographers who collect data through interviews, focus groups and participant observations can undertake cross-validity checks of these methods against one another to ensure the data collected are accurate and unprejudiced. In other words, the ethnographer can cross-validate interview data against participant observation data or data collected through documents. Another way that reliability and validity can be demonstrated in ethnographic research is ensuring that interviews are audio or video recorded. This ensures that other researchers can access the audio or video tape to verify the accuracy of the research report. It is also recommended that the ethnographer's field notes and observations should be submitted to community members for confirmation of accuracy of the record.

Data analysis techniques

In ethnography, the researcher not only collects data but also provides rich descriptions that help us to understand the characteristics of the researched group, community or organisation, as well as their cultural practices. In this way, description becomes a vital tool of ethnography. Ethnographic descriptions must be based on clear and meaningful interpretations. Interpretation requires providing meanings and insights into the findings, providing detailed explanations, making inferences and drawing conclusions, as well as dealing with conflicting evidence (Patton, 1990). Ethnographers also use other tools for analysis of data, such as themes that emerge in the data. Other tools of analysis include metaphors, photos, maps, illustrations, proverbs and triangulation.

Ethnographic researchers use inductive methods to analyse data – that is, they examine data to determine and to classify themes and trends that are evident in the data. In this regard, reflexivity is seen as a major aspect of ethnographic research because the researcher interacts with participants and groups and observes ethical protocols that underpin their relationship with the groups (Reeves et al., 2008). Ethnographic data analysis requires the researcher to use 'thick' or in-depth description to present personal observations and the results of numerous interviews with sources. As part of data analysis, ethnographers engage in triangulation to cross-validate, for example, data generated through participant observations with interview data. This is designed to improve the quality and reliability of the data collected. It is necessary, as what people tell the researcher about their practices during interviews might differ from their actual practices. This is why it is highly recommended that ethnographic researchers should complement personal interviews with participant observations.

Unit of analysis

In analysing ethnographic data, it is important to define the unit of analysis. If, for example, the ethnographer is researching the impact of age and educational status on an African community member's ability to adopt new technologies, the unit of analysis should be defined as the individual respondent and his or her relationship with new technologies. The relationship could be established through in-depth interviews, focus groups and participant observations. A collective portrait of each village or community should be provided to facilitate potential inferences or assessments.

In analysing interview data, the ethnographer must adopt a systematic and gradual process. First, the interview responses should be converted into coded categories. Thereafter, the researcher should group the responses into cases that are similar and those that are strikingly different. This categorisation should be based on the extent to which the interview responses are distinctive or similar. Those responses that are not within the coded categories should be written out into descriptive accounts with the aim of identifying themes, patterns or trends in order to determine the factors that inform willingness to adopt new technologies or factors that inform resistance to technology. The ethnographer could also use simple statistics such as frequency counts, mean and standard deviation to describe the interview data. It may not be necessary, however, for the ethnographer to undertake higher levels of statistical analysis such as chi-square, factor analysis or correlation analysis, as the research is purely qualitative.

Field notes and participant observations should be analysed principally through thick descriptions and interpretations (Denzin, 1989). This requires the ethnographer to provide detailed description of his or her observations. The researcher should undertake cross-validity checks of the specific methods used to collect data. This is where triangulation is required. The next section therefore discusses triangulation of ethnographic data.

Triangulation

In ethnographic research, 'triangulation of different research methods is a valuable means of developing rich accounts of social life and supplementing, for example, broad quantitative accounts with deep qualitative ones' (Plows, 2008, p. 1527). Triangulation involves the combination of different methods for purposes of verification. By using different methods for analysis, each method therefore serves as a complement to others. Denzin (1978) presents four types of triangulation that are regarded as valuable in verifying and validating qualitative data. The triangulation methods are:

- Methods triangulation, which is used to examine the consistency of results obtained through different data collection methods;
- Triangulation of sources, which involves finding out the consistency of different data sources within a particular method;

- Analyst triangulation, which means using many analysts to review results; and
- Theory triangulation, which involves using multiple perspectives to interpret data.

Ethical challenges in traditional ethnography

There are ethical challenges that confront researchers who undertake participant observation. The first concerns the amount of information the researcher should disclose about themselves and what it is they are doing. Mack et al. (2005) advise that the researcher should be careful when disclosing information about who they are and what they are doing. Essentially, the researcher should be clear enough to allay the participants' worry that the researcher's presence might undermine their confidentiality. It all depends on the circumstances. In some situations, the researcher might see no sense in informing the participants about the researcher's presence. In some other situations, it might be sensible for the researcher to identify himself or herself and the reason for their presence. 'You should never be secretive or deliberately misleading about the research project or your role in it. If someone asks directly what you are doing, always provide a truthful response, using your judgment to gauge how exactly to handle a given situation' (Mack et al., 2005, p. 17).

With regard to confidentiality of the research participants, the researcher is advised to safeguard the privacy and identities of the research participants. For example, when the researcher is recording or documenting information, care must be taken to avoid recording information that might identify the research participants either through their names or their residential addresses. Protecting the identities of research participants also includes not disclosing information that will allow anyone to infer the identities of the participants (Mack et al., 2005). Other categories of activities that should be observed during participant observation include: appearance (such as clothes, gender and physical appearance); verbal behaviour (such as forms of communication – who speaks, for how long and to whom, the languages used in conversation, tone of voice, who starts the conversation, etc.); physical behaviour (activities that people engage in, who performs what role, who interrelates with whom, who is isolated, etc.); personal space (the space people maintain when communicating or sitting together); and so on (Mack et al., 2005).

Cultural sensitivity and ethical protocols are at the centre of ethnographic research. They are also important in other forms of research. Bostock (1997), among other researchers, has addressed these issues. The literature on ethnographic research identifies a number of ethical guidelines for ethnographic research. These include: the researcher should validate his or her field notes by submitting the notes to community elders for approval; and the researcher should respect the sensitivity of the people, group or community from which data was collected. In some communities, it is important that the ethnographer should make contact with local leaders to seek clarification about the protocols that researchers have to observe before, during and after the study.

In some Indigenous communities in Australia, Canada and New Zealand, researchers are required to receive prior approval before they can enter the communities for research purposes. This is to ensure, for example, that community rules governing sacred sites are not violated. This is why researchers are required to recognise and respect all protocols relating to proper conduct within the research sites. Sometimes it is valuable to engage the services of a local community member as a research assistant. Not only will the person have good knowledge of community rules and practices but also the presence of the local person serving as research assistant helps to create confidence in community members that the research will be useful to their community. Sharing the outcomes of the research with community members is another important way the researcher can show respect and appreciation to the community, and also demonstrate how the study has made important contributions to knowledge of the community.

Having examined issues involved in conducting ethnographic research in the natural world, the next section discusses the newer form of ethnography – online ethnography or netnography. Following that discussion will be an examination of the ethical challenges that confront ethnographers who conduct research in the online world.

Ethnography in an online environment

While ethnography is recognised as a valid tool of research, there is also growing recognition and awareness that online ethnography is as important as the traditional forms of ethnography otherwise known as 'offline' ethnography. Online ethnography has been described as 'netnography' by researchers such as Kozinets (2010). Kozinets (2002, p. 2) defines netnography or ethnography on the Internet as 'a new qualitative research methodology that adapts ethnographic research techniques to the study of cultures and communities emerging through computer-mediated communications'. Online ethnography recognises that human interaction and social worlds extend also to computer-mediated communication environments such as the Internet, email, chat rooms, instant messaging, online discussion forums and groups, social media (e.g., Facebook, Twitter, YouTube), new media and other digital technologies. Essentially, people live lives in the online world as they do in our everyday world.

Researchers such as Garcia, Standlee, Bechkoff and Cui (2009) and Hallet and Barber (2014) have observed that many ethnographers tend to overlook the significance of online spaces in the daily lives of people they study. Hallet and Barber (2014) state quite categorically that studying people in their natural environment should also include their online world. One suggestion they offer is for ethnographic researchers to consider how physical connections people have may coincide with their online relationships. According to them, 'studying a group in their "natural habitat" now includes their "online habitat"' (Hallet and Barber, 2014, p. 306) because people occupy both online and natural spaces and it is important that ethnographic researchers should study people in their physical spaces as well as in their online world. Ethnographers should reflect on the values of studying people in their digital spaces just like the traditional way of studying people in their natural environment. Hallet and Barber (2014) make the point that a majority of ethnographers in the 21st century frequently ignore the significance of the online world, which could enhance knowledge and understanding of the people they study. They argue:

> it is no longer imaginable to conduct ethnography without considering online spaces...Online spaces no longer rest at the periphery of life, but are central to and have fundamentally transformed the ways people around the world go about their daily business. Emails, instant-messaging, and Facebook posts replace handwritten letters. Blogs and websites have become more common sources of information than printed magazines and newspapers. Twitter allows people to post instantaneous and seemingly mundane updates about life. These spaces have also become sources of global news and political organization.
>
> (Hallet and Barber, 2014, p. 307)

Computer-mediated communication facilitates easier and more rapid communication with many people. Modern technologies provide people with the tools to construct their identities and communities. Online spaces affect how people live their lives and this means that researchers should also examine people's social life in the online world. Garcia et al. (2009) reviewed approaches to conducting ethnographic research in an online world, including the challenges that online research poses. This differs, for example, from the traditional ethnographic research in which the researcher conducts participant observation through physical observation of the participants.

Garcia et al. (2009) note the differences between 'offline' (traditional) and online ethnographic research procedures and protocols. For instance, while participant observation is one of the key methods adopted in traditional ethnographic research, online ethnography does not permit researchers to engage in direct observation of research participants. Sometimes the interaction between the online researcher and participants can be anonymous. In online ethnography, direct relationship between researchers and participants is substituted by textual data on computers, including 'visual, aural, and kinetic components' (Garcia et al., 2009, p. 52). In this context, ethnographic researchers, whether involved in offline or online research, must recognise and include the Internet and aspects of computer-mediated communication in their research in order to sufficiently capture the social world of participants in modern society. This implies that ethnographic researchers must change their research methods to reflect changes in a globalised world. Garcia et al. (2009) cite three reasons for their recommendation.

First, online ethnographic researchers recognise that they cannot physically interact with their research participants; their interpersonal and professional skills will not apply in terms of helping the researchers to gain access to and understand the multiple realities that exist in the world. This means that ethnographic researchers should acquire skills in examination of textual and visual data. Second, owing to lack of physical interaction between the researcher and the research participants in an online world, ethnographic researchers are encouraged to master how to coordinate their identity and their self in visual and textual media through communication channels such as email, chat and instant messaging. Third, ethical issues emerge as a result of the lack of clarity between the private and the public in an online environment. One challenge is how the researcher should protect privacy and confidentiality. This is crucial because online situations are significantly different from face-to-face situations, particularly where the research has been designed and planned with the offline context in mind (Garcia et al., 2009, p. 25).

Despite growing scholarly attention to online ethnography, there remain questions about the boundary between the virtual world and the 'real world' with regard to the research setting. Garcia et al. (2009, p. 54) insist that regardless of the differences, 'there is one social world which contains both traditional and technologically advanced modes of communication and sites of social activity.…' As they put it, the virtual world is not quite distinct from other features of human activity but is a part of that human world. As the online ethnographic researcher can only connect with and access their research participants through computer-mediated communication channels, it is imperative that the researcher should examine the social world of the participants by investigating their online conduct (Garcia et al., 2009, p. 55). One reason why online ethnographers should incorporate computer-mediated communication in the definition of the research setting or site is that most of the communication that used to be conducted through face-to-face means is also conducted electronically in offices, organisations or institutions. For example, anyone who wants to understand how work is performed in an organisation cannot overlook email messages, mobile phones and the organisation's intranet (Garcia et al., 2009).

There is no doubt that technological transformations have affected the way researchers conduct ethnographic enquiry. There is growing recognition that our natural environment has been significantly affected by computer-mediated communication channels. For this reason, researchers have realised they cannot understand all the factors that affect human behaviour and the construction of the social world without incorporating people's social interactions on the Internet and other activities that take place in their technological world. Kozinets (2009, p. 1) uses the term 'netnography' to refer to a unique type of ethnography that is tailored to understand the various kinds of interactions that people have in their technologically mediated world. Netnography therefore refers to an ethnographic method that pertains to the analysis of online cultures and communities (Kozinets, 2009).

Increasing recognition of the impact of new technologies on human societies has spawned this new form of ethnographic research designed to study and understand human interactions in the online world. As Kozinets explains, 'Online connections and alignments are increasingly affecting our social behaviour as citizens, as consumers, as friends and family, and as social beings' (2009, p. 13). Membership of online communities has become a major preoccupation of many people. Kozinets argues that membership of online communities is important to those who belong to the communities.

As more people use the Internet, they use it as a highly sophisticated communications device that enables and empowers the formation of communities. These communities, like the Internet itself, are being found by many to be indispensable. They are becoming 'places' of belonging, information, and emotional support that people cannot do without. Chatting and checking with one's fellow online community members before a purchase, a doctor's visit, a parenting decision, a political rally, or a television show is becoming second nature. Online communities are not virtual. The people that we meet online are not virtual. They are real communities populated with real people, which is why so many end up meeting in the flesh. The topics that we talk about in online communities are important topics, . . .

(Kozinets, 2009, p. 15)

To understand our social and cultural worlds, researchers are now focusing on the impact of computer-mediated communication on our social life. As Garcia et al. (2009) argue, Kozinets (2009) has also given an unequivocal denial to the question about whether there is a difference between people's online social life and their natural social world. He says the two worlds have fused into one, 'the world of real life, as people live it. It is a world that includes the use of technology to communicate, to commune, to socialize, to express, and to understand' (Kozinets, 2009, p. 2). To buttress his argument, he states that no one can present a detailed ethnography of the work life of doctors or lawyers without referring to and examining the contents of online discussion, electronic mail, instant messages and the groups' websites. Similarly, we cannot understand the social world of youths or teenagers without referring to and analysing their mobile phone ownership patterns and communication, SMS text messaging, electronic mail and social networking sites (Kozinets, 2009). This explains why netnography is designed to assist researchers to examine and understand not just 'forums, chat, and newsgroups but also blogs, audiovisual, photographic, and podcasting communities, virtual worlds, networked game players, mobile communities, and social networking sites' (Kozinets, 2009, p. 3).

Kozinets presents three ways that traditional ethnography differs from netnography. In the first instance, the process of going into the online culture or community is different. With regard to accessibility and method, netnography differs from a face-to-face approach. Also, participation in person carries a different meaning from online participation. The same applies to the concept of 'observation'. In the second place, there are novel challenges and opportunities that confront the researcher in the process of gathering cultural data and examining them. The quantity of data collected through netnography also varies.

Similarly, the fact that the data collected in netnography is in digital form ultimately changes the processes of analysis and the tools used to analyse the data. Also, data can be handled differently. In the third instance, 'there are few, if any, ethical procedures for in-person fieldwork that translate easily to the online medium. The abstract guidelines of informed consent are open to wide degrees of interpretation' (Kozinets, 2009, p. 5).

Lyman and Wakeford (1999) identify seven ways in which researchers are grappling with gathering and analysing data through new digital and networked technologies. These include but are not limited to: locating the boundaries and networks in the interconnections between the cyberspace and other platforms; framing identity in unknown and 'pseudononymous' social worlds; comprehending how a feeling of place is framed online and offline; seeing technological objects as creations as well as belongings; and 'using technology to study technology' (Lyman and Wakeford, 1999, p. 361).

In relation to differences in interviews conducted by netnographers and those conducted by traditional ethnographers, Kozinets (1998) identifies some important variations. Netnographic interviews vary from ethnographic interviews in that, in netnography, the interviews appear to be already written down and thus are not susceptible to the uncertainties of memory. Bartl (2009) says that one of the main strengths of netnography is the ability to collect impartial information that has not been sorted or filtered from very experienced users. Kozinets (2002, p. 1) also says that netnography is 'faster, simpler, less expensive than traditional ethnography, and more naturalistic and unobtrusive than focus groups or interviews'. However, netnography has some limitations. One of them is its narrow emphasis on online communities, the requirement that the researcher must possess interpretation skills and 'the lack of informant identifiers present in the online context that leads to difficulty generalizing results to groups outside the online community sample' (Kozinets, 2002, p. 3).

Developing and maintaining relationships in the online world has also resulted in development of new online language. Hallet and Barber (2014, p. 309) cite examples such as people saying 'Facebook me about the party this weekend'. People also 'friend' and 'unfriend' one another in their online world. According to them, 'People incorporate these acronyms into everyday verbiage as well as electronic conversations, revealing the extent to which online and offline worlds overlap. Language continues to develop in order to provide words capable of explaining how digital spaces influence life' (Hallet and Barber, 2014,

p. 310). It is not only languages that are emerging as a result of interactions in people's online world. Social behaviours are also changing, such as people feeling nervous or concerned when they misplace or lose their mobile phones or when they lose connectivity to the Internet (Hallet and Barber, 2014).

There are other ways that online spaces affect people's physical lives. One example is when business organisations use computer-mediated communication to link up with their likely clients through the use of 'pop-up ads, email campaigns, and company websites to reach geographically distant individuals' (Hallet and Barber, 2014, p. 311). For these reasons, Hallet and Barber (2014, p. 313) suggest that 'Understanding contemporary cultures requires acknowledging, respecting, and studying the multiple overlapping spaces where people spend time.' Thus, the use of conventional ethnographic methods to understand the social world of people is now seen as insufficient as people differ when they are in online spaces (Hallet and Barber, 2014).

Despite the usefulness of online ethnography, it should not be assumed that, in a digital world, everyone has access to new technologies. That is not the case, particularly in developing countries where a whole range of factors define and determine those who have access to technologies and those who lack access.

Interviewing in online ethnography

There are various forms of interviewing strategies available to online ethnographic researchers. These include online and offline interviews. Which option is used depends on the purpose of the research. Traditional interviewing methods allow the ethnographic researcher to cross-check data collected online. Similarly, offline interviews help to identify gaps in online data gathering. They also help to clear uncertainties. Online interviews can be constructed in different ways from interviews conducted face-to-face.

It has been argued that online interview data may be more truthful than those collected through offline interviews. In an online interview setting, respondents might feel more free to ask researchers questions than they would in a face-to-face situation (Garcia et al., 2009). In the electronic environment, there are opportunities to conduct research through videoconferencing or by web cameras. Similar problems confront traditional and online ethnographic researchers with regard to gaining access to the research environment, developing a bond with research participants and recruiting volunteers for interviews. In an online setting, the means of gaining access vary because ethnographers cannot depend on their physical presence, appearance or communication style to assist them to gain access. In online research, members of some communities may resist requests or attempts to study them. This may or may not be the case with research participants in a face-to-face situation.

Online observations

Among the textual data readily accessible to online ethnographers are email messages, chat room communication, online sites and other computer-mediated communication channels (Garcia et al., 2009). For example, a researcher investigating emotions or feelings expressed in email communication might look at emoticons which could reveal aspects of the person's identity and personal relationships, including how they present their self, how they describe and view the world (Garcia et al., 2009). However, the point has been made that it is dangerous to draw conclusions about research participants on the basis of how they use emoticons, their method of communication, their writing capabilities, or how they spell words (Garcia et al., 2009; Markham, 2004).

Garcia et al. (2009) provide one important clarification about what observation entails in online research. In their view, 'Observation in online research involves watching text and images on a computer screen rather than watching people in offline settings. However, the technologically mediated environment still provides direct contact with the social world the ethnographer is studying, since participants in that setting communicate through online behavior' (Garcia et al., 2009, p. 58). They distinguish between observation in the online world and observation in an offline environment.

Observation in offline ethnography requires the researcher to be physically present while in the online environment observation can take place discreetly. They use the term 'lurking' to describe one example of a way that a researcher can undertake observation online. They also point out that in some instances, the researcher can engage in 'lurking' without being detected. However, in other contexts, the researcher's presence may be detected but his or her identity may not be easily revealed.

Ethical challenges of researching the online world

Garcia et al. (2009, p. 57) suggest that the approaches adopted in 'offline' participant observation should be modified in an online ethnographic research setting. The suggestion is based on a number of factors. The first is that, as the online ethnographer is unable to physically observe the research participants, it is imperative that the strategies of observation should change. The second factor is that the approaches to field notes and how the results are reported should also change, because of the new ways of recording events with technologies, new methods of interaction between the researcher and the participants, and new research settings. The third is that, as online data consist mostly of textual and visual information, a different set of abilities will be required to make sense of the data and to interpret them. The fourth reason is that current forms of ethnography tend to favour materials that are text-based over visual material. The fifth factor is that there is little research on use of sound and movement on the web (Garcia et al., 2009). Hallet and Barber (2014) also note the ethical challenges that confront online ethnographers, such as issues relating to privacy in social media and how to receive approval from people in distant locations, as well as anonymity or secrecy.

Lurking in online ethnography raises a number of ethical problems. While some researchers find it useful to start observation by lurking, others find it unacceptable. Reference is made to Kozinets and Handelman (1998), who lurked in order to gather data about the conduct of consumers refusing to purchase goods. Kozinets and Handelman used the information they collected to construct interview questions (Garcia et al., 2009). Researchers opposed to lurking as a strategy for collecting observation data in online research argue that it should not be regarded as a form of participation as it is one-directional and does not yield as good results as interactive participation does. Some researchers argue that lurking may jeopardise research participants' privacy and secrecy and could disrupt natural behaviour of the participants (e.g., Soukup, 1999). LeBesco (2004) reports that in her own research, participants believed they were spied on when she lurked. Whatever happens, it would be helpful if researchers who lurked exhibited cultural sensitivity and knowledge of the cultural norms of the research participants. While some site users will not mind if researchers are lurking, others vigorously object to the practice. Garcia et al. (2009) advise ethnographers to endeavour to experience the online site in the same way that authentic participants regularly feel it.

One of the challenges that confront both online and offline ethnographers relates to how they should present observation data and field notes to the readers, especially as there is a belief among research participants and other members of society that online contact and exchanges are not quite authentic. Garcia et al. (2009, p. 65) argue that 'Because of the multimodal nature of online communication, ethnographers often find themselves trying to describe visual, aural, and kinetic observational data in verbal form.' Overall, they state that online ethnographic researchers must discover how to conduct participant observation without being physically present at the site. They must also understand how to build up new capabilities and processes for data collection and analysis, documenting their field notes and presenting the outcomes of their study. This is based on the understanding that existing online ethnographic research leans toward use of textual data and fails to sufficiently incorporate visual, aural and kinetic material (Garcia et al., 2009).

Another challenge that confronts online ethnographers is how to confirm the identity of the research participants. Owing to anonymity that the Internet provides to everybody, it is easy for research participants to hide their true identity. In this context, 'anonymity makes it difficult for researchers to verify information about participants' (Garcia et al., 2009, p. 68). To overcome this problem, Garcia et al. (2009, p. 77) suggest that 'the ethnographer must have an understanding of how the technology operates to be aware of all of the potential threats to privacy and anonymity'. Nevertheless, the data generated online could still be valuable to ethnographers, regardless of the difficulty of verifying the authenticity of the research participants.

Conclusion

This chapter examined systematically the ethnographic research methods of social inquiry. Ethnography as one of the strategies of qualitative research was analysed. Specific ethnographic methods of research such as participant observations, interviews and document analysis that also embraces print and digitally stored documents were examined. The disadvantages of ethnography were outlined, including ethical challenges that confront ethnographers. There is growing recognition that online spaces facilitated by computer-mediated communication constitute an important part of our social life and therefore should be incorporated into contemporary ethnographic research.

While traditional forms of ethnographic research that seek to understand the social world of research participants continue to be used, more scholars are integrating into their study other digital forms of human interaction such as email, chat rooms, instant messaging, blogging and online discussion forums. These online spaces offer as much insight into the social world of research participants as studies of the natural world of research participants do. Although online ethnography or netnography is beginning to gain popularity among ethnographers, there are ethical challenges that arise as a result of conducting online research. Netnography also has its drawbacks, just as traditional ethnographic research has. Despite these drawbacks, online ethnography is gaining more recognition among ethnographic researchers.

9
Mobile Phones Transforming Public Communication in Africa

Introduction

The introduction of mobile phones in Africa is having a profound impact on modes of communication and how people interact. Mobile phones are transforming not only the way African people communicate but also the way they do business, the way teachers and students interrelate and the way news and entertainment are disseminated. Mobile phones have reduced or removed the physical distance between people who reside in rural and remote communities and those who live in cities. Part of the reason why mobile phones have been adopted in Africa is because the technology has many communication benefits. Indeed, mobile phones have filled a niche in people's lives. This chapter analyses the everyday uses of mobile phones in different contexts by men and women, teenagers and adults, as well as urban and rural residents in Africa and other developing regions of the world. The chapter examines how mobile phones contribute to economic development and the factors that drive the uptake of mobile phones, as well as the various challenges that they have brought to people in Africa.

Kelly (2004) states that the unprecedented growth of the mobile phone in Africa demonstrates the usefulness of mobile technology and its capacity to transform the social world of the people, including their economic, political and cultural activities. He observes that 'After years of being an ICT laggard relative to other developing regions of the world, mobile communications have pushed Africa to the forefront in a new information revolution.' This positive assessment reflects the impressive adoption rate of mobile technology in Africa. Bailard (2009, p. 334) reports that one immediate consequence of the uptake of mobile phones in Africa is that 'buyers and sellers can now connect more readily, creating more efficient markets. Small business owners and individual vendors are also now less dependent on middlemen, reducing their susceptibility to extortion or simply bad information.' While some studies assert that mobile phones have helped Africans to enhance productivity (e.g., Donner, 2008), other studies found that mobile phones have helped people to find work (e.g., Samuel, Shah and Hadingham, 2005).

Growth of mobile phones in Africa

The International Telecommunication Union (ITU) predicts that by the end of 2014, the mobile-cellular penetration rate in Africa will reach 69 per cent (ITU, 2014, p. 3). Africa and the Asia Pacific region are projected as the regions with 'the strongest mobile-cellular growth (and the lowest penetration rates)' (ITU, 2014, p. 3). Tortora and Rheault (2011) cite a GALLUP study showing that 57 per cent of the adult population (more than an estimated 151 million people) surveyed in 17 sub-Saharan African countries in 2010 have mobile phones. 'The percentage of adults with mobile phones ranges from a high of 84% in South Africa to a low of 16% in Central African Republic, signaling the potential for tremendous growth in the industry on the sub-continent.' The study showed that Nigeria was the country with the second highest adult population that had mobile phones (71 per cent) and Botswana was third with 62 per cent. Despite the impressive figures in sub-Saharan Africa, the GALLUP report notes that 'penetration still remains relatively low in several countries where adoption rates have been more sluggish, including Burkina Faso (19%), Niger (18%), and the Central African Republic (16%)' (Tortora and Rheault, 2011).

Independent research and consultancy company BuddeComm (2014), which focuses on the 'telecommunications market and its role within the digital economy', reports that 'Nigeria is Africa's largest mobile market with more than 125 million subscribers and a market penetration of around 75% in early 2014.' However, that achievement has come at a cost, such as 'problems with network congestion and quality of service'. These problems have compelled the national regulatory authority, the National Communications Commission (NCC), to enforce penalties against network operators.

The growth of mobile phones in Africa has surpassed all predictions. According to Chéneau-Loquay (2010, p. 1), 'From 51.4 million in 2003, the number of subscribers grew to 264.5 million in 2007 and 375 million by the end of 2008, seven times the growth seen in fixed telephone lines.' This report, which was prepared for the ITU and the French

Ministry of Foreign and European Affairs, shows that the number of telephones rose from 4.19 per 100 people in 2002 to 27.5 in 2007 and 32 per 100 people in 2008. This makes Africa the continent with the fastest rate of growth of mobile phone in the world, namely 77 per cent between 2005 and 2006 (Chéneau-Loquay, 2010). However, the report also shows that, within Africa, inequalities exist owing to variations in penetration rates. For example, while Gabon has 90 phones per 100 inhabitants, Ethiopia has a poor penetration rate of fewer than two phones per 100 people as of 2008. The figures should be treated with caution, though, because one person could own more than one phone while another person could share one phone with their family members (Chéneau-Loquay, 2010).

One implication of the rapid growth of mobile phones in Africa is that they are definitely not a tool accessible only to the rich and fortunate members of society. Mobile phones are now accessible to both privileged and underprivileged Africans. Obviously mobile phone users understand the usefulness of the technology, which is why demand is growing fast, regardless of the cost. The rapid rise of mobile phones in developing regions of the world must be attributed to factors such as the development of cheaper models that sell for under US$20, a burgeoning and active used-phone market, and the initiative of mobile phone manufacturers and operators who are skilled at producing phones that match the specific needs, services and requirements of each society (Chéneau-Loquay, 2010). Take, for example, the development of the prepaid mobile phone system that is used by about 98 per cent of phone users who buy prepaid cards at a cost of about US$2 in West African countries. This facilitates the 'use of online electronic system of credit transfer from phone to phone' (2010, p. 4). Also, sending text messages has proved to be a more convenient way of sending and receiving information (Chéneau-Loquay, 2010). In West African capital cities, it is possible for mobile phone owners to acquire phones that can take more than one SIM card, thus enabling them to access different rates charged by different telephone operators.

Initially, the introduction of the mobile phone to Africa was slow because telecommunications service providers were not interested in the African market. However, the introduction and rapid adoption of the mobile phone has proved all negative projections wrong. It is no wonder that Africa is now regarded as 'the world's fastest-growing mobile phone market, as the number of subscribers rose from 10 to 647 million from 2000 to 2011, with a 66% growth rate in 2005 alone' (cited in Carmody, 2013, p. 24; see also LaFraniere, 2005; Pierskalla and Hollenbach, 2013).

How did Africa make such a great and impressive leap in the adoption and use of mobile phones? LaFraniere (2005) offers an explanation: 'when African nations began to privatize their telephone monopolies in the mid-1990s, and fiercely competitive operators began to sell air time in smaller, cheaper units, cellphone use exploded'. Nine years ago, it was estimated that one in 11 Africans owned a mobile phone. That estimate must be regarded as obsolete in light of the speed of mobile phone adoption in Africa. The demand for mobile phones was so huge that in 2002 and 2003, telecommunications service providers in Nigeria had to defer the sale of their SIM cards (subscriber identity module cards) to enable them to bolster their networks (LaFraniere, 2005). Even in war-torn Liberia, which is now recovering from 15 years of civil strife, adoption and use of mobile phones is growing at an astonishing rate.

Unlike other studies that found that mobile phones are used predominantly for maintenance of social relations in Africa and the Caribbean (e.g., Carmody, 2013; Kalba, 2008; Laguerre, 2013; Slater and Kwami, 2005), Best, Smyth, Etherton and Wornyo (2010) found in their study of mobile phone use in post-conflict Liberia that security and emergency emerged as the main reasons for the use of mobile phones. As the researchers found, 'the safety and security of self, of loved ones, and of personal property are still a major concern in Liberia' (Best et al., 2010, p. 105). This is not surprising, given the recent history of a long civil war in Liberia.

Pierskalla and Hollenbach (2013) state that with an annual growth rate of about 20 per cent and a projected 732 million subscribers by 2012, Africa is regarded as the largest growing market for mobile phones across the world. In their view, 'What makes Africa special in this context is that cell phones not only provide a new way for communication, but in many areas are the only way for interpersonal, direct communication over distance. Many areas that are now covered by cell phone networks were never connected to land lines' (Pierskalla and Hollenbach, 2013, p. 208; see also Best et al., 2010).

Kalba (2008, p. 632) suggests that mobile phones have grown across the world to the point that they 'have out-diffused virtually every prior technology, whether TV sets, radios, wrist watches, wallets, wireline phones, or bicycles, and have done so in the past 25 years'. He states that in the Democratic Republic of Congo the rate of mobile phone adoption moved from 10,000 fixed phone lines in 2000 to a record figure of close to three million mobile phone subscriptions in 2005. Nigeria recorded an even more stunning achievement, moving from approximately one million fixed phone lines to about 19 million mobile phones. The same pattern has been recreated in other African countries such as Ghana, Kenya, Mali, Angola, Morocco, Tanzania and Uganda (Kalba, 2008). Three reasons have been offered to explain this trend. The first is growing public awareness of the usefulness of mobile phones compared to fixed line telephones. The second is expanding opportunities to make calls through mobile phones. The third is that more fixed telephone lines suggest a stronger network foundation that facilitates the use of mobile networks (Kalba, 2008). Additionally, the growth and popularity of mobile phones in developing countries was made possible by the introduction of prepaid calling cards and SIM cards. Another factor that is often forgotten is the impact of competition on the diffusion of mobile phones (Kalba, 2008).

Experience shows that, in markets that are serviced by a single mobile phone operator, prices are much higher than in markets in which there are multiple operators. This is not surprising. Monopoly breeds high prices. It is a supplier's market in which the supplier is the king or queen. Buyers are at the mercy of the supplier, owing to a lack of alternative goods or products. When there is competition, prices tend to go down and low prices tend to drive demand for mobile phones. However, it is not always the case that competition drives down prices in all markets. Despite widespread optimism about the diffusion of mobile phones across the world, we must never forget that a significant number of people around the world do not yet have access to mobile technologies owing to financial, structural, infrastructural and cultural problems, as well as complex geographical terrains and complications of new technologies.

In Africa, Hahn and Kibora (2008) note that the rise of mobile phone adoption and use in Burkina Faso is much higher than the experience in western countries, which suggests the extent to which mobile phone technology is widely appreciated in that country regardless of the economic conditions of the mobile phone owners and users. For example, research suggests that up to 42 per cent of the population of rural dwellers in Burkina Faso live below the internationally accepted poverty line. It is not only in the urban centres of Africa that mobile phones are booming. Mobile phones are also highly regarded and used in rural areas. The comparative uses and relevance of mobile phones in western and non-western countries have been identified by Hahn and Kibora (2008). For example, while mobile phones are perceived as mere technological tools in western societies, in developing countries mobile phones open up spaces previously unavailable for long distance communication.

Why are mobile phones having a global impact? Hahn and Kibora (2008) offer an explanation. Telecommunications development, in particular the uptake of mobile phones, is regarded as evidence of modernity. Mobile phones enjoy high prestige across cultures because of the role they play in facilitating communication across long distances. This explains why the mobile phone is perceived as a symbol of globalisation, wide-reaching communication and interconnections across borders. 'The ubiquitous presence of the phone, and the constant expectancy of being called up and immediately becoming part of the global communication network, is at the root of the image of this technology as a generally accepted symbol of globalisation' (Hahn and Kibora, 2008, p. 89). Train stations, airports and trade fairs serve as 'spaces of globalisation' where mobile phones are more commonly used (Hahn and Kibora, 2008, p. 89).

The introduction of the mobile phone in Burkina Faso has spawned other businesses associated with the mobile phone. Hahn and Kibora report that young business people from Burkina Faso travel overseas to search for and import cheap handsets. The United Arab Emirates and Dubai serve as sources for cheap new phones that are imported into Burkina Faso. However, France is the source country for low-cost, used and damaged phones that are repaired once they arrive in Burkina Faso. Used phones imported from France are known commonly as 'goodbye France'. Migrant workers and students have helped to sustain the trade in used phones in Burkina Faso (Hahn and Kibora, 2008). The various ways in which mobile phones are used in urban and rural areas of Burkina Faso have been described in detail, including a social practice known as 'flashing', which means calling a number, letting it ring once or twice and hanging up before the intended receiver picks up the call (Hahn and Kibora, 2008, p. 95):

> a friend can be flashed in order to let him know that one has already arrived at the appointed place – yet to be called back is not necessarily expected. An elder brother may flash any of his younger relatives, who must react immediately, because the latter expects to receive some information and, of course, because it is the right of the elder to ask his younger sibling to pay for the call. Whoever receives a flash from his village of origin must react as a matter of urgency by returning the call.
>
> (Hahn and Kibora, 2008, p. 95)

In Burkina Faso, there is a booming business in the sale of calling cards which creates job opportunities for many unemployed youth. Thus, the mobile phone has become an income generating tool that allows unemployed people to earn income to help their poorer parents and relatives (Hahn and Kibora, 2008). The growth of the mobile phone in Burkina Faso has also given rise to a different kind of business in which imported phones are modified and given a new life in the country. Suddenly, a new business line has emerged through the growing involvement of youth in the repair of mobile phones. The motivating force behind the adaptations of the mobile phone is the need to sustain social relations and to communicate with family members and relatives (Hahn and Kibora, 2008).

A study of mobile phones in Ghana shows that the phones are used to maintain social relationships at the family level (Slater and Kwami, 2005). Thus, mobile phones are perceived as tools for sustaining social networks, particularly in situations in which family members are separated by geographic distance (Slater and Kwami, 2005). This is consistent with results of studies conducted in the Caribbean countries of Jamaica, Trinidad and Haiti, as well as studies by Laguerre (2013) and Carmody (2013) which show that mobile phones are used mainly to cultivate social relations such as contacting family members and friends. This implies specifically that in the Caribbean, mobile phones are not used for development purposes. Laguerre (2013) and Carmody (2013) also cite studies which show that people in various parts of the developing world use a good portion of their income to pay for mobile phone services. This relates to how poor people in Tanzania spend up to 22 per cent of their monthly income on mobile phone services (Carmody, 2013).

Usefulness of mobile phones

Research shows different ways that Africans use the mobile phone. In Kenya, for example, the mobile phone service provider has made it possible for phone users to call and for the phone to ring for a long period so that the intended recipient would know that they are expected to return the call. As Chéneau-Loquay (2010, p. 4) argues,

> it is the local context that determines the way in which the telephone is used, and all manner of stratagems are applied to minimize the cost of communications – beeping someone, pooling, making use of SMS in preference to calls, using more than one chip or device – but also to allow the users to identify themselves and help one another.

One example of such practices is the widespread use in Africa of 'beeping' or 'flashing' whereby a call is made solely in order to make the addressee's phone ring, without waiting for a reply or even expecting one. One retailer selling credit in Mali explained that 'beeping' was like tapping someone on the shoulder just to remind him you are friends... In Mali, Senegal or Burkina Faso, a beep sent to someone who is financially better off is often not just a mark of friendship but a request to be called back and thereby avoid the cost of the call.

(Chéneau-Loquay, 2010, pp. 4–5)

Another practice that is common among African mobile phone users is the transfer of phone credit, which has been extended to the transfer of cash from one person to another. Aker and Mbiti (2010) point out that despite low levels of investment in infrastructure, access to and use of mobile phones in sub-Saharan Africa has grown rapidly over the past decades. This rapid growth has generated widespread optimism about the impact of mobile phones on the economic development of Africa. No less a personality than Rwandan President Paul Kagame was reported to have expressed such optimism when he said: 'In 10 short years, what was once an object of luxury and privilege, the mobile phone, has become a basic necessity in Africa' (cited in Aker and Mbiti, 2010, p. 208). As mobile phones are being adopted and used rapidly across Africa, many people regard the telephone as a facilitator of socioeconomic development. The increase in mobile phone adoption and use comes against a backdrop of grinding poverty in parts of Africa, as well as the cost of mobile phone handsets and services (Aker and Mbiti, 2010).

An earlier profile of mobile phone users in Africa shows that they are mostly male, educated, young and wealthy, and they live in urban centres. By 2009, the profile has changed to include more poor people, old people and people who reside in rural areas (Aker and Mbiti, 2010, pp. 212–213). De Silva, Ratnadiwakara and Zainudeen (2011) found in their study that mobile phone adoption was associated with or influenced by perceived benefits of its use. They also found that social influence played a major role in people's decision to adopt mobile phone. They conclude that mobile phones have the potential to extend social services to rural dwellers and disadvantaged groups, thereby helping to address economic deprivation and inequity in society. According to the researchers, 'Mobiles provide a direct channel to provide services (e.g., telemedicine, election information, hazard warnings) directly to BoP-type markets that can further social policy objectives' (de Silva et al., 2011, p. 13). In South Africa, for example, farmers in one region are able to use their phones to learn about current prices of goods. This knowledge empowers them when they negotiate with middlemen and middlewomen (LaFraniere, 2005). Similarly, medical workers in the southeast part of South Africa use the mobile phone to call up ambulances during emergency. LaFraniere (2005) reports how the mobile phone is proving valuable to farmers in rural parts of Africa:

> One woman living on the Congo River, unable even to write her last name, tells customers to call her cellphone if they want to buy the fresh fish she sells. 'She doesn't have electricity, she can't put the fish in the freezer,' said Mr. Nkuli of Vodacom. 'So she keeps them in the river,' tethered live on a string, until a call comes in. Then she retrieves them and readies them for sale.

Donner (2010) cites two instances in which mobile phones are used for money transfer services in Kenya and South Africa. In Kenya, M-PESA has grown so popular that the services are being extended to Tanzania and South Africa. Donner (2010, p. 7) states that

> MPESA allows individuals to cash in (exchange hard currency for electronically stored money linked to their SIM card), transfer funds between users and cash out. Millions use it as a safer, more reliable and lower cost alternative to existing remittance systems, sending money to friends and family throughout the country.

M-PESA is operated by Safaricom, the largest mobile phone service provider in Kenya. In South Africa, there is the MXit, a social networking service that operates in the country. Donner (2010, p. 8) states that MXit 'works on the common "feature" phones in South Africa, with basic Internet access via a GPRS connection and the ability to run mobile Java applications'. The two services are deemed successful because of a number of reasons. According to Donner (2010, p. 8), both M-PESA and MXit have been enormously successful because

> Each presents low barriers to adoption, high observability, easy trialability (low risks and low startup costs), simplicity and high value relative to alternatives. Both take advantage of network effects and become more useful as a higher proportion of a community adopts them ... They are woven into everyday life, because each brings a function taken for granted by the world's 'top billion'.

Ogunlesi (2012) identifies seven ways in which mobile phones have changed African lives. These are:

- through transformations in banking (e.g., the M-PESA mobile money transfer service provided by Safaricom to Kenyans);
- promotion of social activism (e.g., the popular demonstrations or protests that erupted in north Africa and the Arab world in 2011);
- access to formal education and significant changes to Africa's problematic education system; popularisation of entertainment through mobile phones (e.g., in Nigeria, where radio listeners are able to call in and participate in talk shows, as well as downloading and distribution of popular songs, photos and videos);
- using mobile phone disaster management tools that enable displaced people in refugee camps to re-establish links with family members;
- boosting agricultural production and empowering farmers by providing them with valuable information relating to weather and market prices that enables them to make informed decisions resulting in increased production; and
- promoting healthcare through spreading messages relating to improved health and lifestyle forms, and through the use of telemedicine to extend medical services to people in remote and rural areas of Africa where there is no access to modern medical facilities.

Similarly, Etzo and Collender (2010) observe that mobile phones facilitate the collection of health data, support the analysis and treatment of ailments and help to disseminate health related messages to people in rural areas.

> Examples include daily text message reminders sent to tuberculosis patients, and Uganda's Text to Change project, which raises HIV/AIDS awareness via a text message-based quiz. Access to mobile phones has been credited with preventing women dying in childbirth in Amensie, in south-central Ghana, as villagers can now call the ambulance when it is needed.
>
> (Etzo and Collender, 2010, p. 663)

In a study of the role of mobile phones in improvements in rural livelihoods and poverty alleviation in a region of Tanzania, Sife, Kiondo and Lyimo-Macha (2010) found that the most significant benefit of using mobile phones was in the reinforcement and development of social networks such as relationships with friends and relatives. This is consistent with studies by Slater and Kwami (2005), Carmody (2013), Laguerre (2013), Donner (2008), Barendregt (2008), Hahn and Kibora (2008) and Kalba (2008). In their study, Sife et al. (2010) also found that mobile phones enhanced the ability of the people in the region of Tanzania to respond to emergencies.

In his assessment of the value of mobile phones to humanity, welfare economic scholar Amartya Sen (2010) explained how the telephone serves as a liberating tool and a facilitator of communication among people.

> A telephone owned by a person helps others to call the person up, as well as to receive calls from him or her, and so the increased freedom of the phone owner adds to the freedom of others. In contrast, a gun owned by one can easily reduce the freedom of others, if the gun is pointed at them . . . .
>
> (Sen, 2010, p. 1)

In other words, a telephone enhances freedom rather than restricts it. Of course, the telephone can also be used for negative purposes, such as to organise a terrorist action, to infringe on a person's right to privacy and to connive with some other person to commit a crime (Sen, 2010). On the other hand, with specific reference to Mozambique, Aker, Collier and Vincente (2013) found that mobile phones were used to educate voters in order to step up voter participation during elections.

Beyond facilitating communication, the mobile phone, according to Sen (2010), also helps with resistance against repression. From this point of view, the mobile phone can be seen as a tool of emancipation. This is an interesting point. While authoritarian regimes in some countries have tried and to some extent succeeded in shutting down mobile phone towers in order to silence the voices of dissent from radical members of social organisations that campaign for political change and social justice, the mobile phone also serves as an instrument of liberation used by ordinary people to resist repression by despotic rulers. References are often made to the role that mobile phones and other digital technologies play in sustaining popular uprisings against dictatorships in Tunisia, Egypt, Libya, Syria and Yemen. While authoritarian leaders see the mobile phone as a tool of destabilisation because it enables ordinary people to challenge the state (the status quo), ordinary people see the mobile phone as an instrument of liberation.

Pierskalla and Hollenbach (2013) draw on research to provide examples of instances in which mobile phones have assisted in the organisation of protest rallies, such as in China in 1999 when Falun Gong members protested in a government building; in Manilla (Philippines), in 2001; and in Kiev, Ukraine, during the so-called Orange Revolution (Pierskalla and Hollenbach, 2013). While acknowledging that mobile phone technology has been used to organise peaceful protests around the world, Pierskalla and Hollenbach (2013, p. 209) argue that 'improved communication through cell phones can facilitate organization and coordination of groups for the purpose of violent collective action'. With regard to the violence that erupted soon after the 2007 presidential election in Kenya, Zuckerman (2009) notes the double-edged nature of new technologies such as the mobile phone, arguing that the Kenyan experience has shown that the same technologies that were used successfully to report on the post-election violence and to promote peace were also used to instigate violence.

There are other ways that mobile phones have proved beneficial to people. They include improved 'access to health care and health information, particularly among hard-to-reach populations; improved ability to diagnose and track diseases; more timely, actionable public health information; and expanded access to ongoing medical education and training for health workers' (Bravo, Valero and Pau, 2012, p. 207). To illustrate the positive role that mobile phones play in different parts of the world, Sen (2010) cited a poignant example of how the mobile phone helped to change public attitudes to abuses of women by the Taliban in Pakistan's Swat Valley. A young woman who was being beaten by the Taliban was video-recorded by a human rights activist who used his mobile phone to record the incident. The video was circulated to television stations across Pakistan with the support of human rights activists in the country. The Pakistani civil society watched the video in shock. The appalling video compelled newspaper organisations to take a critical position against the Taliban in Pakistan. Within months, public opinion had swelled against the Taliban. The government was also moved by the incident that was captured on video. As Sen (2010, p. 3) observed,

It was no longer easy to ignore what was happening in remote Swat, because the Swat Valley atrocities came home in Punjab, Sind, and elsewhere...The government and the military were able to move against the Pakistani Taliban on the basis of public anger at the activities of the Taliban...The changed perception was all brought about by a mobile phone with the additional capability to photograph and take video. It was the technology that made this exposure possible, and it was another feature of that technology – the combination of a video recorder with a telephone – that made it possible for the courageous human rights activist to catch the picture without being detected by the murderous Taliban.

(Sen, 2010, p. 3)

Impact of mobile phones on economic activities

A study of the impact of mobile phones on the fisheries industry in Kerala, India, found that mobile phone coverage encouraged a major reduction in discrepancies in the prices of fish sold across various markets. It also helped to reduce the waste in fish. This invariably led to improvements in the wellbeing of fish farmers and consumers. A study by Abraham (2007) of the fishing community in Kerala shows that mobile phones enable fish farmers to respond faster to demands, which in turn helps them to avoid wasting a lot of fish. Prior to the adoption of mobile phones, farmers wasted a lot of fish, as fish is a perishable item that cannot be stored overnight in any place other than in cold storage facilities that are not available to impoverished farmers. He also found that mobile phones helped the fish farmers to manage supply and demand, as the free flow of price information enabled them to respond to demands in markets in which there was an undersupply of fish. Mobile phones help to reduce the risk and uncertainty suffered by fish farmers prior to the advent of the technology. A similar experience was reported by Aker (2010), who found that the introduction of mobile phones in the grain market in Niger helped to lower the disparity of grain prices across the market by up to 10 per cent.

In terms of further impact on economic and business activities, research shows that mobile phones enable buyers and sellers to link up, leading to a more economical market. Mobile phones enable small business proprietors to rely less on intermediaries who buy goods from them and sell to retailers, thus eliminating their exposure to extortion or misinformation (Bailard, 2009). Research by Abraham (2007), Jensen (2007) and Samuel, Shah and Hadingham (2005) shows that mobile phones help to reduce inconsistencies in prices of goods; they help the unemployed to find jobs, as well as helping to enhance the wellbeing of product manufacturers and consumers. One advantage of mobile phones to the unemployed is that it enables them to leave their phone numbers with employers rather than waiting endlessly till there is a job vacancy. This also gives them the space to engage in other economic activities while waiting for the outcomes of interviews they attended (Carmody, 2013).

Vincent and Cull (2013) show in their research how mobile phones have aided development in women-led farming cooperatives in Lesotho. In their study, they found that mobile phone adoption and use had tremendous impact on the farmers by increasing their ability to communicate, which also resulted in economic growth. Increased communication helped the women farmers to lower their cost of transactions and at the same time helped them to increase sales. The research found that mobile phone use helped to empower the women in the farming cooperatives. On account of the findings, Vincent and Cull (2013) state that 'The empowerment advantages of having mobiles extend beyond individual feelings of self-esteem and confidence' (2013, p. 43). Ownership and use of mobile phones helped the women to learn the fundamentals of the English language and mathematics because their mobile phones aided in their knowledge of how to count (i.e., to add and subtract) and their ability to understand the guidelines on their mobile phones. The women also felt empowered because of a sense of belonging to a flourishing farming cooperative.

According to Vincent and Cull (2013, p. 43), 'empowerment has resulted from the way mobiles have facilitated access to networks and relevant expertise. Such networks have now been recognized as an asset, that of social capital'. Additionally, mobile phones have empowered the women farmers by making it possible for them to gain access to proper education. Drawing on research evidence, the researchers identify various ways in which female education drives empowerment in developing countries. These include

> knowledge autonomy (women have a wider world view and a greater capacity to question authority), decision-making autonomy (education strengthens women's say in decision making), physical autonomy (educated women have more contact with the outside world and the opportunities it brings), emotional autonomy (women shift their loyalties from extended kin to the conjugal family, and they also have more egalitarian relationships between spouses and between parents and children), and economic and social autonomy and self-reliance (education increases a woman's self-reliance in economic matters and the self-reliance that is required for social acceptance and status...).
> (cited in Vincent and Cull, 2013, p. 44)

Among the various benefits associated with the adoption and use of new information and communication technologies in developing countries are growth in knowledge of market information, enhancement of management of transportation, particularly during emergencies, and improving the efficiency of development action (Martin and Abbott, 2011). In Uganda, which is ranked 156 out of 179 countries in the United Nations Human Development Index, education, spending capacity and income are quite low in a country with a population of about 32 million and an HIV prevalence rate of 5.4 per cent among people aged between 15 and 49. In this situation, agriculture is fundamental to the development of the economy.

In Uganda, over 80 per cent of the working population live below the poverty line (Martin and Abbott, 2011). According to the researchers, mobile phone subscription between 2004 and 2008 rose from 776,200 to more than 8.5 million in Uganda. The literature on mobile phone use for agricultural development shows that mobile phones can support socioeconomic development objectives. Martin and Abbott (2011) report on a study in Kenya which showed how mobile phones were used for the identification and organisation of livestock illnesses and to organise attendance and involvement in organisation meetings. In the study, farmers suggested that mobile phones decreased their transportation costs by allowing them to access information relating to agriculture and support of group members.

In a study of the effects of mobile phones on traders of consumable food in Tanzania, Molony (2008) found that mobile phones did not affect the level of confidence between the traders and the buyers of their products, who also serve as their creditors. This means the traders are powerless to use mobile phones to access information on existing prices offered in the market. This finding is inconsistent with the outcomes of Jensen's (2007) study of the adoption of mobile phones by fish farmers in the Indian state of Kerala. He found that with the mobile phone, a significant number of fish farmers were able to move beyond their market zone to market their fish. The mobile phone also enabled the fish farmers to reduce wastage. In a related study, Aker (2010) found in her study of grain sellers in the Republic of Niger that mobile phones enabled the traders to search for and market their products at lower cost across a number of markets. These studies show how mobile phones enabled traders to determine market prices and the level of demand for their products.

Molony (2008, p. 639) identifies a gap in the studies by Jensen (2007) and Aker (2010) which he said related to lack of 'requisite detail about the shape of interpersonal networks and the resilience of face-to-face communication in the light of these new technologies'. He concludes that his study of the sale of perishable food by traders shows that confidence and the necessity for direct personal contact are a common experience in the way most medium-scale enterprises are conducted in Africa, regardless of the availability of mobile phones. This implies that some traditional features that underpin African business practices will persist, regardless of the introduction of new technologies such as the mobile phone. He also states that the mobile phone rather than the Internet is the most frequently used new technology by traders in Tanzania.

Molony (2008, p. 645) identifies a range of advantages that mobile phones offer to agricultural farmers, such as assisting farmers and buyers to acquire knowledge of demand, and enhancement of buyers' management of supply. Additionally, mobile phones facilitate dependable and much quicker transmission of information, and increase the capacity of traders to monitor or track the movement of goods that are in transit. In Molony's (2008, p. 646) view, mobile phones make possible a reduction in time and money spent on travel, as well as a reduction in risks associated with travel.

> While the cost of making a call using a mobile phone is still high in Tanzania, it is far lower than having no reliable access and having to travel personally to Dar es Salaam, or the risk of sending somebody else to make decisions that could just as easily be made in the village.
>
> (Molony, 2008, p. 646)

Molony (2008) concludes by asserting that mobile phones are becoming a part of Tanzania's agricultural business culture owing to the vital role they play in enhancing the exchange of information relating to supply and demand between farmers and the general market. This information empowers farmers and helps them to avoid sending their produce to the market without knowledge of prices. Subsequently, farmers are able to decide whether they should redirect produce to other markets where they can earn a small profit rather than lose everything in Dar es Salaam.

In terms of healthcare delivery, Aker and Mbiti (2010, p. 222) report how mobile phones are being used in Kenya, Malawi and South Africa to transmit reminders each day to HIV-positive patients in relation to their medication timetable. Mobile phones also allowed community health officials to forward information relating to the status of HIV patients. In general, mobile phones have proved instrumental to the administration of telehealth in remote and rural areas of developed and developing countries. In terms of politics, mobile phones are being used by political candidates during election campaigns to monitor elections and campaigns. Aker and Mbiti (2010) show how mobile phones have been used to promote enlightenment of voters and to engage citizens in monitoring elections. One good example was in Kenya after the 2007 controversial presidential election, in which 'citizen-based monitoring was mapped via a software called "Ushahidi" ("testimony" in Swahili) to allow Kenyans to report post-election unrest via voice, text message, and Internet and to map it, in real time, to the entire world' (Aker and Mbiti, 2010, p. 223).

There is abundant research evidence that mobile phones enhance economic growth in developing countries. In their study of the impact of mobile phones on economic growth in Africa, Waverman, Meschi and Fuss (2005, p. 10) argue that 'Investment in telecoms generates a growth dividend because the spread of telecommunications reduces costs of interaction, expands market boundaries, and enormously expands information flows.' Abraham (2007, p. 15) found in his study of an Indian fishing community that mobile phones help to serve the oral tradition that most community people are comfortable with. Nine years before Abraham's study was published, Obijiofor (1998) had noted that, owing to the high value placed on interpersonal and kin relationships in Africa, the telephone would be easily adopted there because of its ability to promote and sustain interpersonal relationships and also because of the oral nature of communication in Africa. As he argued, 'the telephone will promote orality of communication in Africa and also sustain kinship relationships. With the telephone, information will be diffused faster to greater distances and destinations' (Obijiofor, 1998, p. 458). Nevertheless, Obijiofor notes that the adoption of the telephone as a means of communication in Africa will have consequences for existing sociocultural practices:

> in Africa as in other societies, knowledge is usually associated with power. The greater diffusion of information through the telephone implies that community information will become public knowledge. Local events will be easily diffused and widely reported. The power and influence wielded by the elders, community leaders, and the gongmen will be displaced, in my opinion, by the telephone because the telephone will promote more openness in the dissemination of information. The perception of elders as repositories for knowledge would be untenable as secret knowledge becomes public knowledge.
>
> (Obijiofor, 1998, p. 458)

Some aspects of mobile phone use can have a negative impact on the poor. Carmody (2013, p. 28) points to Tanzania in which 'the poorest 75% of the population who use mobile phones spend an average of 22% of their monthly incomes on them'. This represents evidence of the flow of money from impoverished people to mobile phone companies that are based overseas but have offices in Africa. So, while the mobile phone plays important roles for Africans and people in developing regions by facilitating the transfer of money and mobile banking (Donner and Tellez, 2008), the mobile phone also worsens the level of poverty among the less privileged members of society, as Carmody (2013) showed in Tanzania.

Critique of mobile phone use in Africa

While many scholars celebrate the swift diffusion of mobile phones in Africa, they seem to overlook the problems that hinder efficient use of the mobile phone in some parts of Africa. Among the problems that impede effective use of mobile phones are defective network connectivity and poor quality of service. It is these and other problems that Obijiofor (2008) highlights with regard to telecommunications services provided to Nigerians by a leading service provider in the country. Recalling his experiences in Nigeria, Obijiofor (2008) reports:

> Anyone who was in Nigeria in December 2007 and much of January 2008 would have experienced the worst telecommunications service provided by a company since the introduction of mobile telephony in Nigeria. Here are some of the bizarre experiences. You dial a mobile phone number and the call goes to an unintended receiver. You speak with someone on your mobile phone and you hear other people discussing on the same line. This is not something that is associated with mobile phone business in this age of new technologies.

> With MTN Nigeria, anything is possible. You dial a mobile phone number and before you complete the dialling, one of the following messages flashes across your mobile phone screen: 'Call end. No response'; 'Call end. Dropped'; 'Call end. No answer', etc. Add to these the phenomenon of your receiver's voice dropping off constantly. In the first decade of the 21st century, customers of MTN Nigeria should not have to put up with this nonsense.

Poor telecommunications service delivery is not limited to MTN Nigeria. To overcome the problems of network connectivity and poor service delivery, many Nigerian citizens have opted to own two or more mobile phones. With all the advancements in telecommunications technology, it must seem absurd that poor service delivery and connectivity problems have hindered mobile phone subscribers in Nigeria from harnessing the benefits associated with mobile telephony.

Despite the growing climate of optimism and enthusiasm about the impact of mobile phones on Africa's socioeconomic development, Wasserman (2010) argues that much of the discussion on the impact of mobile phones in Africa seems to be based on the old linear model of communication for development that presented technology as a modernising tool that would transform Africa. He argues that attention ought to be devoted to the ways in which mobile phone technologies are domesticated by Africans (Wasserman, 2010, p. 9). In his view, 'mobile phones do pose new opportunities and challenges to democratic life in Africa. At the same time these technologies are taken up by people, in a varied, heterogeneous African context that in many ways is dissimilar from contexts in the developed world' (2010, p. 9). Wasserman contends that statistics on mobile phone penetration in Africa and the projected future growth of the continent's economy as a result of mobile phone uptake do not provide insights into how users engage with mobile phones in their daily lives.

While Wasserman's critique is valid to some extent, it must be stressed that there are studies that examine specifically how Africans use mobile phones for improvements in their socioeconomic conditions (examples include Aker, 2010; Aker and Mbiti, 2010; Burrell, 2010; Carmody, 2013; Chéneau-Loquay, 2010; Hahn and Kibora, 2008; Martin and Abbott, 2011).

While mobile phone diffusion and use across Africa has been acknowledged, and while mobile phones continue to stimulate the socioeconomic development of Africa even in areas where Internet access is restricted, debate persists about the use of mobile phones for political activism in Africa. Zuckerman (2010), for example, argues that while the economic advantages of mobile phones should not be discounted and indeed should be encouraged, there may well be inherent flaws in using mobile phones 'as a platform for activism and political speech, as well as for future technical innovation' (Zuckerman, 2010, p. 100). He states that, as mobile phone networks are generally centralised in many developing countries, they are easier and more susceptible to control by governments. He cites an example in Ethiopia in which the government switched off SMS services in June 2005 following worries that students were mobilising to protest against falsified election results (Zuckerman,

2010, p. 101). In contrast, SMS text messages were used in Kenya to stage protests and to fan inter-ethnic hatred following the contested presidential election results of 2007. Days after the electoral commission pronounced the sitting president the winner of the election, mobile phone operators disabled SMS services to prevent rapid transmission of hateful messages to a large segment of the population. Zuckerman argues that while switching off SMS services may have been a smart and laudable move by mobile phone operators in Kenya, the action deprived the opposition of an important tool it could have used to organise political protests (Zuckerman, 2010). He also raised another problem that has emerged with the advent of mobile phones.

Governments across the world are opposed to mobile phone companies withholding personal details of mobile phone owners. This is probably why it is mandatory in some countries for anyone wishing to buy SIM cards to disclose their personal details. Theoretically, this goes against the freedom of information that is guaranteed in Article 19 of the United Nations Universal Declaration on Human Rights. The challenge is how to protect individual rights to privacy and at the same time protect the security interests of the state against terrorist activities. There is no easy way out of this dilemma. New technology such as the mobile phone brings with it new challenges.

Another example of the use of mobile phones for political activism is the contested role that mobile phones played in engineering the popular uprisings that toppled governments in 2011 in countries such as Tunisia, Egypt, Libya and Yemen. Pierskalla and Hollenbach (2013) have asked whether the propagation of mobile phones across Africa has contributed to an increase in planned and violent conflicts. Their study deviates from established research on the usefulness of mobile phones to human societies in terms of socioeconomic development (see, for example, Abraham, 2007; Africa Partnership Forum, 2008; Aker and Mbiti, 2010).

In many research investigations, mobile phones and other new technologies are presented as tools that promote democracy, socioeconomic development, transparency and accountability (Pierskalla and Hollenbach, 2013). Nevertheless, Pierskalla and Hollenbach take a different path by arguing that 'While the quick and cheap spread of communication technology can improve political accountability through various mechanisms, private communication technology (and cell phones specifically) may also facilitate organized violence' (Pierskalla and Hollenbach, 2013, p. 207). This may be the case. Scholars have long identified negative ways in which the telephone could be put to use by criminal groups and individuals. Aronson (1971, p. 158) outlined decades ago the negative uses of the telephone:

> The existence of organized, corporate crime as we are afflicted with it today, is just as inconceivable without the telephone as more morally acceptable corporate empires. Gambling of all types...prostitution...and drug dealing could probably not exist at their present levels of activity and profitability in the absence of the telephone. And if legitimate brokers and salesmen solicit customers over the telephone so do swindlers, 'conmen' and 'boiler-room' operators of all sorts. The telephone as an instrument of communication is morally neutral, though the uses to which it is put are surely not.

Similarly, Spence and Smith (2010, p. 11) point to the negative ways that mobile phones have been used and are being used such as 'mobile phones being used to fan violence, cyber crime, and terrorism'. This is an important point. No one should be led to believe that the telephone is a tool that is free from human abuses. The telephone itself, as a communication tool, is not capable of causing harm. We must look at the ways the telephone is used in different cultures by different people.

Etzo and Collender (2010) make an important point about the lack of access to technology in many parts of Africa. They argue that despite successes associated with mobile phone adoption and use in Africa, mobile phones remain inaccessible to many Africans who are unable to enjoy the benefits of mobile phones owing to obstacles such as high cost of mobile phones, cost of calls and the absence of regulatory policies. They argue that 'Mobile telephony may contribute to widening the gap between the poor and the poorest, leading to what Manuel Castells has defined as the "fourth world" – a non-consuming and non-producing marginalized group which is "structurally irrelevant in the current structure of the global economy"' (Etzo and Collender, 2010, p. 665).

While the adoption of mobile phones is growing in Africa, those who do not own or do not have access to the technology feel they have been barred from socioeconomic progress. As Hahn (2012, p. 184) explains, 'Individuals without a mobile can be marked as being backward and hindering development.' He cites research by Hahn and Kibora (2008), who note in their study of mobile phone introduction and adoption in Burkina Faso that mobile phone owners felt their country would lag behind the rest of the world if people did not own and use mobile technologies.

Digital divide in Africa

Martin and Abbott (2011) argue that while a lot is known about the digital divide between rich and poor countries, little is known about the level of digital divide that exists within countries. For example, owing to low levels of education, high rates of illiteracy and lack of assets, women comprise a majority of the world's poorest (Martin and Abbott, 2011, p. 20). These impediments may affect the ability of women to use mobile phones to make improvements in agriculture. In their study of farmers in rural Uganda, Martin and Abbott (2011, p. 31) found that

> Farmers strongly believe that the mobile phone increases efficiency and money savings by avoiding wasted travel; that it increases effectiveness of operations due to access to improved agricultural resources; and that it increases the ability to reach new information, such as market prices, agricultural advice, and financial opportunities. Men, unlike women, view transportation efficiency and access to new contacts and opportunities to be major impacts, suggesting that women are less mobile and may have less exposure to new contacts and opportunities.

Donner (2008, p. 145) draws on the literature on mobile phone adoption to show how researchers have framed the digital divide in Africa to express concerns that liberalisation and rising competition may not be adequate to guarantee worldwide access to mobile phones in many developing countries, notwithstanding the fact that some scholars have projected the mobile phone as a 'more accessible, less expensive means' to reduce the digital divide (Donner, 2008, p. 145). He argues that when some scholars refer to the digital divide, more often than not they use the concept to differentiate between 'mobile phone users and nonusers, or between telephone users and nonusers' (Donner, 2008, p. 145). Still, other scholars use the concept of digital divide to draw attention to questions about access to telephones and computer technology as an important facilitator of economic development and poverty reduction (Donner, 2008).

Blumenstock and Eagle (2012) provide research evidence to show the degree of disparities in mobile phone access and use in Rwanda. Equity in access to and use of new technologies has dominated the literature on mobile phone adoption and use in Africa. Scott, McKemyey and Batchelor (2004) found in their study of the use of telecommunications services in three African countries, namely Botswana, Uganda and Ghana, that gender differences did not significantly affect technology use in terms of how men and women used telecommunications services. The same similarity exists not only with regard to fixed and mobile phone use but also in relation to areas of public access such as phone shops and public booths (2004). However, the research found disparities with regard to use of Internet and SMS text messaging. The research showed that men and women have different attitudes and concerns that inform the way they use telecommunication services. These differences are gender-based (Scott et al., 2004).

With specific reference to how gender affected the use of phone by men and women in Ghana, Scott et al. (2004, p. 200) report that

> men are more likely to use the phone to communicate with friends, to make business and work-related calls, and to make calls relating to religious affairs, although this is still only a relatively minor use. On the other hand, a greater proportion of women make family calls relating to financial matters.

In Rwanda, however, Blumenstock and Eagle (2012, p. 14) report that 'it is the privileged, male members of Rwandan society who disproportionately own and use mobile phones'. This is consistent with the findings reported by Burrell (2010) about mobile phones in rural Uganda. In fact, Burrell (2010) notes the problem of access to mobile phones for women in rural Uganda, so much so that the public phone has become a space where rural women can assert their independence in their communication.

Public phone services also offer rural women the chance 'to inquire privately about work opportunities, health matters and other concerns' (Burrell, 2010, p. 246). Similar to the problem of access to mobile phones is also the question about the lack of infrastructure that will support mobile phone use. This is another of the impediments that mobile phone owners have to grapple with in Africa. One example has to do with erratic supply of electricity. How do mobile phone owners who reside in rural and remote parts of Africa that have an unstable supply of electricity charge their phones? This is an important question. While the literature suggests that people in remote areas without access to electricity charge their phones through car batteries, it is important to note that car batteries are not easily accessible in some remote locations.

Theoretical frameworks on mobile phone adoption

Different theoretical frameworks have been applied to studies of mobile phone adoption and use. Pedersen and Ling (2002) identify three principal schools of thought that have been used to study mobile phone adoption. These are diffusion, adoption and domestication theories. Adoption theory draws on three models that are applied in studies of technology adoption. These are the Technology Acceptance Model (TAM) which was first advanced by Davis (1989), the Theory of Reasoned Action (TRA) which was first outlined by Fishbein and Ajzen (1975), and the expansion of TRA into a model of planned behaviour (cited in Pedersen and Ling, 2002).

Domestication theory is a useful framework to examine mobile phone adoption and use in Africa and other parts of the world. The theory is associated with consumption of technology. In domestication, 'the emphasis is on consumption rather than mere use. So attention has been given to what ICTs mean to people, how they experience them and the roles ICTs can come to play in their lives' (Haddon, 2001, p. 3). Silverstone and Hirsch (1994) see domestication as a process through which unfamiliar objects are made familiar in human societies. Berker, Hartmann, Punie and Ward (2006, p. 1) point out that domestication helps 'to describe and analyse processes of (media) technology's acceptance, rejection and use'. They state that domestication investigates 'the complexity of everyday life and technology's place within its dynamics, rituals, rules, routines and patterns' (Berker et al., 2006, p. 1). Domestication looks at what people do with technology and the circumstances in which they do it (Haddon, 2001). Domestication therefore provides us with knowledge of how mobile phones fit into the everyday practices of people in the context of other competing activities in their lives. Domestication examines the symbolic meanings that owners of mobile phones attach to the technology.

Haddon notes that the term 'domestication' was designed 'to suggest the "taming of the wild" as ICTs are acquired from the public domain but then made personal, or, in these early studies of the domestic context, made to be a part of the home' (Haddon, 2001, p. 4). He cautions against any assumption that domestication is always beneficial and gives instances of people being unsure of technology but still feeling they need it:

> People use ICTs but can feel ambivalent about them. ICTs can appear to get out of hand (and this is true of established ones like TV which

can seem to dominate life too much, let alone mobile telephony which can make us feel too reachable). Even users can perceive them as leading to a lifestyle which they feel to be questionable, for instance in terms of enhancing dependency on the technologies or actually facilitating more stress. They can be tolerated, but not necessarily embraced – as in the case of people who do not like answering machines, but nevertheless feel the need to have one in their circumstances. Their place in life can be bounded, as when they are only used for certain purposes in certain circumstances compared to what others might see as their fuller potential. And they can be abandoned, or even rejected at an early stage after adoption.

(Haddon, 2001, p. 4)

A very important point that Haddon makes about adoption and use of technology in domestication theory is that there are non-users who influence the decision of others to adopt or not to adopt technology. These non-users of technology often serve as 'gatekeepers'. In households, some ICTs are seen as communal acquisitions (e.g., main television set in the house, fixed line telephones). According to Haddon (2001, p. 5), the way individuals use technology and the strategies for controlling use of technology occur in a setting in which members of the household have 'commitments, routines and general demands on time and space as well as values, hopes and concerns which all interact and in so doing shape consumption'.

Despite its usefulness in facilitating understanding of how people adopt, use and appropriate technologies, domestication as a framework for understanding the social uses of technology has been criticised by a number of scholars. Sorensen (2006) and Punie (2005) point out the complex processes that inform technology use and practice. Domestication acknowledges that technology is not only an object that is represented but also a medium that incorporates with it useful principles, functions and connotations. Thus, technologies carry public meanings into the private domain of the household (Hartmann, 2006). Bakardjieva (2006) argues that domestication ignores the social processes of production. She contends that when new technologies are adopted into the household, they should not be seen as the consumption of technology and content but a collection of production practices such as a working instrument and not a leisure item. Haddon (2007, 2004) points out that some aspects of domestication theory tend to concentrate on the use of technology at family, household or home level but hardly go beyond the domestic environment. Other disadvantages of domestication theory include its inability to deal with issues relating to access to technology, skills required to use technology and the content of technology.

While Hahn and Kibora (2008, p. 91) argue that it is not enough to understand mobile phones as tools that are 'domesticated', Oudshoorn and Pinch (2003) contend that the importance of mobile phones lies in the uses to which they are put and the contexts in which they are used rather than the technology through which the mobile phone operates.

Two other theories that contribute to our knowledge and understanding of mobile phone adoption and use in Africa are information and communication technologies for development and the diffusion of innovations perspective (Martin and Abbott, 2011). Another theoretical framework that is used to examine the impact of mobile phones on human society is Amartya Sen's (1999) capability approach (CA). This approach looks at human development as a 'process of expanding the real freedoms that people enjoy' (Sen, 1999, p. 1). Sen (1999) argues that human development should be assessed on the basis of the capabilities that individuals and groups of people have which refer to the freedom that people have to do the things they cherish. This framework differs from other models that concentrate on earnings.

Sen's framework for assessment of human development is wide-ranging, including political, social, cultural, economic and other indices. With specific reference to mobile phones, Smith, Spence and Rashid (2011, p. 78) state that 'Mobiles and their networks alter users' capability sets through the changing of their positions in relation to important development resources in at least two ways: (1). increased access to timely and/or relevant **information**, and (2) expanded possibilities for **connectedness** between people.' However, they point out that mobile phones can serve as tools for constraining human capability through their use for purposes such as violent conflicts (see Pierskalla and Hollenbach, 2013; and Zuckerman, 2009, for examples of how mobile phones were used to perpetuate violence in Africa).

The literature on mobile phone use shows there are different ways in which the technology has been used to expand human capabilities. These include the use of mobile phones to sustain social and family relations, to respond to emergency situations, to save time and travel costs, to communicate and to interact, and for economic benefits (see Abraham, 2007; Jensen, 2007; Aker and Mbiti, 2010).

Smith et al. (2011, p. 82) identify one important way through which mobile phones enhance human capability and freedom:

a significant impact of mobile phones, and in particular, mobiles enabled with camera or video capacity, is the way they work to increase the general awareness and mindset of people, particularly youth, as well as to enhance the situational awareness of protestors, the international community, the military, and even the authoritarian regime, of the events occurring on the ground. This systemic self-awareness is a critical input that enhances the possibility for self-organizing that can propel and sustain protest movements without a central organizing structure.

Smith et al. (2011) also point to how the mobile phone facilitated citizen participation in election monitoring (such as in Kenya in 2007 and 2013, and in Nigeria between 2011 and 2013 during state, parliamentary and council elections).

Donner (2008) identifies a third theoretical framework that is used to evaluate mobile phone use in developing countries. This is the diffusion of innovations model outlined by Rogers (2003) that also serves to assess the processes of introduction, adoption and use of new technologies. Diffusion of innovations explains how new ideas, objects or behaviour are spread in a given population. There are five elements that determine the success or failure of the innovation. Other important theories include the TAM used to explain mobile phone adoption and use in Nigeria and Kenya (Meso, Musa and Mbarika, 2005, cited in Donner, 2008), and the TRA that was used in studies conducted in Guinea (Kaba, Diallo, Plaisent, Bernard and N'Da, 2006, cited in Donner, 2008). According to Legris, Inghamb and Collerette (2003, p. 192), 'A key purpose of TAM is to provide a basis for tracing the impact of external variables on internal beliefs, attitudes, and intentions.' The TRA, developed by Fishbein and Ajzen (1975), argues that human behaviour is determined by the intention to act.

Mobile phone contribution to rural development

There is a range of literature showing that mobile phones contribute to rural development and poverty alleviation in developing countries (Donner, 2008; Hudson, 2006). Other areas where mobile phones are believed to influence socioeconomic development include: acquiring information for solid decision making, such as distribution and repossession of market information relating to buying and selling; organisation of transportation during emergency situations; and meeting people and making contacts to facilitate information exchange and improvements in farm yields (Martin and Abbott, 2011, p. 20). Carmody (2012) states that a great deal of the literature that examines the impacts of mobile phone on socioeconomic development in Africa tends to assume that Africa missed out on the globalisation bandwagon. Mobile phones are regarded as a tool to reduce poverty by connecting the people in Africa to the rest of the world and also to other Africans (Carmody, 2012). He criticises the literature on the impact of mobile phones on socioeconomic development, stating that the literature tends to be 'too shallowly "geographical", focusing on spatial diffusion and connection..., rather than on the impacts on socioeconomic structures' (Carmody, 2012, p. 3). According to Carmody (2012), this particular literature overlooks the unfavourable international system and focuses on physical distance as a basis for arguing that Africa is underdeveloped owing to geographical distance. It is this concept of a digital divide that has placed too much emphasis on technology and drawn attention away from other inadequacies and inequalities that hinder development (Carmody, 2012).

While scholars have identified the various ways that mobile phones have contributed to poverty alleviation, little attention has been paid to other ways in which mobile phones contribute to poverty. The idea that mobile phones contribute to poverty in Africa is not particularly dealt with in the literature. Carmody's article provides important insights into how a technology that is believed to empower the rich and poor across the world is believed also to contribute to poverty in Africa. His study deserves further systematic investigation to understand the conditions under which mobile phones create poverty and the conditions under which mobile phones aid socioeconomic development. This is an unresolved argument that requires further research attention.

Conclusion

There is abundant research evidence that shows that mobile phones enhance economic growth in developing countries in Africa and other parts of the world. For this reason, mobile phones are regarded as tools that promote democracy, socioeconomic development, transparency and accountability in Africa. While the uptake of mobile phones is growing in Africa, there are people who do not own or do not have access to the technology. These people feel in one way or another that they have been excluded from benefiting from mobile phones. While the rapid diffusion of mobile phones in Africa has been acknowledged, some scholars seem to overlook impediments to public use of the mobile phone in some parts of Africa. Among the problems that impede effective use of mobile phones are defective network connectivity, poor quality of service and unstable supply of electricity.

On the political front, debate continues about the use of mobile phones for political activism in Africa. There are instances in which governments have stepped in to control and monitor mobile phone use by citizens on the grounds that the security of the citizens and the state is more important than individual freedoms. At another level, governments across the world are opposed to mobile phone companies withholding personal details of mobile phone subscribers and owners. For this reason, people wishing to buy SIM cards in many countries are required to disclose their personal details. Theoretically, this goes against everyone's right to privacy but governments have argued that in the age of terrorism, this is one way to protect the security interests of citizens and the state. To what extent do governments have the right to intrude on the freedom of individuals by insisting that telecommunications service providers must disclose the personal details of mobile phone subscribers? While everyone values freedom, everyone is also concerned about threats to their security. The challenge is how to protect individual rights to privacy and at the same time protect the security interests of citizens and the state.

While scholars have analysed how mobile phones contribute to poverty alleviation, little scholarly attention has been paid to how mobile phones engender poverty. The idea that mobile phones promote poverty in Africa rather than help to reduce the problem is not something that many people have considered. The issue has not received adequate scholarly and research attention. It is important for us to understand the different conditions under which the mobile phone could encourage poverty and the conditions under which mobile phones facilitate socioeconomic development.

Bibliography

Aboriginal Peoples Television Network (2005) Factsheet, http://aptn.ca/corporate/facts.php. Accessed on 15 October 2014.

Abraham, Reuben (2007) 'Mobile phones and economic development: Evidence from the fishing industry in India', *Information Technologies & International Development*, 4(1), pp. 5–17.

Adam, Lishan and Frances Wood (1999) 'An investigation of the impact of information and communication technologies in sub-Saharan Africa', *Journal of Information Science*, 25(4), pp. 307–318.

Adelman, Mara B. and Larry R. Frey (1997) *The fragile community: Living together with AIDS*, Mahwah, NJ, Lawrence Erlbaum Associates, Inc., Publishers.

Adesanmi, Pius (2011) 'Social media, the public sphere, and the anxieties of power in Nigeria', Lecture delivered at the Keynote Speaker Series of the African Students Association, State University of New York at Oswego, 2 November 2011, http://www.nigeriavillagesquare.com/pius-adesanmi/social-media-the-public-sphere-and-the-anxieties-of-power-in-nigeria-1.html. Accessed on 17 August 2014.

Adomi, Esharenana E., Rose B. Okiy and Josiah O. Ruteyan (2003) 'A survey of cyber cafés in Delta State, Nigeria', *The Electronic Library*, 21(5), pp. 487–495.

Africa Partnership Forum (2008) 'ICT in Africa: Boosting economic growth and poverty reduction', Tenth Meeting of the Africa partnership forum, Tokyo, Japan, 7–8 April 2008, http://www.africapartnershipforum.org/meetingdocuments/40314752.pdf. Accessed on 18 March 2014.

Agbobli, Christian (2008) 'Internet and development in Senegal: Towards new forms of use', *Africa Media Review*, 16(2), pp. 11–28.

Ahlers, Douglas (2006) 'News consumption and the new electronic media', *The Harvard International Journal of Press/Politics*, 11(1), pp. 29–52.

Airhihenbuwa, Collins O., Bunmi Makinwa and Rafael Obregon (2000) 'Toward a new communications framework for HIV/AIDS', *Journal of Health Communication*, 5(Supplement 1), pp. 101–111.

Airhihenbuwa, Collins O. and J. DeWitt Webster (2004) 'Culture and African contexts of HIV/AIDS prevention, care and support', *Sahara-J: Journal of Social Aspects of HIV/AIDS*, 1(1), pp. 4–13.

Airhihenbuwa, Collins O. and Rafael Obregon (2000) 'A critical assessment of theories/models used in health communication for HIV/AIDS', *Journal of Health Communication*, 5(Supplement 1), pp. 5–15.

Aker, Jenny C. (2010) 'Information from markets near and far: Mobile phones and agricultural markets in Niger', *American Economic Journal: Applied Economics*, 2(3), pp. 46–59.

Aker, Jenny C. and Isaac M. Mbiti (2010) 'Mobile phones and economic development in Africa', *Journal of Economic Perspectives*, 24(3), pp. 207–232.

Aker, Jenny C., Paul Collier and Pedro C. Vicente (2013) 'Is information power? Using mobile phones and free newspapers during an election in Mozambique', http://www.pedrovicente.org/cell.pdf. Accessed on 20 March 2014.

Akinfemisoye, Motilola Olufenwa (2013) 'Challenging hegemonic media practices: Of "alternative" media and Nigeria's democracy', *Ecquid Novi: African Journalism Studies*, 34(1), pp. 7–20.

Alao, Isiaka Atunde and Abubakar Lanre Folorunsho (2008) 'The use of cyber cafés in Ilorin, Nigeria', *The Electronic Library*, 26(2), pp. 238–248.

Albert, Isaac Olawale (2010) 'Whose deliberative democracy? A critique of online public discourses in Africa', http://www.social.nigeriavillagesquare .com/articles/guest-articles/whose-deliberative-democracy-a-critique-of-online -public-discourses-in-africa.html. Accessed on 17 August 2014.

Allan, Benjamin Joseph (2004) 'Everybody's a comedian (or a journalist?): Investigating claims for personal publishing on the Internet as "journalism" and as a new form of public sphere'. Unpublished Master's thesis, University of Canterbury, Christchurch, New Zealand.

Alozie, Nicholas O., Patience Akpan-Obong and William A. Foster (2011) 'Sizing up information and communication technologies as agents of political development in sub-Saharan Africa', *Telecommunications Policy*, 35(8), pp. 752–763.

Anderson, Cokie Gaston (2003) 'American Indian tribal web sites: A review and comparison', *The Electronic Library*, 21(5), pp. 450–455.

Anderson, Keith J. (2001) 'Internet use among college students: An exploratory study', *Journal of American College Health*, 50(1), pp. 21–26.

Andrade, Antonio Díaz and Cathy Urquhart (2010) 'The affordances of actor network theory in ICT for development research', *Information Technology & People*, 23(4), pp. 352–374.

Ani, Okon Edet, Chika Uchendu and Emmanuel U. Atseye (2007) 'Bridging the digital divide in Nigeria: A study of Internet use in Calabar metropolis, Nigeria', *Library Management*, 28(6/7), pp. 355–365.

Annan, Kofi A. (2003) 'Information and communication technologies: A priority for Africa's development', in Joseph O. Okpaku (ed.) *Information and communication technologies for African development: An assessment of progress and challenges ahead*, pp. xiii–xv. New York, The United Nations ICT Task Force.

Anunobi, Chinwe V. (2006) 'Dynamics of Internet usage: A case of students of the Federal University of Technology, Owerri (FUTO), Nigeria', *Educational Research and Reviews*, 1(6), pp. 192–195.

Aoki, Kumiko and Edward J. Downes (2003) 'An analysis of young people's use of and attitudes toward cell phones', *Telematics and Informatics*, 20(4), pp. 349–364.

Aronson, Sidney H. (1971) 'The sociology of the telephone', *International Journal of Comparative Sociology*, 12(3), pp. 153–167.

Article 19 (2006) *Broadcasting pluralism and diversity: Training manual for African regulators*, London, Article 19.

Atton, Chris (2002) *Alternative media*, London, Sage Publications Ltd.

Atton, Chris and Hayes Mabweazara (2011) 'New media and journalism practice in Africa: An agenda for research', *Journalism: Theory, Practice and Criticism*, 12(6), pp. 667–673.

Atton, Chris and James Frederick Hamilton (2008) *Alternative journalism*, London, Sage Publications Ltd.

Australian Associated Press (AAP, 2009) 'One in three people with HIV do not know', http://au.news.yahoo.com/a/-/world/6391310/one-in-three-people-with-hiv-do-not-know/. Accessed on 27 October 2009.

AVERT (n.d.) http://www.avert.org/africa-hiv-aids-statistics.htm. Accessed on 28 November 2014.

Avgerou, Chrisanthi (2010) 'Discourses on ICT and development', *Information Technologies & International Development*, 6(3), pp. 1–18.

Awoleye, O. Michael, W. Owolabi Siyanbola and O. Francisca Oladipo (2008) 'Adoption assessment of Internet usage amongst undergraduates in Nigerian universities: A case study approach', *Journal of Technology Management & Innovation*, 3(1), pp. 84–89.

Bailard, Catie Snow (2009) 'Mobile phone diffusion and corruption in Africa', *Political Communication*, 26(3), pp. 333–353.

Bakardjieva, Maren (2006) 'Domestication running wild: From the moral economy of the household to the mores of a culture', in Thomas Berker, Maren Hartmann, Yves Punie and Katie J. Ward (eds) *Domestication of media and technology*, pp. 62–78. London, Open University Press.

Balnaves, Mark and Peter Caputi (1997) 'Technological wealth and the evaluation of information poverty', *Media International Australia*, 83, pp. 92–102.

Banda, Fackson (2010) *Citizen journalism and democracy in Africa: An exploratory study*, Grahamstown, South Africa, Highway Africa.

Banda, Fackson (2007) 'An appraisal of the applicability of development journalism in the context of public service broadcasting (PSB)'. Paper presented during the South African broadcasting corporation's 'News Content Planning' workshop on 21 October 2006, held at the Birchwood Executive Hotel, in Boksburg, South Africa, *Communicatio: South African Journal for Communication Theory and Research*, 33(2), pp. 154–170.

Banda, Fackson (2006) 'Key issues in public service broadcasting in sub-Saharan Africa'. Paper commissioned by the Open Society Institute (OSI) and presented at a meeting in London, UK, on 31 October 2006, as part of the organisation's proposed research project on public service broadcasting in sub-Saharan Africa.

Bandura, Albert (2002) 'Social cognitive theory of mass communication', in Jennings Bryant and Dolf Zillmann (eds) *Media effects: Advances in theory and research*, 2nd edition, pp. 121–153. Mahwah, NJ, Lawrence Erlbaum Associates, Inc., Publishers.

Bandura, Albert (1997) *Self-efficacy: The exercise of control*, New York, Freeman.

Bandura, Albert (1994) 'Social cognitive theory and exercise of control over HIV infection', in Ralph J. DiClemente and John L. Peterson (eds) *Preventing AIDS: Theories and methods of behavioural interventions*, pp. 25–60. New York, Plenum Press.

Barber, Karin (1987) 'Popular arts in Africa', *African Studies Review*, 30(3), pp. 1–78.

Barder, Owen (2012) 'What is development?' Centre for global development, http://www.cgdev.org/blog/what-development. Accessed on 15 July 2014.

Bardoel, Jo (2002) 'The Internet, journalism and public communication policies', *Gazette: The International Journal for Communication Studies*, 64(5), pp. 501–511.

Barendregt, Bart (2008) 'Sex, cannibals, and the language of cool: Indonesian tales of the phone and modernity', *The Information Society*, 24(3), pp. 160–170.

Barendt, Eric (1993) *Broadcasting law: A comparative study*, Oxford, Clarendon Press.

Barnard, Ian (2006) 'The language of multiculturalism in South African soaps and sitcoms', *Journal of Multicultural Discourses*, 1(1), pp. 39–59.

Barrantes, Roxana (2007) 'Analysis of ICT demand: What is digital poverty and how to measure it?' in Hernan Galperin and Judith Mariscal (eds) *Digital poverty: Latin American and Caribbean perspectives*, pp. 29–54. Warwickshire, UK and Ottawa, Practical Action Publishing.

Bartl, Michael (2009) 'Netnography – Utilizing online communities as source of innovation', http://www.michaelbartl.com/article/netnography/. Accessed on 4 October 2014.

Batty, Philip (1993) 'Singing the electric: Aboriginal television in Australia', in Tony Dowmunt (ed.) *Channels of resistance: Global television and local empowerment*, pp. 106–125. London, BFI Publishing in association with Channel Four Television.

Baxter, Leslie A. and Earl Babbie (2004) *The basics of communication research*, Southbank, Victoria, Thomson Wadsworth.

BBC (2009) http://news.bbc.co.uk/2/hi/africa/8180475.stm. Accessed on 7 March 2013.

Beckett, Charlie (2010) The value of networked journalism. Presented at the value of networked journalism conference at the London School of Economics, 11 June 2010, http://www.lse.ac.uk/media@lse/POLIS/documents/Polis%20papers/ValueofnetworkedJournalism.pdf. Accessed on 27 April 2014.

Berger, Guy (2011) 'Empowering the youth as citizen journalists: A South African experience', *Journalism: Theory, Practice and Criticism*, 12(6), pp. 708–726.

Berger, Guy (2009) 'How the Internet impacts on international news: Exploring paradoxes of the most global medium in a time of "hyperlocalism"', *International Communication Gazette*, 71(5), pp. 355–371.

Berker, Thomas, Maren Hartmann, Yves Punie and Katie J. Ward (2006) *Domestication of media and technology*, London, Open University Press.

Best, Michael L., Thomas N. Smyth, John Etherton and Edem Wornyo (2010) 'Uses of mobile phones in post-conflict Liberia', *Information Technologies & International Development*, 6(2), pp. 91–108.

Blumenstock, Joshua Evan and Nathan Eagle (2012) 'Divided we call: Disparities in access and use of mobile phones in Rwanda', *Information Technologies & International Development*, 8(2), pp. 1–16.

Blumler, Jay G. (1993) 'Making money with mission: Purity versus pragmatism in public broadcasting', *European Journal of Communication*, 8(4), pp. 403–424.

Bostock, Lester (1997) *The greater perspective: Protocol and guidelines for the production of film and TV on Aboriginal and Torres Strait Islander communities*, Sydney, SBS Publications.

Bourgault, Louise M. (1993) 'Press freedom in Africa: A cultural analysis', *Journal of Communication Inquiry*, 17(2), pp. 69–92.

Brants, Kees (2005) 'Guest Editor's Introduction: The Internet and the public sphere', *Political Communication*, 22(2), pp. 143–146.

Bravo, Sury, Miguel A. Valero and Ivan Pau (2012) 'A tele-health communication and information system for underserved children in rural areas of Nicaragua', *Information Technologies & International Development*, 8(4), pp. 205–221.

Brewer, John D. (2001) 'The ethnographic critique of ethnography: Sectarianism in the RUC', in Alan Bryman (ed.) *Ethnography*, Volume IV, pp. 100–113. London, Sage Publications Ltd.

Breytenbach, Johan, Carina de Villiers and Martina Jordaan (2013) 'Communities in control of their own integrated technology development processes', *Information Technology for Development*, 19(2), pp. 133–150.

Brinkman, Inge, Siri Lamoureaux, Daniela Merolla and Mirjam de Bruijn (2011) 'Local stories, global discussions: Websites, politics and identity in African contexts', in Herman Wasserman (ed.) *Popular media, democracy and development in Africa*, pp. 236–252. London, Routledge.

Broadcasting Research Unit (1986) *The public service idea in British broadcasting: Main principles*, London, British Film Institute Publications.

Brown, William J and Arvind Singhal (1993) 'Ethical considerations of promoting prosocial messages through the popular media', *Journal of Popular Film and Television*, 21(3), pp. 92–99.

Bruns, Axel (2005) *Gatewatching: Collaborative online news production*, New York, Peter Lang.

Brush, Stephen B. (1996) 'Whose knowledge, whose genes, whose rights?' in Stephen B. Brush and Doreen Stabinsky (eds) *Valuing local knowledge: Indigenous people and intellectual property rights*, pp. 1–21. Washington, DC, Island Press.

Buchtmann, Lydia (2000) 'Digital Songlines: The use of modern communication technology by an Aboriginal community in remote Australia', *Prometheus*, 18(1), pp. 59–74.

Bucy, Erik P., Walter Gantz and Zheng Wang (2007) 'Media technology and the 24-hour news cycle', in Carolyn A. Lin and David J. Atkin (eds) *Communication technology and social change: Theory and implications*, pp. 143–163. Mahwah, NJ, Lawrence Erlbaum Associates, Inc., Publishers.

BuddeComm (2014) 'Nigeria – Mobile Market – Insights, Statistics and Forecasts', http://www.budde.com.au/Research/Nigeria-Mobile-Market-Insights-Statistics -and-Forecasts.html. Accessed on 1 December 2014.

Burns, Maureen (2012) 'Protecting the brand: A history of ABC online news-as-commodity', in Maureen Burns and Niels Brügger (eds) *Histories of public service broadcasters on the web*, pp. 49–61. New York, Peter Lang.

Burns, Maureen Elizabeth (2008) 'Public service broadcasting meets the Internet at the Australian Broadcasting Corporation (1995–2000)', *Continuum: Journal of Media & Cultural Studies*, 22(6), pp. 867–881.

Burrell, Jenna (2010) 'Evaluating shared access: Social equality and the circulation of mobile phones in rural Uganda', *Journal of Computer-Mediated Communication*, 15(2), pp. 230–250.

Bussiek, Hendrik (ed.) (2013) *Public broadcasting in Africa series: An overview*, Johannesburg, South Africa, AfriMAP.

Calhoun, Craig (1992) 'Introduction: Habermas and the public sphere', in Craig Calhoun (ed.) *Habermas and the public sphere*, pp. 1–48. Cambridge, MA, The MIT Press.

Campbell, W. Joseph (2003) 'African cultures and newspapers', in Shannon E. Martin and David A. Copeland (eds) *The function of newspapers in society: A global perspective*, pp. 31–46. Westport, Connecticut, Praeger.

Carmody, Pádraig (2013) 'A knowledge economy or an information society in Africa? The integration and the mobile phone revolution', *Information Technology for Development*, 19(1), pp. 24–39.

Carmody, Pádraig (2012) 'The informationalization of poverty in Africa? Mobile phones and economic structure', *Information Technologies & International Development*, 8(3), pp. 1–17.

Castells, Manuel (2000) *The rise of the network society: The information age: Economy, society and culture*, Volume 1, New Jersey, Wiley-Blackwell.

Chachage, Bukaza Loth (2001) 'Internet cafés in Tanzania: A study of the knowledge and skills of end-users', *Information Development*, 17(4), pp. 226–232.

Chalaby, Jean K. (1996) 'Journalism as an Anglo-American invention: A comparison of the development of French and Anglo-American journalism, 1830s–1920s', *European Journal of Communication*, 11(3), pp. 303–326.

Chambers, Simone and Anne Costain (2000) 'Introduction', in Simone Chambers and Anne Costain (eds) *Deliberation, democracy, and the media*, pp. xi–xiv. Lanham, MD, Rowman & Littlefield Publishers, Inc.

Charney, Tamar and Bradley S. Greenberg (2001) 'Uses and gratifications of the Internet', in Carolyn A. Lin and David J. Atkin (eds) *Communication technology and society: Audience adoption and uses*, pp. 379–407. Cresskill, NJ, Hampton Press, Inc.

Chavula, Hopestone Kayiska (2013) 'Telecommunications development and economic growth in Africa', *Information Technology for Development*, 19(1), pp. 5–23.

Chéneau-Loquay, Annie (2010) *Innovative ways of appropriating mobile telephony in Africa*, Geneva, French Ministry of Foreign and European Affairs and the International Telecommunication Union.

Chetty, Matthew (n.d.) Information and communications technologies (ICTs) for Africa's development, http://www.ansa-africa.net/uploads/documents/publications/ICT_for_Africas_development.pdf. Accessed on 12 July 2014.

Chikonzo, Agnes (2006) 'The potential of information and communication technologies in collecting, preserving and disseminating indigenous knowledge in Africa', *The International Information & Library Review*, 38(3), pp. 132–138.

Christensen, Toke H. and Inge Røpke (2010) 'Can practice theory inspire studies of ICTs in everyday life?' in Birgit Bräuchler and John Postill (eds) *Theorising media and practice (Anthropology of media, Volume 4)*, pp. 233–258. Oxford, Berghahn Books.

Conradie, D. P., C. Morris and S. J. Jacobs (2003) 'Using information and communication technologies (ICTs) for deep rural development in South Africa', *Communicatio: South African Journal for Communication Theory and Research*, 29(1–2), pp. 199–217.

Contractor, Noshir S., Arvind Singhal and Everett M. Rogers (1988) 'Metatheoretical perspectives on satellite television and development in India', *Journal of Broadcasting and Electronic Media*, 32(2), pp. 129–148.

Convention Establishing the World Intellectual Property Organization (1967), signed at Stockholm on 14 July 1967, http://www.wipo.int/treaties/en/text.jsp?file_id=283854. Accessed on 11 October 2014.

Couldry, Nick (2004) 'Theorising media as practice', *Social Semiotics*, 14(2), pp. 115–132.

Council of Europe (1992) *European charter for regional or minority languages*, http://conventions.coe.int/Treaty/en/Treaties/Html/148.htm. Accessed on 13 March 2013.

Crang, Mike A. and Ian Cook (2007) *Doing ethnographies*, London, Sage Publications Ltd.

Curran, James, David Elstein and Todd Gitlin (2002) 'Open democracy: Public service media – thinking for our time', cited in Fourie, Pieter (2003) 'The future of public service broadcasting in South Africa: The need to return to basic principles', *Communicatio: South African Journal for Communication Theory and Research*, 29(1–2), pp. 148–181.

Daes, Erica-Irene A. (2004) 'The impact of globalization on Indigenous intellectual property and cultures', Lecture delivered by Professor Erica-Irene A. Daes, 25 May 2004, Sydney, Museum of Sydney, https://www.humanrights.gov .au/news/speeches/impact-globalization-indigenous-intellectual-property-and -cultures. Accessed on 23 July 2014.

Dahlberg, Lincoln (2007) 'The Internet, deliberative democracy, and power: Radicalizing the public sphere', *The International Journal of Media and Cultural Politics*, 3(1), pp. 47–64.

Dahlberg, Lincoln (2004) 'The Habermasian public sphere: A specification of the idealized conditions of democratic communication', *Studies in Social and Political Thought*, 10, pp. 2–18.

Dahlberg, Lincoln (2001) 'Democracy via cyberspace: Mapping the rhetorics and practices of three prominent camps', *New Media & Society*, 3(2), pp. 157–177.

Dahlgren, Peter (2005) 'The Internet, public spheres, and political communication: Dispersion and deliberation', *Political Communication*, 22(2), pp. 147–162.

Dahlgren, Peter (1991) 'Introduction', in Peter Dahlgren and Colin Sparks (eds) *Communication and citizenship: Journalism and the public sphere*, pp. 1–24. London, Routledge.

Davis, Fred D. (1989) 'Perceived usefulness, perceived ease of use, and user acceptance of information technologies', *MIS Quarterly*, 13(3), pp. 319–340.

Davis, Michael (n.d.) 'Indigenous peoples and intellectual property rights', Research paper 20, http://www.aph.gov.au/About_Parliament/Parliamentary _Departments/Parliamentary_Library/pubs/rp/RP9697/97rp20. Accessed on 25 July 2014.

Davis, Susan Schaefer (2007) 'Empowering women weavers? The Internet in rural Morocco', *Information Technologies & International Development*, 4(2), pp. 17–23.

de Bruin, Marjan (2006) 'Blind spots and wasted effort in Caribbean HIV/AIDS policy making: Communication and behaviour change', *New Glocal Times*, 4, http://ojs.ub.gu.se/ojs/index.php/gt/article/view/2628/2346. Accessed on 23 April 2014.

Delgado-P., Guillermo (2002) 'Solidarity in cyberspace: Indigenous peoples online; have new electronic technologies fulfilled the promise they once seemed to hold for indigenous peoples? The answers are yes, and no', *NACLA Report on the Americas*, 35(5), pp. 49–52, http://web4 .infotrac.galegroup.com/itw/infomark/690/1/54401884w4/purl=rc. Accessed on 10 September 2004.

Denzin, Norman K. (1989) *Interpretive interactionism*, Newbury Park, CA, Sage Publications Ltd.

Denzin, Norman K. (1978) *The Research Act: A theoretical introduction to sociological methods*, New York, McGraw-Hill Publishers.

Dervin, Brenda and David Schaefer (1999) 'Peopling the public sphere', *Peace Review*, 11(1), pp. 17–23.

De Silva, Harsha, Dimuthu Ratnadiwakara and Ayesha Zainudeen (2011) 'Social influence in mobile phone adoption: Evidence from the bottom of the pyramid in emerging Asia', *Information Technologies & International Development*, 7(3), pp. 1–18.

Deuze, Mark (2007) *Media Work*, Cambridge, UK, Polity.

Deuze, Mark (2003) 'The web and its journalisms: Considering the consequences of different types of news media online', *New Media & Society*, 5(2), pp. 203–230.

Dixon, Robyn (2015) 'Ebola vaccine heads to Liberia for tests even as crisis eases', *Los Angeles Times*, 23 January 2015. http://www.latimes.com/world/africa/la-fg -wn-liberia-ebola-vaccine-20150123-story.html. Accessed on 25 January 2015.

Dobos, Jean (1992) 'Gratification models of satisfaction and choice of communication channels in organizations', *Communication Research*, 19(1), pp. 29–51.

Donner, Jonathan (2010) 'Framing M4D: The utility of continuity and the dual heritage of "mobiles development"', *The Electronic Journal on Information Systems in Developing Countries*, 44(3), pp. 1–16.

Donner, Jonathan (2008) 'Research approaches to mobile use in the developing world: A review of the literature', *The Information Society*, 24(3), pp. 140–159.

Donner, Jonathan and Camilo Andres Tellez (2008) 'Mobile banking and economic development: Linking adoption, impact, and use', *Asian Journal of Communication*, 18(4), pp. 318–332.

Elendureports, http://www.elendureports.com/. Accessed on 18 October 2014.

Emeagwali, Philip (2007) 'Technology widens rich-poor gap', http://www .guardiannewsngr.com/editorial_opinion/article04. Accessed on 14 July 2014.

Etzo, Sebastiana and Guy Collender (2010) 'The mobile phone "revolution" in Africa: Rhetoric or reality?' *African Affairs*, 109(437), pp. 659–668.

European Union's Amsterdam Treaty (1997) *Treaty of Amsterdam amending the treaty on European Union, The treaties establishing the European communities and certain related acts*, Luxembourg, Office for Official Publications of the European Communities, http://www.europarl.europa.eu/topics/treaty/pdf/ amst-en.pdf. Accessed on 13 November 2014.

Facebook, https://www.facebook.com/. Accessed on 18 October 2014.

Fejes, Fred (1981) 'Media imperialism: An assessment', *Media, Culture & Society*, 3(3), pp. 281–289.

Fenton, Natalie (2010) 'Drowning or waving? New media, journalism and democracy', in Natalie Fenton (ed.) *New media, old news: Journalism and democracy in the digital age*, pp. 3–16. London, Sage Publications Ltd.

Ferree, Myra Marx, William A. Gamson, Jurgen Gerhards and Dieter Rucht (2002) 'Four models of the public sphere in modern democracies', *Theory and Society*, 31(3), pp. 289–324.

Figueres, José María (2003) 'Preface', in Joseph O. Okpaku (ed.) *Information and communication technologies for African development: An assessment of progress and challenges ahead*, pp. ix–xi. New York, The United Nations ICT Task Force.

Fine, Gary Alan (1993) 'Ten lies of ethnography: Moral dilemmas of field research', *Journal of Contemporary Ethnography*, 22(3), pp. 267–294.

Finlayson, Rosalie and Mbulungeni Madiba (2002) 'The intellectualisation of the indigenous languages of South Africa: Challenges and prospects', *Current Issues in Language Planning*, 3(1), pp. 40–61.

Fishbein, Martin and Icek Ajzen (1975) *Beliefs, attitude, intention, and behavior: An introduction to theory and research*, Reading, MA, Addison-Wesley.

Fishman, Joshua A. (ed.) (1972) *Advances in the sociology of language*, The Hague, Netherlands, Mouton.

Flanagin, Andrew J. and Miriam J. Metzger (2001) 'Internet use in the contemporary media environment', *Human Communication Research*, 27(1), pp. 153–181.

Flor, Alexander G. (2001) 'ICT and poverty: The indisputable link'. Paper presented at the Third Asia Development Forum on "Regional Economic Cooperation in Asia and the Pacific", Bangkok, 11–14 June 2001, http://www.academia.edu/2011146/ICT_and_poverty_The_indisputable_link. Accessed on 15 July 2014.

Fonseca, Clotilde (2010) 'The digital divide and the cognitive divide: Reflections on the challenge of human development in the digital age', *Information Technologies & International Development*, 6(Special edition), pp. 25–30.

Forsey, Martin Gerard (2010) 'Ethnography as participant listening', *Ethnography*, 11(4), pp. 558–572.

Fourie, Pieter J. (2004) 'Leapfrogging into the market approach: The loss of public service broadcasting for development and nation building', http://ripeat.org/wp-content/uploads/2010/03/Fourie.pdf. Accessed on 7 March 2014.

Fourie, Pieter J. (2003) 'The future of public service broadcasting in South Africa: The need to return to basic principles', *Communicatio: South African Journal for Communication Theory and Research*, 29(1–2), pp. 148–181.

Freimuth, Vicki S. (1992) 'Theoretical formulations of AIDS media campaigns', in Timothy Edgar, Mary Anne Fitzpatrick & Vicki S. Freimuth (eds) *AIDS: A communication perspective*, pp. 9–110. Hillsdale, NJ, Lawrence Erlbaum Associates, Inc., Publishers.

Frey, Lawrence R., Mara B. Adelman, Lyle J. Flint, & Jim L. Query (2000) 'Weaving meanings together in an AIDS residence: Communicative practices, perceived health outcomes, and the symbolic construction of community', *Journal of Health Communication*, 5(1), pp. 53–72.

Friedman, Samuel R., Don C. Des Jarlais & Thomas P. Ward (1994) 'Social models for changing health-relevant behavior', in Ralph J. DiClemente and John L. Peterson (eds) *Preventing AIDS: Theories and methods of behavioral interventions*, pp. 95–116. New York, Springer US.

Fuchs, Christian (2008) 'The implications of new information and communication technologies for sustainability', *Environment, Development and Sustainability*, 10(3), pp. 291–309.

Furuholt, Bjørn, Stein Kristiansen and Fathul Wahid (2008) 'Gaming or gaining? Comparing the use of Internet cafés in Indonesia and Tanzania', *The International Information & Library Review*, 40(2), pp. 129–139.

Galavotti, Christine, Katina A. Pappas-DeLuca and Amy Lansky (2001) 'Modeling and reinforcement to combat HIV: The MARCH approach to behaviour change', *American Journal of Public Health*, 91(10), pp. 1602–1607.

Garcia, Angela Cora, Alecea I. Standlee, Jennifer Bechkoff, and Yan Cui (2009) 'Ethnographic approaches to the Internet and computer-mediated communication', *Journal of Contemporary Ethnography*, 38(1), pp. 52–84.

Garnham, Nicholas (1992) 'The media and the public sphere', in Craig Calhoun (ed.) *Habermas and the public sphere*, pp. 359–376. Cambridge, MA, The MIT Press.

Geldof, Marije (2011) 'Earphones are not for women: Gendered ICT use among youths in Ethiopia and Malawi', *Information Technologies & International Development*, 7(4), pp. 69–80.

Gillman, Helen, Maria Elisa Pinzon and Roxanna Samii (2003) 'Fighting rural poverty: The role of ICTs', International Fund for Agricultural Development (IFAD). Paper presented as a side event during the World Summit on the

Information Society, Geneva, December 2003, http://www.ifad.org/events/ wsis/phase1/synthesis/. Accessed on 11 July 2014.

Gillwald, Alison (2010) 'The poverty of ICT policy, research, and practice in Africa', *Information Technologies & International Development*, 6(Special edition), pp. 79–88.

Gladstone, Mark (2014) 'Social media could be used to track HIV', *Houston Chronicle*, 26 February 2014, http://blog.chron.com/healthzone/2014/02/social -media-could-be-used-to-track-hiv/. Accessed on 19 April 2014.

Glaser, Barney G. and Anselm L. Strauss (1967) *The discovery of grounded theory: Strategies for qualitative research*, Chicago, IL, Aldine Publishing Company.

Golding, Peter (1977) 'Media professionalism in the third world: The transfer of an ideology', in James Curran, Michael Gurevitch and Janet Woollacott (eds) *Mass Communication and Society*, pp. 291–314. London, Edward Arnold (Publishers) Ltd.

Goldstein, Susan, Shereen Usdin, Esca Scheepers and Garth Japhet (2005) 'Communicating HIV and AIDS, what works? A report on the impact evaluation of *Soul City*'s fourth series', *Journal of Health Communication*, 10(5), pp. 465–483.

Gordon, Ronald D. (2007) 'Beyond the failures of Western communication theory', *Journal of Multicultural Discourses*, 2(2), pp. 89–107.

Gray, Marianne (2013) 'Can public service broadcasting endure in South Africa? *The South African.com*, http://www.thesouthafrican.com/news/can-public -service-broadcasting-endure-in-south-africa.htm. Accessed on 7 March 2014.

Greaves, Thomas (1996) 'Tribal rights', in Stephen B. Brush and Doreen Stabinsky (eds) *Valuing local knowledge: Indigenous people and intellectual property rights*, pp. 25–37. Washington, DC, Island Press.

Grossman, Lawrence K. (1996) *The electronic republic: Reshaping democracy in the information age*, New York, Penguin.

Guermazi, Boutheina and David Satola (2005) 'Creating the "right" enabling environment for ICT', in Robert Schware (ed.) *E-development: From excitement to effectiveness*, pp. 23–46. Washington, DC, Global Information and Communication Technologies Department, The World Bank Group.

Gumuchio-Dagron, Alfonso (2003) 'Take five: A handful of essentials for ICTs in development', in Bruce Girard (ed.) *The one to watch: Radio, new ICTs and interactivity*, pp. 25–43. Rome, The Food and Agriculture Organisation.

Gunter, Barrie (2000) *Media research methods: Measuring audiences, reactions and impact*, London, Sage Publications Ltd.

Habermas, Jürgen (1989) *The structural transformation of the public sphere: An enquiry into a category of bourgeois society*, Cambridge, MA, MIT Press.

Haddon, Leslie (2007) 'Roger Silverstone's legacies: Domestication', *New Media & Society*, 9(1), pp. 25–32.

Haddon, Leslie (2004) *Information and communication technologies in everyday life: A concise introduction and research guide*, Oxford, Berg.

Haddon, Leslie (2001) 'Domestication and mobile telephony'. Paper presented at the conference 'Machines that Become Us', Rutgers University, NJ, 18–19 April 2001, http://www.lse.ac.uk/media@lse/whosWho/ AcademicStaff/LeslieHaddon/Domestication%20and%20mobile.pdf. Accessed on 21 March 2014.

Hahn, Hans Peter (2012) 'Mobile phones and the transformation of society: Talking about criminality and the ambivalent perception of new ICT in Burkina Faso', *African Identities*, 10(2), pp. 181–192.

Hahn, Hans Peter and Ludovic Kibora (2008) 'The domestication of the mobile phone: Oral society and new ICT in Burkina Faso', *The Journal of Modern African Studies*, 46(1), pp. 87–109.

Hallet, Ronald E. and Kristen Barber (2014) 'Ethnographic research in a cyber era', *Journal of Contemporary Ethnography*, 43(3), pp. 306–330.

Hamilton, John Maxwell and Eric Jenner (2003) 'The new foreign correspondence', *Foreign Affairs*, 82(5), pp. 131–138.

Hammersley, Martyn (1992) *What's wrong with ethnography? Methodological explorations*, London and New York, Routledge.

Hartmann, Maren (2006) 'The triple articulation of ICTs: Media as technological objects, symbolic environments and individual texts', in Thomas Berker, Maren Hartmann, Yves Punie and Katie J. Ward (eds) *Domestication of media and technology*, pp. 80–99. London, Open University Press.

Haythornthwaite, Caroline (2001) 'Introduction: The Internet in everyday life', *American Behavioral Scientist*, 45(3), pp. 363–382.

Heath, Carla W. (2001) 'Regional radio: A response by the Ghana Broadcasting Corporation to democratization and competition', *Canadian Journal of Communication*, 26(1), http://search.proquest.com.ezproxy.library.uq.edu.au/docview/219530168?accountid=14723. Accessed on 8 March 2014.

Hendrickson, Richard D. (2006) 'Publishing e-mail addresses ties readers to writers', *Newspaper Research Journal*, 27(2), pp. 52–68.

Henten, Anders, Morten Falch and Amos Anyimadu (2004) 'Telecommunications development in Africa: Filling the gap', *Telematics and Informatics*, 21(1), pp. 1–9.

Ho, Kong Chong, Zaheer Baber and Habibul Khondker (2002) ' "Sites" of resistance: Alternative websites and state-society relations', *British Journal of Sociology*, 53(1), pp. 127–148.

Hofstede, Geert (2001) *Culture's consequences: Comparing values, behaviours, institutions, and organizations across nations*, 2nd edition, London, Sage Publications Ltd.

Hofstede, Geert (1997) *Cultures and organizations: Software of the mind*, New York, McGraw-Hill.

Hosman, Laura and Elizabeth Fife (2008) 'Improving the prospects for sustainable ICT projects in the developing world', *International Journal of Media and Cultural Politics*, 4(1), pp. 51–69.

Houston, Renée and Michele H. Jackson (2009) 'A framework for conceptualizing technology in development', in Thomas L. McPhail (ed.) *Development communication: Reframing the role of the media*, pp. 99–122. West Sussex, MA, Blackwell Publishing Ltd.

Howard, Philip E. N., Lee Rainie and Steve Jones (2001) 'Days and nights on the Internet: The impact of a diffusing technology', *American Behavioral Scientist*, 45(3), pp. 383–404.

Hudson, Heather (2006) *From rural village to global village: Telecommunications for development in the information age*, London, Routledge.

Hudson, Heather (1978) 'The role of telecommunications in socio-economic development.' *Issues in Communications*, No. 2. London, International Institute of Communications, pp. 45–54.

Hurwitz, Roger (1999) 'Who needs politics? Who needs people? The ironies of democracy in cyberspace', *Contemporary Sociology*, 28(6), pp. 655–661.

International Telecommunication Union (2014) *The world in 2014: ICT facts and figures*, Geneva, International Telecommunication Union.

Internet Live Stats, http://www.internetlivestats.com/internet-users/. Accessed on 27 November 2014.

Internet World Stats, http://www.internetworldstats.com/stats1.htm. Accessed on 27 November 2014.

Iroh, Eddie (2006) 'Public funds and public broadcasting: An examination of the funding model for public broadcasting in the West African sub-region.' Paper presented at the SABC conference on funding of public broadcasting, Johannesburg, South Africa, 24 March 2006.

Jagboro, Kofoworola Omolara (2003) 'A study of Internet usage in Nigerian universities: A case study of Obafemi Awolowo University, Ile-Ife, Nigeria', *First Monday*: Peer-reviewed journal on the Internet, 8(2–3), http://firstmonday.org/htbin/cgiwrap/bin/ojs/index.php/fm/article/view/1033/954. Accessed on 6 July 2009.

Jain, Priti and Stephen M. Mutula (2001) 'Diffusing information technology in Botswana: A framework for Vision 2016', *Information Development*, 17(4), pp. 234–240.

James, Jennifer (2013) 'Young Zambian women and their fight against HIV/AIDS', http://www.impatientoptimists.org/Posts/2013/07/Why-Young-Zambian-Women. Accessed on 25 April 2014.

Janke, Terri (2003) Minding culture: Case studies on intellectual property and traditional cultural expressions, Geneva, World Intellectual Property Organization, http://www.wipo.int/export/sites/www/freepublications/en/tk/781/wipo_pub_781.pdf. Accessed on 31 July 2014.

Jansen, H. and G. Bentley (2004) *Ontario's Far North study: Broadband best practices and benefits in Fort Severn and Big Trout Lake*. Submitted to: Connect Ontario: Broadband Regional Access (COBRA) Management Board Secretariat and Broadband for Rural and Northern Development (BRAND) Industry Canada, http://knet.ca/documents/ON-far-north-study-Broadband-Best-Practices-Benefits-Fort-Severn.pdf. Accessed on 11 March 2015.

Jeffrey, Bob and Geoff Troman (2004) 'Time for ethnography', *British Educational Research Journal*, 30(4), pp. 535–548.

Jegede, Olugbemiro J. (1995) 'Indigenous African mode of thought and its implications for educating future world citizens', *The Journal of Afro-Latin American Studies and Literature*, 3(1), pp. 93–120.

Jensen, Mike (2002) 'The African Internet: A status report', http://www3.sn.apc.org/africa/afstat.htm. Accessed on 2 October 2007.

Jensen, Robert (2007) 'The digital provide: Information (technology), market performance, and welfare in the South Indian fisheries sector', *The Quarterly Journal of Economics*, 122(3), pp. 879–924.

Jones, Steve, Camille Johnson-Yale, Sarah Millermaier and Francisco Seoane Perez (2009) 'Everyday life, online: US college students' use of the Internet', *First Monday* (Peer-Reviewed Journal on the Internet), 14(10), 5 October 2009, http://firstmonday.org/ojs/index.php/fm/article/view/2649/2301. Accessed on 5 August 2014.

Jordaan, Marenet (2013) 'Poke me, I'm a journalist: The impact of Facebook and Twitter on news routines and cultures at two South African weeklies', *Ecquid Novi: African Journalism Studies*, 34(1), pp. 21–35.

Juma, Calestous and Norman Clark (2002) 'Technological catch-up: Opportunities and challenges', SUPRA occasional paper, research centre for the social sciences, University of Edinburgh, http://www.pte.pl/pliki/2/21/Technological%20Catch-Up.%20Opportunities%20and%20Challenges%20for%20Developing%20Countries%202002.pdf. Accessed on 10 July 2014.

Kaba, Bangaly, Amadou Diallo, Michel Plaisent, Prosper Bernard and Koffi N'Da (2006) 'Explaining the factors influencing cellular phones use in Guinea', *Electronic Journal of Information Systems in Developing Countries*, 28(3), pp. 1–7.

Kalba, Kas (2008) 'The adoption of mobile phones in emerging markets: Global diffusion and the rural challenge', *International Journal of Communication*, 2, pp. 631–661.

Kalichman, Seth C., K. J. Sikkema and A. Somlai (1996) 'People living with HIV infection who attend and do not attend support groups: A pilot study of needs, characteristics and experiences', *AIDS Care: Psychological and Sociomedical Aspects of AIDS/HIV*, 8(5), pp. 589–599.

Kamira, Robyn (2003) 'Te Mata o te Tai – the edge of the tide: Rising capacity in information technology of Maori in Aotearoa – New Zealand', *The Electronic Library*, 21(5), pp. 465–475.

Kandell, Jonathan J. (1998) 'Internet addiction on campus: The vulnerability of college students', *CyberPsychology & Behavior*, 1(1), pp. 11–17.

Katz, Jack (2002) 'From how to why: On luminous description and causal inference in ethnography (Part 2)', *Ethnography*, 3(1), pp. 63–90.

Kaye, Barbara K. (2007) 'Blog use motivations: An exploratory study', in Mark Tremayne (ed.) *Blogging, citizenship, and the future of media*, pp. 127–148. New York, Routledge.

Kaye, Barbara K. and Thomas J. Johnson (2004) 'A web for all reasons: Uses and gratifications of Internet components for political information', *Telematics and Informatics*, 21(3), pp. 197–223.

Kelly, Tim (2004) 'Mobile communications in Africa', *African Technology Development Forum*, http://www.atdforum.org/spip.php?article89/. Accessed on 16 October 2014.

Kiggundu, John (2007) 'Intellectual property law and the protection of Indigenous knowledge', in Isaac N. Mazonde and Pradip Thomas (eds) Indigenous knowledge systems and intellectual property in the twenty-first century: Perspectives from Southern Africa, pp. 26–47. Dakar, Senegal, Council for the Development of Social Science Research in Africa.

Koo, Kevin, Jennifer D. Makin and Brian W. C. Forsyth (2013) 'Barriers to male-partner participation in programs to prevent mother-to-child HIV transmission in South Africa', *AIDS Education and Prevention*, 25(1), pp. 14–24.

Kozinets, Robert V. (2010) *Netnography: Doing ethnographic research online*, Los Angeles, Sage Publications Ltd.

Kozinets, Robert V. (2009) 'Cultures and communities online', http://www.sagepub.com/upm-data/31333_01_Kozinets_Ch_01.pdf. Accessed on 4 October 2014.

Kozinets, Robert V. (2002) 'The field behind the screen: Using netnography for marketing research in online communities', *Journal of Marketing Research*, 39(1), pp. 61–72.

Kozinets, Robert V. (1998) 'On netnography: Initial reflections on consumer research investigations of cuberculture', *Advances in Consumer Research*, 25(1), pp. 366–371.

Kozinets, Robert V. and Jay Handelman (1998) 'Ensouling consumption: A netnographic exploration of the meaning of boycotting behavior', *Advances in Consumer Research*, 25(1), pp. 475–480.

Kubey, Robert W., Michael J. Lavin and John R. Barrows (2001) 'Internet use and collegiate academic performance decrements: Early findings', *Journal of Communication*, 51(2), pp. 366–382.

Kupe, Tawana (2004) 'An agenda for researching African media and communication contexts', *Ecquid Novi: African Journalism Studies*, 25(2), pp. 353–356.

Kutty, P. V. Valsala G. (2002) *National experiences with the protection of expressions of folklore/traditional cultural expressions: India, Indonesia and the Philippines*, Geneva, World Intellectual Property Organization, http://www.wipo.int/tk/en/studies/cultural/expressions/study/kutty.pdf. Accessed on 31 July 2014.

Kwansah-Aidoo, Kwamena and Levi Obijiofor (2006) 'Patterns of Internet use among university students in Ghana', in O. Felix Ayadi (ed.) *African development: What role for business? Proceedings of the international academy of African business and development conference*, Vol. 7, pp. 359–365. Accra, Ghana (23–27 May 2006), Ghana Institute of Management and Public Administration.

LaFraniere, Sharon (2005) 'Cellphones catapult rural Africa to 21st century', *The New York Times*, 25 August 2005, http://www.nytimes.com/2005/08/25/international/africa/25africa.html?_r=0&pagewanted=print. Accessed on 18 March 2014.

Laguerre, Michel (2013) 'Information technology and development: The Internet and the mobile phone in Haiti', *Information Technology for Development*, 19(2), pp. 100–111.

LeBesco, Kathleen (2004) 'Managing visibility, intimacy, and focus in online critical ethnography', in Mark D. Johns, Shing-Ling Chen and G. Jon Hall (eds) *Online social research: Methods, issues and ethics*, pp. 63–79. New York, Peter Lang.

Lee, Sarah (1999) 'Private uses in public spaces: A study of an Internet café', *New Media & Society*, 1(3), pp. 331–350.

Legris, Paul, John Inghamb and Pierre Collerette (2003) 'Why do people use information technology? A critical review of the technology acceptance model', *Information & Management*, 40(3), pp. 191–204.

Lerner, Daniel (1958) *The passing of traditional society: Modernizing the Middle East*, Glencoe, IL, The Free Press.

Lewis, Susan Jane and Andrew James Russell (2011) 'Being embedded: A way forward for ethnographic research', *Ethnography*, 12(3), pp. 398–416.

Lie, Rico (2008) 'Rural HIV/AIDS communication/intervention: From using models to using frameworks and common principles', in Jan Servaes (ed.) *Communication for development and social change*, pp. 279–295. New Delhi, Sage Publications India Pvt Ltd.

Littlejohn, Stephen W. (1992) *Theories of human communication*, 4th edition, Belmont, CA, Wadsworth Publishing Company.

Livingston, Steven (2007) 'The Nokia effect: The reemergence of amateur journalism and what it means for international affairs', in David D. Perlmutter and John Maxwell Hamilton (eds) *From pigeons to news portals: Foreign reporting and the challenge of new technology*, pp. 47–69. Baton Rouge, Louisiana State University Press.

Lloyd, Jan M., Laura A. Dean and Diane L. Cooper (2007) 'Students' technology use and its effects on peer relationships, academic involvement, and healthy lifestyles', *NASPA Journal*, 44(3), pp. 481–495.

Loudon, Melissa and B. Theo Mazumdar (2013) 'Media representations of technology in Egypt's 2011 pro-democracy protests, *Ecquid Novi: African Journalism Studies*, 34(1), pp. 50–67.

Louw, Eric (2001) *The media and cultural production*, London, Sage Publications Ltd.

Lyman, Peter and Nina Wakeford (1999) 'Introduction: Going into the (virtual) field', *American Behavioral Scientist*, 43(3), pp. 359–376.

Mabweazara, Hayes Mawindi (2011) 'Between the newsroom and the pub: The mobile phone in the dynamics of everyday mainstream journalism practice in Zimbabwe', *Journalism: Theory, Practice and Criticism*, 12(6), pp. 692–707.

Mabweazara, Hayes Mawindi, Okoth Fred Mudhai and Jason Whittaker (eds) (2013) *Online journalism in Africa: Trends, practices and emerging cultures*, London, Routledge.

Mack, Natasha, Cynthia Woodsong, Kathleen M. MacQueen, Greg Guest and Emily Namey (2005) *Qualitative research methods: A data collector's field guide*, North Carolina, USA, Family Health International.

Madon, Shirin (2000) 'The Internet and socioeconomic development: Exploring the interaction', *Information Technology & People*, 13(2), pp. 85–101.

Maingard, Jacqueline (1997) 'Transforming television broadcasting in a democratic South Africa', *Screen*, 38(3), pp. 260–274.

Mansell, Robin and Uta Wehn (1998) *Knowledge societies: Information technology for sustainable development*, New York, United Nations Publications and Oxford University Press.

Mare, Admire (2013) 'A complicated but symbiotic affair: The relationship between mainstream media and social media in the coverage of social protests in southern Africa', *Ecquid Novi: African Journalism Studies*, 34(1), pp. 83–98.

Marker, Phil, Kerry McNamara and Lindsay Wallace (2001) *The significance of information and communication technologies for reducing poverty*, London, Programme for Policy Studies, Development Policy Department, http://www.itu.int/ITU-D/resmob/documents/ICT_Collaboration_Jan2002/15-DFID-UK.pdf. Accessed on 15 July 2014.

Markham, Annette N. (2004) 'Representation in online ethnographies: A matter of context sensitivity', in Mark D. Johns, Shing-Ling Chen and G. Jon Hall (eds) *Online social research: Methods, issues and ethics*, pp. 141–155. New York, Peter Lang.

Martin, Brandie Lee and Eric Abbott (2011) 'Mobile phones and rural livelihoods: Diffusion, uses, and perceived impacts among farmers in rural Uganda', *Information Technologies & International Development*, 7(4), pp. 17–34.

Masoga, Mogomme Alpheus (2007) 'Contesting space and time: Intellectual property rights and Indigenous knowledge systems research – A challenge', in Isaac N. Mazonde and Pradip Thomas (eds) *Indigenous knowledge systems and intellectual property in the twenty-first century: Perspectives from Southern Africa*, pp. 3–11. Dakar, Senegal, Council for the Development of Social Science Research in Africa.

May, Julian Douglas (2012) 'Digital and other poverties: Exploring the connection in four East African countries', *Information Technologies & International Development*, 8(2), pp. 33–50.

Mazonde, Isaac N. (2007) 'Introduction', in Isaac N. Mazonde and Pradip Thomas (eds) *Indigenous knowledge systems and intellectual property in the twenty-first century: Perspectives from Southern Africa*, pp. 1–2. Dakar, Senegal, Council for the Development of Social Science Research in Africa.

McAnany, Emile G. (2012) *Saving the world: A brief history of communication for development and social change*, Urbana, IL, University of Illinois Press.

McConaghy, Cathryn (2000) 'The web and today's colonialism', *Australian Aboriginal Studies*, 2000(1 & 2), pp. 48–55.

McGonagle, Tarlach (2004) 'Regulating minority-language use in broadcasting: International law and the Dutch national experience', *16 Mediaforum*, 5, pp. 155–160.

McGonagle, Tarlach, Bethany Davis Noll and Monroe Price (eds) (2003) *Minority-language related broadcasting and legislation in the OSCE*, Study commissioned by the OSCE High Commissioner on National Minorities, London, Programme in Comparative Media Law and Policy (PCMLP), Centre for Socio-Legal Studies and Oxford University.

McManus, John H. (2009) 'The commercialization of news', in Karin Wahl-Jorgensen and Thomas Hanitzsch (eds) *The handbook of journalism studies*, pp. 218–233. New York, Routledge.

McNair, Brian (2011) 'Managing the online news revolution: The UK experience', in Graham Meikle and Guy Redden (eds) *News online: Transformations and continuities*, pp. 38–52. London, Palgrave MacMillan.

McPhail, Thomas L. (2009) 'Introduction to development communication', in Thomas L. McPhail (ed.) *Development communication: Reframing the role of the media*, pp. 1–20. West Sussex, MA, Blackwell Publishing Ltd.

McQuail, Denis (2005) *McQuail's mass communication theory*, 5th edition, London, Sage Publications Ltd.

Meadows, Michael (2000) 'The indigenous broadcasting sector', in *Productivity Commission 2000, Broadcasting, Report no. 11*, AusInfo, Canberra.

Melkote, Srinivas R., Sundeep R. Muppidi and Divakar Goswami (2000) 'Social and economic factors in an integrated behavioural and societal approach to communication in HIV/AIDS', *Journal of Health Communication*, 5(Supplement 1), pp. 17–27.

Merrigan, Gerianne and Carole Logan Huston (2004) *Communication research methods*, Southbank, Victoria, Thomson Wadsworth.

Meso, Peter, Philip Musa and Victor Mbarika (2005) 'Towards a model of consumer use of mobile information and communication technology in LDCs: The case of sub-Saharan Africa', *Information Systems Journal*, 15(2), pp. 119–146.

Michaels, Eric (1994) *Bad aboriginal art: Tradition, media and technological horizons*, St Leonards, NSW, Allen and Unwin.

Michaels, Eric (1986) *Aboriginal invention of television: Central Australia 1982–86*, The Institute Report Series, Canberra, Australian Institute of Aboriginal and Torres Strait Islander Studies.

Michaels, Eric (1985a) 'Ask a foolish question: On the methodologies of cross-cultural media research', *Australian Journal of Cultural Studies*, 3(2), pp. 45–59.

Michaels, Eric (1985b) 'New technologies in the outback and their implications', *Media Information Australia*, 38, pp. 69–72.

Michaels, Eric (1984) 'Aboriginal "Air Rights"', *Media Information Australia*, 34, pp. 51–57.

Middleton, Julie (2010) '*Ka Rangona te Reo*: The development of Maori-language television broadcasting in Aotearoa New Zealand', *Te Kaharoa*, 3(1), pp. 146–176.

Miike, Yoshitaka (2010) 'An anatomy of Eurocentrism in communication scholarship: The role of Asiacentricity in de-Westernizing theory and research', *China Media Research*, 6(1), pp. 1–11.

Miike, Yoshitaka (2006) 'Non-western theory in western research? An Asiacentric agenda for Asian communication studies', *The Review of Communication*, 6(1–2), pp. 4–31.

Mirandilla, Mary Grace P. (2007) 'Community telecenters as a development tool: Employing a participatory approach to determine how ICTs can help transform rural communities in the Philippines.' Paper presented at the international conference on living in the information society: ICT on people, work and communities in Asia, Renaissance Hotel, Makati, Manilla, Philippines, 23–24 April 2007.

Moahi, Kgomotso H. (2007) 'Copyright in the digital era and some implications for indigenous knowledge', in Isaac N. Mazonde and Pradip Thomas (eds) *Indigenous knowledge systems and intellectual property in the twenty-first century: Perspectives from Southern Africa*, pp. 66–77. Dakar, Senegal, Council for the Development of Social Science Research in Africa.

Molony, Thomas (2008) 'Running out of credit: The limitations of mobile telephony in a Tanzanian agricultural marketing system', *The Journal of Modern African Studies*, 46(4), pp. 637–658.

Morolong, Siamisang (2007) 'Protecting folklore under modern intellectual property regimes: Limitations and alternative regimes for protection', in Isaac N. Mazonde and Pradip Thomas (eds) *Indigenous knowledge systems and intellectual property in the twenty-first century: Perspectives from Southern Africa*, pp. 48–65. Dakar, Senegal, Council for the Development of Social Science Research in Africa.

Morphy, Howard (1984) *Journey to the crocodile's nest: An accompanying monograph to the film Madarrpa funeral at Gurka'wuy*, Canberra, Australian Institute of Aboriginal Studies.

Morris, Merrill and Christine Ogan (1996) 'The Internet as mass medium', *Journal of Communication*, 46(1), pp. 39–50.

Morris, Mike L. and Stavros E. Stavrou (1993) 'Telecommunication needs and provision to underdeveloped black areas in South Africa', *Telecommunications Policy*, 17(7), pp. 529–539.

Moyo, Dumisani (2009) 'Citizen journalism and the parallel market of information in Zimbabwe's 2008 election', *Journalism Studies*, 10(4), pp. 551–567.

Moyo, Dumisani (2007) 'Alternative media, diasporas and the mediation of the Zimbabwe crisis', *Ecquid Novi: African Journalism Studies*, 28(1 & 2), pp. 81–105.

Moyo, Last (2011) 'Blogging down a dictatorship: Human rights, citizens journalists and the right to communicate in Zimbabwe', *Journalism: Theory, Practice and Criticism*, 12(6), pp. 745–760.

Moyo, Last (2009a) 'The digital divide: Scarcity, inequality and conflict', in Glen Creeber and Royston Martin (eds) *Digital cultures: Understanding new media*, pp. 122–130. Maidenhead, Open University Press/McGraw-Hill Education.

Moyo, Last (2009b) 'Digital democracy: Enhancing the public sphere', in Glen Creeber and Royston Martin (eds) *Digital cultures: Understanding new media*, pp. 139–150. Berkshire, England, Open University Press/McGraw-Hill Education.

Mudhai, Okoth Fred (2013) *Civic engagement, digital networks, and political reform in Africa*, New York, Palgrave Macmillan.

Mudhai, Okoth Fred (2011) 'Immediacy and openness in a digital Africa: Networked-convergent journalisms in Kenya', *Journalism: Theory, Practice and Criticism*, 12(6), pp. 674–691.

Mudhai, Okoth Fred (2004) 'Researching the impact of ICTs as change catalysts in Africa', *Ecquid Novi: African Journalism Studies*, 25(2), pp. 313–335.

Mugabe, John (2007) 'Intellectual property protection and traditional knowledge: An exploration in international policy discourse', *Intellectual Property and Human Rights: Proceedings of a panel discussion, organized by the World Intellectual Property Organization in collaboration with the Office of the United Nations High Commissioner for Human Rights*, on 9 November 1998, to commemorate the 50th anniversary of the proclamation of the Universal Declaration of Human Rights, pp. 97–122. Geneva, World Intellectual Property Organization.

Mutula, Stephen M. (2008) 'Digital divide and economic development: Case study of sub-Saharan Africa', *The Electronic Library*, 26(4), pp. 468–489.

Mutula, Stephen M. (2003) 'Cyber café industry in Africa', *Journal of Information Science*, 29(6), pp. 489–497.

Mwesige, Peter G. (2004) 'Cyber elites: A survey of Internet café users in Uganda', *Telematics and Informatics*, 21(1), pp. 83–101.

Myhre, Sonja L. and June A. Flora (2000) 'HIV/AIDS communication campaigns: Progress and prospects', *Journal of Health Communication*, 5(Supplement 1), pp. 29–45.

Neto, Isabel, Charles Kenny, Subramaniam Janakiram and Charles Watt (2005) 'Look before you leap: The bumpy road to e-development', in Robert Schware (ed.) *E-development: From excitement to effectiveness*, pp. 1–22. Washington, DC, The World Bank Group.

Newman, Nic (2009) 'The rise of social media and its impact on mainstream journalism: A study of how newspapers and broadcasters in the UK and US are responding to a wave of participatory social media, and a historic shift in control towards individual consumers'. *Working paper*. Reuters Institute for the Study of Journalism. Oxford, University of Oxford, https://reutersinstitute.politics.ox.ac.uk/fileadmin/documents/Publications/The_rise_of_social_media_and_its_impact_on_mainstream_journalism.pdf. Accessed on 4 May 2014.

Nigeria Village Square, http://www.nigeriavillagesquare.com/index.php. Accessed on 18 October 2014.

Norris, Pippa (2001) *Digital divide: Civic engagement, information poverty, and the Internet worldwide*, Cambridge, Cambridge University Press.

Nyamnjoh, Francis B. (2005a) *Africa's media, democracy and the politics of belonging*, London, Zed Books.

Nyamnjoh, Francis B. (2005b) 'Journalism in Africa: Modernity, Africanity', *Rhodes Journalism Review*, 25, pp. 3–6.

Nyamnjoh, Francis B. (1999) 'African cultural studies, cultural studies in Africa: How to make a useful difference', *Critical Arts: A Journal of Cultural Studies in Africa*, 13(1), pp. 15–39.

Nyíri, Kristóf (ed.) (2003) *Mobile democracy: Essays on society, self and politics*, Vienna, Passagen Verlag.

OAU (2001) 'Abuja Declaration on HIV/AIDS, tuberculosis and other related infectious diseases', African Summit on HIV/AIDS, Tuberculosis and other related infectious diseases, Abuja, Nigeria, 24–27 April 2001.

Obijiofor, Levi (2012) 'Death of the gatekeeper: Foreign news reporting and public sphere participation in Africa', in Judith Clarke and Michael Bromley (eds) *International news in the digital age: East-West perceptions of a new world order*, pp. 41–59. London, Routledge.

Obijiofor, Levi (2011) 'New technologies as tools of empowerment: African youth and public sphere participation', in Herman Wasserman (ed.) *Popular media, democracy and development in Africa*, pp. 207–219. London, Routledge.

Obijiofor, Levi (2009a) 'Mapping theoretical and practical issues in the relationship between ICTs and Africa's socioeconomic development', *Telematics and Informatics*, 26(1), pp. 32–43.

Obijiofor, Levi (2009b) 'Journalism in the digital age: The Nigerian press framing of the Niger Delta conflict', *Ecquid Novi: African Journalism Studies*, 30(2), pp. 175–203.

Obijiofor, Levi (2009c) 'Perceptions and use of Internet and email technologies by Nigerian university undergraduate students.' Paper presented at the African Council for Communication Education (ACCE) conference – Communication Education and Practice in Africa: A Social Contract for the 21st Century? – University of Ghana, Accra, 11–13 August 2009.

Obijiofor, Levi (2008) 'MTN: It's time to go', *Nigeria village square*, http://www.nigeriavillagesquare.com/articles/levi-obijiofor/mtn-its-time-to-go.html. Accessed on 17 October 2014.

Obijiofor, Levi (2001) 'Cultural barriers to reporting HIV/AIDS'. Paper presented at a workshop sponsored by the Commonwealth Press Union, London, and the Centre for International Journalism, University of Queensland, Australia, 29 November 2001.

Obijiofor, Levi (1998) 'Africa's dilemma in the transition to the new information and communication technologies', *Futures*, 30(5), pp. 453–462.

Obijiofor, Levi (1995) *Mass media and sociocultural phenomena in the process of development: An ethnographic study of two Nigerian communities*. Unpublished PhD thesis, Queensland University of Technology, Brisbane, Australia.

Obijiofor, Levi, Chris Lawe Davies, Brian Connelly, Sandra Haswell, Steve McIlwaine, Nigel McCarthy and Helen Ester (2001) 'Television in a remote aboriginal community: Social justice or injustice'. Paper presented at the Journalism Education Association (JEA) annual conference, *Justice and Journalism*, Sheraton Hotel, Perth, 3–7 December, http://www.uq.edu.au/jrn/jea/full-program.htm. Accessed on 20 March 2002.

Obijiofor, Levi and Folker Hanusch (2011) *Journalism across cultures: An introduction*, Basingstoke, London, Palgrave Macmillan.

Obijiofor, Levi, Sohail Inayatullah and Tony Stevenson (2000) 'Impact of new information and communication technologies (ICTs) on socioeconomic and educational development of Africa and the Asia-Pacific', *Journal of Futures Studies*, 4(2), pp. 21–66.

Odero, Jared (2003) 'Using the Internet café at Technikon Pretoria in South Africa: Views from students'. Paper presented at the Norwegian Network on ICT and Development Annual Workshop, Bergen, Norway, 14–15 November. Cited in Wahid, Fathul, Bjørn Furuholt and Stein Kristiansen (2006) 'Internet for development? Patterns of use among Internet café customers in Indonesia', *Information Development*, 22(4), pp. 278–291.

O'Donoghue, Lowitja (Lois) (1998) www.alia.org.au/press/release/1998.04.30a .html. Accessed on 28 September 2000.

O'Donnell, Susan and Guillermo Delgado (1995) 'Using the Internet to strengthen the Indigenous nations of the Americas', *Media Development*, 3, pp. 36–38.

Ogunlesi, Tolu (2013) 'Youth and social media in Nigeria', *Rhodes Journalism Review*, 33, pp. 20–22.

Ogunlesi, Tolu (2012) 'Seven ways mobile phones have changed lives in Africa', Special report on CNN, http://edition.cnn.com/2012/09/13/world/ africa/mobile-phones-change-africa/index.html. Accessed on 2 October 2012.

O'Hearn, Denis (2009) 'Amartya Sen's development as freedom: Ten years later', *Policy & Practice: A Development Education Review*, http://www .developmenteducationreview.com/issue8-focus1. Accessed on 15 July 2014.

Okpaku, Joseph O. (2003) 'Background on information and communications technologies for development in Africa', in Joseph Ohiomogben Okpaku (ed.) *Information and communication technologies for African development: An assessment of progress and challenges ahead*, pp. 23–46. New York, The United Nations ICT Task Force.

Olatokun, Michael Wole and Ibilola Oluseyi Bodunwa (2006) 'GSM usage at the University of Ibadan', *The Electronic Library*, 24(4), pp. 530–547.

Olokor, Friday (2013) 'Why we oppose use of condom – Catholic church', *Punch* newspaper online, 17 June 2013, http://www.punchng.com/news/why -we-oppose-use-of-condom-catholic-church/. Accessed on 17 June 2013.

Omenugha, Kate Azuka (2009) 'Nigerian students' use of information and communication technology – A blessing or a curse?' Paper presented at the African Council for Communication Education (ACCE) conference – Communication Education and Practice in Africa: A Social Contract for the 21st Century? – University of Ghana, Accra, 11–13 August 2009.

Omotayo, Bukky Olufemi (2006) 'A survey of Internet access and usage among undergraduates in an African university', *The International Information & Library Review*, 38(4), pp. 215–224.

O'Neill, Brian and Michael J. Murphy (2012) 'Canadian content, public broadcasting and the Internet: CBC's online strategy 1995–2000', in Maureen Burns and Niels Brugger (eds) *Histories of public service broadcasters on the web*, pp. 163–173. New York, Peter Lang.

One Laptop per Child, http://one.laptop.org/about/mission. Accessed on 17 July 2014.

Ong, Walter J. (1982) *Orality and literacy: The technologizing of the word*, London, Methuen & Co. Ltd.

Organisation for Security and Cooperation in Europe (OSCE) High Commissioner on National Minorities 2003 (2010) *Guidelines on the use of minority languages in the broadcast media*, The Hague, Netherlands, OSCE High Commissioner on National Minorities, http://www.osce.org/hcnm/32310?download= true. Accessed on 7 March 2014.

Ott, Dana (1998) 'Power to the people: The role of electronic media in promoting democracy in Africa', *First Monday* (Peer-Reviewed Journal on the Internet), 3(4), April 1998, http://firstmonday.org/ojs/index.php/fm/article/ view/588/509. Accessed on 25 April 2014.

Ott, Dana and Melissa Rosser (2000) 'The electronic republic? The role of the Internet in promoting democracy in Africa', *Democratization*, 7(1), pp. 137–156.

Oudshoorn, Nelly and Trevor Pinch (2003) 'How users and non-users matter', in Nelly Oudshoorn and Trevor Pinch (eds) *How users matter*, pp. 1–25. Cambridge, MA, The MIT Press.

Oyelaran-Oyeyinka, Banji and Catherine Nyaki Adeya (2004) 'Internet access in Africa: Empirical evidence from Kenya and Nigeria', *Telematics and Informatics*, 21(1), pp. 67–81.

Oyelaran-Oyeyinka, Banji and Kaushalesh Lal (2003) 'The Internet diffusion in Sub-Saharan Africa: A cross-country analysis', Discussion paper series, The United Nations University, Institute for New Technologies (UNU/INTECH).

Panford, Solomon, Maud Ofori Nyaney, Samuel Opoku Amoah and Nana Garbrah Aidoo (2001) 'Using folk media in HIV/AIDS prevention in rural Ghana', *American Journal of Public Health*, 91(10), pp. 1559–1562.

Papacharissi, Zizi (2002) 'The virtual sphere: The Internet as a public sphere', *New Media & Society*, 4(1), pp. 9–27.

Papacharissi, Zizi and Alan M. Rubin (2000) 'Predictors of Internet usage', *Journal of Broadcasting & Electronic Media*, 44(2), pp. 175–196.

Papa, Michael J., Arvind Singhal, Sweety Law, Saumya Pant, Suruchi Sood, Everett M. Rogers and Corinne L. Shefner-Rogers (2000) 'Entertainment-education and social change: An analysis of parasocial interaction, social learning, collective efficacy, and paradoxical communication', *Journal of Communication*, 50(4), pp. 31–55.

Parker, Brett (2003) 'Maori access to information technology', *The Electronic Library*, 21(5), pp. 456–460.

Parmentier, Mary Jane C. and Sophia Huyer (2008) 'Female empowerment and development in Latin America: Use versus production of information and communications technology', *Information Technologies & International Development*, 4(3), pp. 13–20.

Patel, Viraj V. (2014) 'The promising role of social media in preventing HIV', http://www.kevinmd.com/blog/2014/02/promising-role-social -media-preventing-hiv.html. Accessed on 19 April 2014.

Paterson, Chris (2013) 'Editorial note: Journalism and social media in the African context', *Ecquid Novi: African Journalism Studies*, 34(1), pp. 1–16.

Paterson, Chris and Simone Doctors (2013) 'Participatory journalism in Mozambique', *Ecquid Novi: African Journalism Studies*, 34(1), pp. 107–114.

Patrick, Andrew S., Alex Black and Thomas E. Whalen (1996) 'CBC radio on the Internet: An experiment in convergence', *Canadian Journal of Communication*, 21(1), http://www.cjc-online.ca/index.php/journal/article/ view/926/832. Accessed on 24 January 2015.

Patton, Michael Quinn (1990) *Qualitative evaluation and research methods*, 2nd edition, Newbury Park, CA, Sage Publications Ltd.

Paulussen, Steve and Pieter Ugille (2008) 'User generated content in the newsroom: Professional and organisational constraints on participatory journalism', *Westminster Papers in Communication & Culture*, 5(2), pp. 24–41.

Pavlik, John V. (2003) 'New technology and news flows: Journalism and crisis coverage', in Kevin Kawamoto (ed.) *Digital Journalism: Emerging media and the changing horizons of journalism*, pp. 75–90. Oxford, Rowman & Littlefield.

Pedersen, Per E. and Rich Ling (2002) 'Mobile end-user service adoption studies: A selective review'. Paper submitted to the *Scandinavian Journal of Information Systems*, http://citeseerx.ist.psu.edu/viewdoc/download?doi=10.1.1.20.3402&rep=rep1&type=pdf. Accessed on 30 March 2014.

Perse, Elizabeth M. and John A. Courtright (1993) 'Normative images of communication media: Mass and interpersonal channels in the new media environment', *Human Communication Research*, 19(4), pp. 485–503.

Pew Research Center (2013a) 'Social networking fact sheet', *Pew research internet project*, http://www.pewinternet.org/fact-sheets/social-networking-fact-sheet/. Accessed on 19 April 2014.

Pew Research Center (2013b) 'Emerging nations embrace Internet, mobile technology: Cell phones nearly ubiquitous in many countries', *Pew Research Global Attitudes Project*, http://www.pewglobal.org/2014/02/13/emerging-nations-embrace-internet-mobile-technology/. Accessed on 19 April 2014.

Picard, Robert G. (2004) 'Commercialism and newspaper quality', *Newspaper Research Journal*, 25(1), pp. 54–65.

Pierskalla, Jan H. and Florian M. Hollenbach (2013) 'Technology and collective action: The effect of cell phone coverage on political violence in Africa', *American Political Science Review*, 107(2), pp. 207–224.

Pitroda, Sam (1993) 'Development, democracy, and the village telephone', *Harvard Business Review*, November–December, pp. 66–79.

Plows, Alexandra (2008) 'Social movements and ethnographic methodologies: An analysis using case study examples', *Sociology Compass*, 2(5), pp. 1523–1538.

Poell, Thomas and Erik Borra (2011) 'Twitter, YouTube, and Flickr as platforms of alternative journalism: The social media account of the 2010 Toronto G20 protests', *Journalism: Theory, Practice and Criticism*, 12(6), pp. 695–713.

Posey, Darrell (1994) 'International agreements for protecting indigenous knowledge', in Vicente Sánchez and Calestous Juma (eds) *Biodiplomacy: Genetic resources and international relations*, pp. 119–137. Nairobi, Kenya, ACTS Press.

Pratt, Cornelius B., Louisa Ha and Charlotte A. Pratt (2002) 'Setting the public health agenda on major diseases in Sub-Saharan Africa: African popular magazines and medical journals, 1981–1997', *Journal of Communication*, 52(4), pp. 889–904.

Price, Monroe and Marc Raboy (2001) *Public service broadcasting in transition: A documentary reader*, Brussels, European Commission. Compiled by the Programme in Comparative Media Law and Policy for the European Institute for the Media.

Profita, Hillary (2006) 'Outside voices: Samuel freedman on the difference between the amateur and the pro', http://www.cbsnews.com/news/outside

-voices-samuel-freedman-on-the-difference-between-the-amateur-and-the-pro/
. Accessed on 4 May 2014.

Punch newspaper, http://www.punchng.com/. Accessed on 18 October 2014.

Punie, Yves (2005) 'The future of ambient intelligence in Europe – The need for more everyday life', in Roger Silverstone (ed.) *Media, technology and everyday life in Europe*, pp. 159–177. Aldershot, Ashgate.

Quinn, Stephen and Vincent F. Filak (2005) *Convergent journalism: An introduction – writing and producing across media*, London, Focal Press.

Raboy, Marc (ed.) (1995) *Public broadcasting for the 21st century*, Luton, University of Luton Press.

Ramirez, Ricardo, Helen Aitkin, Rebekah Jamieson and Don Richardson (2004) *Harnessing ICTs: A Canadian First Nations Experience. Introduction to K-Net*, http://www.eldis.org/go/home&id=15899&type=Document# .VQFMaeFUbIW. Accessed on 11 March 2015.

Reeves, Patricia M. (2000) 'Coping in cyberspace: The impact of Internet use on the ability of HIV-positive individuals to deal with their illness', *Journal of Health Communication*, 5(Supplement 1), pp. 47–59.

Reeves, Scott, Ayelet Kuper and Brian David Hodges (2008) 'Qualitative research methodologies: Ethnography', *British Medical Journal*, 337(7668), pp. 512–514.

Robins, Melinda B. (2002) 'Are African women online just ICT consumers?' *Gazette: The International Journal for Communication Studies*, 64(3), pp. 235–249.

Rodríguez, Francisco and Ernest J. Wilson, III (2000) *Are poor countries losing the information revolution?* Washington, DC, World Bank Group.

Rogers, Everett (2003) *Diffusion of innovations*, New York, Simon and Schuster.

Rogers, Everett M. (2000) 'Introduction', *Journal of Health Communication*, 5(Supplement 1), pp. 1–3.

Rogers, Everett M. (1989) 'Inquiry in development communication', in Molefi Kete Asante and William B. Gudykunst (eds) *Handbook of international and intercultural communication*, pp. 67–86. Newbury Park, CA, Sage Publications Ltd.

Rogers, Everett M. with Svenning, Lynne (1969) *Modernization among peasants: The impact of communication*, New York, Holt, Rinehart & Winston, Inc.

Röller, Lars-Hendrik and Leonard Waverman (2001) 'Telecommunications infrastructure and economic development: A simultaneous approach', *American Economic Review*, 91(4), pp. 909–923.

Rooney, Richard Charles (2013) 'Social media and journalism: The case of Swaziland', *Ecquid Novi: African Journalism Studies*, 34(1), pp. 100–106.

Roy, Loriene and Daniel L. Alonzo (2003) 'Perspectives on tribal archives', *The Electronic Library*, 21(5), pp. 422–427.

Roy, Loriene and David Raitt (2003) 'The impact of IT on indigenous peoples', *The Electronic Library*, 21(5), pp. 411–413.

SABC: About the SABC Charter (n.d.) http://www.sabc.co.za/wps/portal/SABC/ SABCCHARTER. Accessed on 15 October 2014.

Saharareporters, http://www.saharareporters.com/. Accessed on 18 October 2014.

Sahay, Sundeep and Geoff Walsham (1995) 'Information technology in developing countries: A need for theory building', *Information Technology for Development*, 6(3–4), pp. 111–124.

Sairosse, Tomas Mauta and Stephen M. Mutula (2004) 'Use of cyber cafés: Study of Gaborone City, Botswana', *Program: Electronic library and information systems*, 38(1), pp. 60–66.

Sambrook, Richard (2010) *Are foreign correspondents redundant? The changing face of international news*, Oxford, Reuters Institute for the Study of Journalism.

Samuel, Jonathan, Niraj Shah and Wenona Hadingham (2005) 'Mobile communications in South Africa, Tanzania and Egypt: Results from community and business surveys', *Vodafone Policy Paper Series*, 2, pp. 44–52.

Satoshi, Ishii (2007) 'A Western contention for Asia-centred communication scholarship paradigms: A commentary on Gordon's paper', *Journal of Multicultural Discourses*, 2(2), pp. 108–114.

Schaniel, William C. (1988) 'New technology and culture change in traditional societies', *Journal of Economic Issues*, XXII(2), pp. 493–498.

Schramm, Wilbur (1964) *Mass media and national development: The role of information in the developing countries*, Stanford, CA, Stanford University Press.

Scott, Nigel, Kevin McKemyey and Simon J. Batchelor (2004) 'The use of telephones amongst the poor in Africa: Some gender implications', *Gender, Technology and Development*, 8(2), pp. 185–207.

Sein, Maung K. and G. Harindranath (2004) 'Conceptualizing the ICT artifact: Toward understanding the role of ICT in national development', *The Information Society*, 20(1), pp. 15–24.

Selwyn, Neil (2003) 'Apart from technology: Understanding people's non-use of information and communication technologies in everyday life', *Technology in Society*, 25(1), pp. 99–116.

Sen, Amartya (2010) 'Reflections from and on the forum: The mobile and the world', *Information Technologies & International Development*, 6(Special edition), pp. 1–3.

Sen, Amartya (1999) *Development as freedom*, Oxford and London, Oxford University Press.

Servaes, Jan (ed.) (2003) *Approaches to development: Studies on communication for development*, Paris, UNESCO.

Servaes, Jan (1999) *Communication for development: One world, multiple cultures.* Cresskill, NJ: Hampton Press, Inc.

Servaes, Jan, Thomas L. Jacobson and Shirley A. White (eds) (1996) *Participatory communication for social change*, Thousand Oaks, CA, Sage Publications Ltd.

Sharma, Chetan, Sarita Sharma and Ujjwala Subhedar (2007) 'Putting ICTs in the hands of the women of Kanpur and the Chikan embroidery workers of Lucknow', *Information Technologies and International Development*, 4(2), pp. 11–16.

Sherry, John L. (1997) 'Prosocial soap operas for development', *Journal of International Communication*, 4(2), pp. 75–101.

Shirky, Clay (2011) 'The political power of social media: Technology, the public sphere, and political change', *Foreign Affairs*, 90(1), pp. 28–41.

Sife, Alfred Said, Elizabeth Kiondo and Joyce G. Lyimo-Macha (2010) 'Contribution of mobile phones to rural livelihoods and poverty reduction in Morogoro region, Tanzania', *The Electronic Journal on Information Systems in Developing Countries*, 42(3), pp. 1–15.

Silverstone, Roger and Eric Hirsch (1994) *Consuming technologies: Media and information in domestic spaces*, London, Routledge.

Singer, Jane B. (2006) 'Stepping back from the gate: Online newspaper editors and the co-production of content in Campaign 2004', *Journalism and Mass Communication Quarterly*, 83(2), pp. 265–280.

Singer, Jane B. (2003) 'Who are these guys? The online challenge to the notion of journalistic professionalism', *Journalism: Theory, Practice and Criticism*, 4(2), pp. 139–163.

Singhal, Arvind and Everett M. Rogers (1999) *Entertainment-education: A communication strategy for social change*, London, Taylor & Francis.

Sissouma, Seydou (2000) *From the rural village to the global village: International Development Research Centre*, http://www.idrc.ca/en/ev-5308-201-1-DO_TOPIC .html. Accessed on 12 November 2007.

Skjerdal, Terje S. (2009) 'Between journalism "universals" and cultural particulars: Challenges facing the development of a journalism programme in an East African context', *Journal of African Media Studies*, 1(1), pp. 23–34.

Slabbert, Sarah, Iske van der Berg and Rosalie Finlayson (2007) 'Jam or cheese? The challenges of a national broadcaster in a multilingual context', *Language Matters*, 38(2), pp. 332–356.

Slater, Don and Janet Kwami (2005) 'Embeddedness and escape: Internet and mobile use as poverty reduction strategies in Ghana', *Information Society Research Group Working Paper 4*, London, University College, http://r4d.dfid.gov.uk/PDF/Outputs/Mis_SPC/R8232-ISRGWP4.pdf. Accessed on 22 March 2014.

Small, Mario Luis (2009) 'How many cases do I need?': On science and the logic of case selection in field-based research', *Ethnography*, 10(1), pp. 5–38.

Smith, Anthony (1998) 'Television as a public service medium', in Anthony Smith and Richard Paterson (eds) *Television: An international history*, pp. 38–54. Oxford, Oxford University Press.

Smith, Matthew L., Randy Spence and Ahmed T. Rashid (2011) 'Mobile phones and expanding human capabilities', *Information Technologies & International Development*, 7(3), pp. 77–88.

Sonaike, S. Adefemi (2004) 'The Internet and the dilemma of Africa's development', *Gazette: The International Journal for Communication Studies*, 66(1), pp. 41–61.

Sørensen, Knut Holtan (2006) 'Domestication: The enactment of technology', in Thomas Berker, Maren Hartmann, Yves Punie and Katie J. Ward (eds) *Domestication of media and technology*, pp. 40–61. London, Open University Press.

Soriano, Cheryll Ruth R. (2007) 'Exploring the ICT and rural poverty reduction link: Community telecenters and rural livelihoods in Wu'an, China'. Paper presented at the international conference on living in the information society: ICT on people, work and communities in Asia, Renaissance Hotel, Makati, Manilla, Philippines, 23–24 April 2007.

Soukup, Charles (1999) 'The gendered interactional patterns of computer-mediated chatrooms: A critical ethnographic study', *Information Society*, 15(3), pp. 161–176.

Spence, Michael (2010) 'Some thoughts on ICT and growth', *Information Technologies and International Development*, 6(Special edition), pp. 5–9.

Spence, Nancy (2010) 'Gender, ICTs, human development, and prosperity', *Information Technologies & International Development*, 6(Special edition), pp. 69–73.

Spence, Randy and Matthew L. Smith (2010) 'ICT, development, and poverty reduction: Five emerging stories', *Information Technologies & International Development*, 6(Special edition), pp. 11–17.

Steemers, Jeanette (2002) Changing channels: The redefinition of public service broadcasting for the digital age, http:/www.essex.ac.uk/ecpr/jointsessions/Manpapers/w24/steemers.pdf. Accessed on 7 March 2014.

Tafler, David (2000) 'The use of electronic media in remote communities', *Australian Aboriginal Studies*, 1 & 2, pp. 27–38.

Tambini, Damian (1999) 'New media and democracy: The civic networking movement', *New Media & Society*, 1(3), pp. 305–329.

Tanner, Eliza (2001) 'Chilean conversations: Internet forum participants debate Augusto Pinochet's detention', *Journal of Communication*, 51(2), pp. 383–403.

Tarawe, John and Roger W. Harris (2007) 'Stories from e-Bario'. Paper presented at the international conference on Living in the Information Society: ICT on people, work and communities in Asia, Renaissance Hotel, Makati, Manilla, Philippines, 23–24 April 2007.

Teer-Tomaselli, Ruth E. (1998) 'The public broadcaster and democracy in transformation: The 1996 Spry Memorial Lecture', *Canadian Journal of Communication*, 23(2), pp. 145–162.

The Guardian newspaper, http://www.ngrguardiannews.com/. Accessed on 18 October 2014.

The World Bank and the African Development Bank (2012) *eTransform Africa: The transformational use of information and communication technologies in Africa*, http://www-wds.worldbank.org/external/default/WDSContentServer/WDSP/IB/2012/12/27/000356161_20121227022850/Rendered/PDF/NonAscii FileName0.pdf. Accessed on 10 July 2014.

Thomas, Pradip and Francis B. Nyamnjoh (2007) 'Intellectual property challenges in Africa: Indigenous knowledge systems and the fate of connected worlds', in Isaac N. Mazonde and Pradip Thomas (eds) *Indigenous knowledge systems and intellectual property in the twenty-first century: Perspectives from Southern Africa*, pp. 12–25. Dakar, Senegal, Council for the Development of Social Science Research in Africa.

Tichenor, Phillip J., George A. Donohue and Clarice N. Olien (1970) 'Mass media flow and differential growth in knowledge', *Public Opinion Quarterly*, 34(2), pp. 159–170.

Tomaselli, Ruth (1989) 'Public service broadcasting in the age of information capitalism', *Communicare*, 8(2), pp. 27–37.

Tortora, Bob (2014) 'Africa continues going mobile: Mobile phone growth outpacing income growth in many countries', *GALLUP*, May 1, 2014, http://www.gallup.com/poll/168797/africa-continues-going-mobile.aspx. Accessed on 27 November 2014.

Tortora, Bob and Magali Rheault (2011) 'Mobile phone access varies widely in Sub-Saharan Africa: Average phone owner is more likely to be male, educated, and urban', *GALLUP*, September 16, 2011, http://www.gallup.com/poll/149519/Mobile-Phone-Access-Varies-Widely-Sub-Saharan-Africa.aspx. Accessed on 1 December 2014.

Treichler, Paula A. (1999) *How to have theory in an epidemic: Cultural chronicles of AIDS*, Durham, Duke University Press.

Tufte, Thomas (2008) 'Fighting AIDS with edutainment: Building on the Soul City experience in South Africa', in Jan Servaes (ed.) *Communication for development and social change*, pp. 325–344. New Delhi, Sage Publications India Pvt Ltd.

Tuinstra, Fons (2004) 'Caught between the Cold War and the Internet', *Nieman Reports*, 58(3), pp. 100–103.

Tungwarara, Ozias (2013) 'Foreword', in Hendrik Bussiek (ed.) *Public broadcasting in Africa series: An overview*, pp. vii–viii. Johannesburg, South Africa, AfriMAP.

Twitter, https://twitter.com/. Accessed on 18 October 2014.

Uchendu, Victor Chikezie (1965) *The Igbo of Southeast Nigeria* (Case Studies in Cultural Anthropology), New York, Holt, Rinehart and Winston.

Ugah, Akobundu Dike and Victoria Okafor (2008) 'Faculty use of a cybercafé for Internet access', *Library Philosophy and Practice* (a Peer-Reviewed Electronic Journal), http://www.webpages.uidaho.edu/~mbolin/lpp.htm. Accessed on 6 July 2009.

Ugboajah, Frank Okwu (1985) '"Oramedia" in Africa', in Frank Okwu Ugboajah (ed.) *Mass Communication, Culture and Society in West Africa*, pp. 165–176. K. G. Saur, Munchen, Germany, Hans Zell Publishers.

UNAIDS (2014) 'UNAIDS and WHO undertake joint mission to Mali to support the response to Ebola', 24 November 2014, http://www.unaids.org/en/resources/presscentre/featurestories/2014/november/20141124_Mali. Accessed on 28 November 2014.

UNAIDS (2013) *Global Report: UNAIDS report on the global AIDS epidemic 2013*, Geneva, Joint United Nations Programme on HIV/AIDS (UNAIDS), http://www.unaids.org/sites/default/files/sub_landing/files/UNAIDS_Global_Report_2013_en_1.pdf. Accessed on 28 November 2014.

UNAIDS (2011a) 'Preventing HIV with social media and mobile phones', http://www.unaids.org/en/resources/presscentre/featurestories/2011/may/20110502sm/. Accessed on 19 April 2014.

UNAIDS (2011b) 'Mobile technologies, social media ignite HIV prevention revolution in Africa', *Infectious Diseases News*, 21 June 2011, http://www.healio.com/infectious-disease/hiv-aids/news/print/infectious-disease-news/%7B2b6d4ea7-1be2-43cb-8738-143fb2eccc9d%7D/mobile-technologies-social-media-ignite-hiv-prevention-revolution-in-africa. Accessed on 19 April 2014.

UNAIDS (2009) *AIDS epidemic update 2009*, Geneva, Switzerland, UNAIDS, http://data.unaids.org/pub/Report/2009/2009_epidemic_update_en.pdf. Accessed on 16 December 2009.

UNICEF (2011a) *From 'What's your ASLR' to 'Do You Wanna Go Private?'* Digital citizenship and safety project, New York, UNICEF, http://www.unicef.org/southafrica/SAF_resources_mxitstudy.pdf. Accessed on 19 April 2014.

UNICEF (2011b) 'UNICEF study explores the social networking habits of young people', http://www.unicef.org/southafrica/education_9718.html. Accessed on 19 April 2014.

United Nations Environment Programme (1992) 'Rio declaration on environment and development, Rio de Janeiro, 3–14 June 1992', http://www.unep.org/Documents.Multilingual/Default.asp?DocumentID=78&ArticleID=1163. Accessed on 11 October 2014.

United Nations General Assembly Declaration on the Rights of Persons Belonging to National or Ethnic, Religious or Linguistic Minorities (1992), http://www.un.org/documents/ga/res/47/a47r135.htm. Accessed on 13 March 2014.

United Nations Human Rights Office of the High Commissioner for Human Rights (1976) International covenant on civil and political rights, http://www.ohchr.org/en/professionalinterest/pages/ccpr.aspx. Accessed on 13 March 2014.

United Nations Millennium Development Goals (n.d.) http://www.un.org/millenniumgoals/. Accessed on 17 July 2014.

Ushahidi.com, http://ushahidi.com/about-us/. Accessed on 18 October 2014.

US National Minority AIDS Council (2011) *HIV prevention goes social: Using social media to create, connect, and come together*, http://www.aidseducation.org/documents/HIV_Prevention_Goes_Social_NMAC_Social_Media_Toolkit1-Sept.2012.pdf. Accessed on 19 April 2014.

Valaskakis, Gail (1992) 'Communication, culture and technology: Satellites and native broadcasting in Canada', in Stephen Harold Riggins (ed.) *Ethnic minority media: An international perspective*, pp. 63–81. California, Sage Publications Inc.

Valente, Thomas W. and Walter P. Saba (1998) 'Mass Media and interpersonal influence in a reproductive health communication campaign in Bolivia', *Communication Research*, 25(1), pp. 96–124.

Vaughan, Peter W., Everett M. Rogers, Arvind Singhal and Ramadhan M. Swalehe (2000) 'Entertainment-education and HIV/AIDS prevention: A field experiment in Tanzania', *Journal of Health Communication*, 5(Supplement 1), pp. 81–100.

Vincent, Katharine and Tracy Cull (2013) ' "Ten seeds": How mobiles have contributed to development in women-led farming cooperatives in Lesotho', *Information Technologies & International Development*, 9(1), pp. 37–48.

Wahid, Fathul, Bjørn Furuholt and Stein Kristiansen (2006) 'Internet for development? Patterns of use among Internet café customers in Indonesia', *Information Development*, 22(4), pp. 278–291.

Wall, Melissa (2009) 'Africa on YouTube: Musicians, tourists, missionaries and aid workers', *International Communication Gazette*, 71(5), pp. 393–407.

Wasserman, Herman (2010) 'Mobile phones, popular media and everyday African democracy: Transmissions and transgressions', Keynote address at the workshop – Mobile phones: The new talking drums of everyday Africa – Africa Studiecentrum, Leiden, Netherlands.

Wasserman, Herman and Arnold S. de Beer (2009) 'Towards de-Westernizing journalism studies', in Karin Wahl-Jorgensen and Thomas Hanitzsch (eds) *The handbook of journalism studies*, pp. 428–438. New York, Routledge.

Wasserman, Herman and Arnold S. de Beer (2005) 'Which public? Whose interest? The South African media and its role during the first ten years of democracy', *Critical Arts*, 19(1), pp. 36–51.

Wasserman, Herman and Patrice Kabeya-Mwepu (2005) 'Creating connections: Exploring the intermediary use of ICTs by Congolese refugees at tertiary educational institutions in Cape Town', *Southern African Journal of Information and Communication*, 6, pp. 94–103.

Waverman, Leonard, Meloria Meschi and Melvyn Fuss (2005) 'The impact of telecoms on economic growth in developing countries', *Vodafone Policy Paper Series*, 2, pp. 10–23.

Webb, Andrew (2004) 'Cell phones, services enrich their market with new teen services', *Knight Ridder Tribune Business News*, 19 June 2004, http://proquest.umi.com/pqdweb?did=653704821&sid=1&Fmt=3&clientId=20806&RQT=309&VName=PQD. Accessed on 26 October 2009.

Weiss, Robert (1994) *Learning from strangers*, New York, Free Press.

Whitehead, Tony L. (2005) 'Basic classical ethnographic research methods', The Cultural Systems Analysis Group (CuSAG), Department of Anthropology, University of Maryland, College Park, Maryland 20742, USA.

Wilkinson, Jeffrey S. and Lu Chen (2001) 'Putonghua-language radio programming in Hong Kong: RTHK and the Putonghua audience', *Canadian Journal of Communication*, 26(1), http://www.cjc-online.ca/index.php/journal/issue/view/95/showToc. Accessed on 24 January 2015.

Willems, Wendy (2011) 'At the crossroads of the formal and popular: Convergence culture and new publics in Zimbabwe', in Herman Wasserman (ed.) *Popular media, democracy and development in Africa*, pp. 46–62. London, Routledge.

Williams, Bruce A. and Michael X. Delli Carpini (2004) 'Monica and Bill all the time and everywhere: The collapse of gatekeeping and agenda setting in the new media environment', *American Behavioral Scientist*, 47(9), pp. 1208–1230.

Wilson, Ernest J. III and Kelvin Wong (2003) 'African information revolution: A balance sheet', *Telecommunications Policy*, 27(1–2), pp. 155–177.

Wilson, William Julius and Anmol Chaddha (2009) 'The role of theory in ethnographic research', *Ethnography*, 10(4), pp. 549–564.

Wolf, R. Cameron, Katherine C. Bond and Linda A. Tawfik (2000) 'Peer promotion programs and social networks in Ghana: Methods for monitoring and evaluating AIDS prevention and reproductive health programs among adolescents and young adults', *Journal of Health Communication*, 5(Supplement 1), pp. 61–80.

World Summit on the Information Society (WSIS) (2003) 'Declaration of principles: Building the information society: A global challenge in the new millennium', https://www.itu.int/wsis/docs/geneva/official/dop.html. Accessed on 5 July 2014.

Young, Sean D., Caitlin Rivers and Bryan Lewis (2014) 'Methods of using real-time social media technologies for detection and remote monitoring of HIV outcomes', *Preventive Medicine*, http://dx.doi.org/10.1016/j.ypmed.2014.01.024. Accessed on 19 April 2014.

YouTube, http://www.youtube.com/. Accessed on 17 October 2014.

Zaffiro, James J. (2000) 'Broadcasting reform and democratization in Botswana', *Africa Today*, 47(1), pp. 86–99.

Zuckerman, Ethan (2010) 'Decentralizing the mobile phone: A second ICT4D Revolution?' *Information Technologies & International Development*, 6(Special edition), pp. 99–103.

Zuckerman, Ethan (2009) 'Citizen media and the Kenyan electoral crisis', in Stuart Allan and Einar Thorsen (eds) *Citizen journalism: Global perspectives*, pp. 187–196. New York, Peter Lang.

Author Index

Subject Index